ETRUSCAN ITALY

ETRUSCAN ITALY

Nigel Spivey and Simon Stoddart

Line drawings by Steven Ashley

B. T. Batsford Ltd, London

© Nigel Spivey and Simon Stoddart 1990
First published 1990

All rights reserved. No part of this publication
may be reproduced, in any form or by any means,
without permission from the Publisher

Typeset by Tradespools Ltd, Frome, Somerset
and printed in Great Britain by The Bath Press, Bath

Published by B. T. Batsford Ltd
4 Fitzhardinge Street, London W1H 0AH

*A CIP catalogue record for this book is
available from the British Library*

ISBN 0 7134 6521 2

To Caroline and Charlotte

CONTENTS

ACKNOWLEDGEMENTS

The authors are grateful to Caroline Stoddart, at whose dinner table this collaboration was first conceived; to all at the British School at Rome, an institution remarkable for its fostering of both scholarship and romance; and to the Masters and Fellows of Emmanuel College and Magdalene College, Cambridge, without whose support this book would not have been written. We would like to thank all those who read earlier versions of the text including Steven Ashley, Chris Hunt, Sheila Clark, Michael Crawford, Claire Pumfrey, Marco Rendeli and Kenneth and Daphne Stoddart. The artist is grateful to Andrew and Julia Rogerson for their hospitality and support during the preparation of these drawings.

We would like to thank the staff at Batsford (particularly Peter Kemmis Betty and Penny Jones) for their help and advice and the efficient production of this book.

Illustrations

Bibliographic sources for adapted line illustrations: Fig. 3: Mazzanti, R. and Pasquinucci, M. 1983. L'evoluzione del littorale lunense pisano fino alla metà del XIX secolo. *Bollettino della Società Geografica Italiana* 10–12, 605–28. Fig. 4: Fedeli, F. 1983. Populonia. Storia e territorio. Firenze, Edizioni all'Insegna del Giglio. Fig. 6: Sestini, A. 1981. Introduzione all'Etruria mineraria: il quadro naturale e ambientale. In Atti del XII convegno di Studi Etruschi ed Italici. Firenze-Populonia-Piombino, 16–20 giugno, 1979. *L'Etruria mineraria*. Firenze, Olschki, 3–21. Fig. 14: di Gennaro, F. 1982. Organizzazione del territorio nell'Etruria meridionale protostorica: applicazione di un modello grafico. *Dialoghi di Archeologia* 4 (2), 102–112. Fig. 15: di Gennaro, G. 1986. Forme di insediamento tra Tevere e Fiora dal Bronzo Finale al principio dell'età del ferro. Firenze, Olschki. Fig. 16: Cassano, S. M. and Manfredini, A. 1978. Torrionaccio (Viterbo). Scavo di un abitato protostorico. *Notizie degli Scavi di Antichità* 32, 1–382. Negroni Catacchio, N. 1981. (ed.) Sorgenti della Nova. Una comunità protostorica e il suo territorio nell'Etruria meridionale. (Catalogo della mostra) Roma, Consiglio delle Ricerche). Fig. 17: Pallottino, M. 1937. Tarquinia. *Monumenti Antichi* 36, 5–594. Fig. 18a: Ward-Perkins, J. B. 1961. The historical geography of the ancient city. *Papers of the British School at Rome* 29, 1–123. Fig. 18b: Guaitoli, M. 1982. Notizie preliminari su recenti ricognizioni svolte in seminari dell'Istituto. *Quaderni dell'Istituto de topografia antica dell'Università di Roma* 9, 79–87. Fig. 19: Tamburini, P. 1986. Il villaggio del Gran Carro: conoscenze attuali e proposte di ricerca. In Carancini, G. L. (ed.) Atti dell'Incontro di Acquasparta 1985. Gli insediamenti perilacustri dell'età del bronzo e della prima età del ferro: il caso dell'antico Lacus Velinus. Palazzo Cesi, 15–17 novembre, 1985. Perugia, Instituto di Archeologia, Università di Perugia, 213–238. Fig. 20: Linington, R. E. 1982. Tarquinia, località Calvario: recenti interventi nella zona del abitato protostorico. In Caporali, G. B. and Sgubini Moretti, A. M. (eds.) *Archeologia nella Tuscia*. (Primo incontro di Studio, Viterbo 1980). Roma, Consiglio Nazionale delle Ricerche, 117–123. Fig. 22: Prayon, F. 1975. Frühetruskische Grab-und Haus-architecktur. Heidelberg. Fig. 23: Walker, L. 1985. The Site at Doganella, in the Albegna valley: Spatial patterns in an Etruscan landscape. In

Malone, C.A.T. and Stoddart, S.K.F. *Papers in Italian Archaeology IV. Vol. 3. Patterns in Protohistory.* (B.A.R. International Series 245) Oxford, British Archaeological Reports, 243–254. Fig. 24: Barker, G. 1988. Archaeology and the Etruscan countryside. *Antiquity* 62, 772–85. Fig. 25: Mansuelli, G. 1972. Marzabotto: dix années de fouilles et de recherches. *Mélanges de l'école française de Rome. Antiquité* 84, 111–44. Fig. 26: Viden, A. 1986. Architettura domestica. Piante delle case. In Wikander, and Roos, P. (eds.) *Architettura etrusca nel Viter bese. (Catalogo della mosica).* Roma, De Luca Editore, 47–56. Fig. 29: Judson, S. and Kahane, A. 1963. Underground drainageways in Southern Etruria and Northern Latium. *Papers of the British School at Rome* 31, 74–99. Fig. 30: Rathje, A. 1983. A banquet service from Latin city of Ficana. Analecta Romana Instituti Danici 13, 7ff. Fig. 31: Scheffer, C. 1981. Acquarossa. Cooking and Cooking Stands in Italy. 1400–400 B.C. *Acta Institi Romani Regni Sueciae.* 4° 38 (2) (1), 9–114. Barker, G. 1981. *Landscape and Society: Prehistoric Central Italy.* London, Academic Press. Fig. 32: Bouloumié Marique, A. 1978. La ceramique comune de Murlo (Poggio Civitate). *Mélanges de l'école française de Rome. Antiquité.* 90, 51–112. Fig. 34: Bartoloni, G., Beijer, A. and De Santis, A. 1985. Huts in the central Tyrrhenian area of Italy during the protohistoric age. In Malone, C. A. T., and Stoddart, S. K. F. (eds.) *Papers in Italian Archaeology IV Vol. 3. Patterns in Protohistory.* (B. A. R. International Series 245) Oxford, British Archaeological Reports, 175–202. Fig. 39: Rathje, A. 1979. Oriental imports in Etruria in the eighth and seventh centuries BC: their origins and implications. In Ridgway, D. and Ridgway, F. (eds.) *Italy before the Romans. The Iron Age, Orientalizing and Etruscan Periods.* London, Academic Press, 143–83. Fig. 40. Martelli Cristofani, M. 1985. I luoghi e i prodotti dello scambio. In Cristofani, M. (ed.) *La Civilta etrusca.* (Catalogo della mostra) Milano, Electa, 175–181. Figs 41–42: Martelli Cristofani, M. 1978. La ceramica greco-orientale in Etruria. In Colloques internationaux du Centre National de la Recherche Scientifique n. 569. Sciences Humaines. *Les Ceramiques de la Grece de l'est et leur diffusion en Occident.* Centre Jean Berard. Institut Francais de Naples, 6–9 Juillet, 1976. Paris – Naples, Editions de Centre National de la Recherche Scientifique – Biblioteque de l'Institut Francais de Naples, 150–212. Fig. 43: Atti 1985. Atti dell'incontro di studio, 5–7 dicembre 1983, Roma. *Il Commercio Etrusco Arcaico.* 5–7 dicembre, 1983. (Quaderni del centro di studio per l'archeologia etrusco-italica) Roma, Consiglio Nazionale delle Ricerche. Fig. 44: Spivey, N. 1987. *The Micali Painter and his followers.* Oxford, Oxford University Press. Fig. 62: Brown, F. 1980. *Cosa. The Making of a Roman Town.* Ann Arbor, University of Michigan Press. Figs. 81 and 85: P. Stary, 'Foreign Elements in Etruscan Arms and Armour', *Proceedings of the Prehistoric Society*, 45, 1979. Fig. 92: Peroni, R. 1963. Dati di scavo sul sepolcreto di Pianello di Genga. *Jahrbuch des deutschen archäologischen Instituts und archäologischer Anzeiger* 78, 361–403. For Toms 1986, see Bibliography. Fig. 93: Potter, T. W. 1979. *The Changing Landscape of South Etruria.* London, Elek. Fig. 94: *Notizie degli Scavi alle antichità* 1970, 178–329. Fig. 98: Prayon, F. 1975. Frühetruskische Grab- und Haus-architecktur. Heidelberg.

All photos are those of the authors unless otherwise acknowledged above.

LIST OF ILLUSTRATIONS

INTRODUCTION

We possess no Etruscan literature. That some sort of Etruscan literature once existed is beyond doubt; that we shall ever find substantial examples of it is unlikely, though not impossible.

The extinction of a direct literary testimony for the Etruscans helps to explain both the academic neglect of their civilization and also their popular image – still sedulously propagated in some quarters – as a mystery people. The study of the classics has always been based upon the study of texts: no texts, no study. Republican Roman schoolboys could be required to construe Etruscan, but modern schoolboys never. This point has become dated, since modern education policies are engineered in such a way as to prevent modern schoolboys learning Latin and Greek. Furthermore, it is true to say that ancient history, as a discipline, has largely avoided Etruscan Italy and has done so for the lack of texts.

What literary record we have of Etruria comes to us second-hand and coloured in various ways. Greek historians, like Herodotus writing in the fifth century BC, were writing for a Greek audience, an audience that would have regarded the Etruscans as *barbaroi*. Or they may be writing from a Greek colonial context: Diodorus Siculus, for example, was Sicilian-nurtured and wrote from the background of a Greek colonial Sicily that had been in more or less continuous conflict with Etruscan interests. And of course the Roman historians were writing for Rome: a city and a culture whose early expansion brought the end of Etruscan Italy. We can no more expect a fair account of Etruscan history from the Romans than we could have expected a fair account of Czechoslovakian history from a Soviet academician. We are not the only historians

with this problem. Those attempting to recover the history of pre-colonial Africa encounter very similar difficulties.

That there were once some Etruscan chronicles (*Tuscae historiae*) is indicated by certain Roman references (and, indirectly, by the well-known but utterly lost 20-volume history of Etruria by the emperor Claudius). The possible cyclic and pseudo-prophetic basis of such annals is the source of some inconclusive scholarship and need not concern us here. We know that individual families and cities must have maintained their own local and particular records: as late as the first century AD a number of families at Tarquinia (by then a city fully absorbed into the Roman sphere) were able to set up *elogia*, inscribed tablets commemorating the deeds of their Etruscan ancestors as far back as the fifth century BC. The fact remains, however, that there is no Etruscan-written history of Etruscan Italy, nor is there any properly impartial history of Etruscan Italy.

We shall address the value of the Roman testimony shortly; before doing so, it is worth noting what effect the lack of texts has had upon our consciousness, in terms of modern literature. The hermetic air of being unknown and undivulged, being sealed into a landscape of fancy and romance – this has, not surprisingly, caught the imaginations of travellers, especially those of a Gothic disposition. One of the most articulate apprehensions of this hermetic air is contained in Nathaniel Hawthorne's *The Marble Faun* (1860), which also encompasses the one-time appeal of the Roman Campagna; but better known and more accessible is D. H. Lawrence's *Etruscan Places* (published in book form only posthumously, in 1932).

There is little that needs saying here about the quality of Lawrence's account. *Etruscan Places* is one of those rare, genuinely inspirational books: its author was dying when he wrote it, dying when he made the difficult and dangerous expeditions to the then malarial sites of Etruria – Cerveteri, Tarquinia, Vulci and Volterra. A sporting, dolphin-like spirit runs through the writing, which not even the impositions of Mussolini can put down. George Orwell (in his essay *Inside the Whale*, 1940) saw what was happening with Lawrence's Etruscans: 'exasperation with the present' had transported Lawrence into a past that was 'safely mythical'. The Etruscans, having no written-down voice, were in no position to answer back: Lawrence could see what he liked, could populate Etruscan Italy with his own ideas. Literally this amounts to an idealization of the past. It remains preferable to a Bloomsbury-style aestheticism (Roger Fry's brief pronouncements on Etruscan art – in his *Last Lectures* (ed. K. Clark) 1939 – are laughable idiocies) but it is proprietorial. The reader of *Etruscan Places* gets D. H. Lawrence's Etruscans, not *the* Etruscans.

Shifts of historical affection are natural enough. The manner in which the Etruscans have been favoured in their own land is instructive: drummed up as forbears during the years of the Risorgimento, played down when the Fascists sought the rebirth of the Roman Empire; and now, in left-leaning, affluent, export-conscious Italy, launched by FIAT as a civilization 'lively in the activities of labourers, merchants and craftsmen; ingenious in works of hydraulic engineering, architecture and medical science'. There is not the space here to give a complete survey of Etruscan fortunes at the hands of those in modern and medieval times who have used and abused their relics and images. We should look, however, at the nature of the Roman history of Etruscan Italy – not least because it is the intention of this book to reject the value of the Roman historians as sources for Etruscan history.

'Rewriting Livy'

Rewriting Livy was the provisional title for this book. It was rejected for two reasons: firstly, too many of our acquaintances alarmed us with the demand, 'Who is Livy?' (a sign of the times); secondly, the title was misleading – it implied that Livy had attempted to write a history of Etruscan Italy, which he never did.

Well, who indeed is Livy? 'One of the greater Roman historians: to him above all we owe our conception of the Roman national character. He is much read in schools and universities . . .' (or at least *was*, before modern politicians decided that he was not worth conserving). Titus Livius (59 BC – AD 17) wrote a history of Rome *ab urbe condita*, from its beginnings as a city. He wrote this history for the Rome of Augustus, for the Rome whose empire has been extended throughout Spain and France, large parts of Germany, Greece, Bulgaria, Turkey, Syria and Palestine, Egypt and the North African coast. Britain was poised to fall. Livy's task was to remind his contemporaries what it meant to be Roman. There was nothing in his brief about doing historical justice to the first victims of Roman expansion. In fact, Livy had every reason for trying to disguise the fact that Rome, when little more than a shanty settlement on the Palatine, had been colonized by the Etruscans, whose period of rule at Rome saw the monumental foundations of the city laid out. This archaeological fact was one to conceal: it contaminated the purity of the race; it spoiled the story. In any case, Livy was writing about the foundation of Rome well after it had happened. It was almost as remote as the Trojan War. Even if Livy had been interested in research, he may not have come up with any results.

Livy was no cad. In the Preface to his History, he concedes that the history of Rome prior to the foundation of the city draws upon traditions 'suitable rather to the fictions of poetry than to the genuine records of history' (*poeticis magis decora fabulis quam incorruptis rerum gestarum monumentis*). He should have added, for honesty's sake, that the same charge could be levelled at his own account of early Rome. And if Livy were absolutely honest, he would have shrugged off the charge, for the scope of this work is didactic. The praise of famous men

1 The Rape of Lucretia *by Titian*
(Fitzwilliam Museum, Cambridge)

was the core principle of all Roman education. History should be exemplary. So it is that Livy weaves into his account of Etruscan Rome 'a series of stories as beautiful as they are unreal' (as Thomas Arnold has it). Let us take one, which according to Livy's chronology ought to have taken place about 530 BC: the Rape of Lucretia by the Etruscan prince Sextus Tarquinius, subsequently celebrated by many poets and artists, including Titian (fig. 1).

Lucretia is a Latin, a proto-Roman lady: she is a beauty, whose *forma* attracts Sextus, son of the then ruling Tarquinius Superbus ('Tarquin the Proud'). Livy presents young Sextus as *amore ardens*, burning with love: one night, playing on the hospitality offered to his rank, he breaks into Lucretia's bedroom, and tries to make love to her; when she repudiates his ardour, Sextus turns nasty and rapes her at knifepoint. Lucretia's husband and his friends find her, terribly distressed: she seems less upset by the rape itself than by the implications of adultery (her phrase, '*Vestigia viri alieni, Collatine, in lecto sunt tuo*' – 'Another man's traces, Collatinus, are in your bed' – may contain echoes of legal phraseology, from actions *de adulterio*). She then kills herself, in front of the men: and one of them, Brutus (a forbear of the Brutus who killed Julius Caesar), thereupon swears to rid Rome of the Tarquins.

In Livy's narrative, the purpose of this story is to explain, in part, the historical event, i.e., the expulsion of the Tarquins from Rome. There is also a secondary, moral lesson: unlike some high-standing women contemporaries Livy could mention, Lucretia could not live with her injured chastity (*amissa pudicitia*). The story of the rape is repeated by a number of other historians: Dionysius of Halicarnassus, Dio Cassius, Valerius Maximus and Zonaras; but, interestingly, it is cast into poetic form in the *Fasti* of Ovid. In Ovid's account, the *forma* of Lucretia is again the point of departure: Ovid's Tarquinius, like Livy's, *ardet*, and then grows violent (*instat amans hostis precibus, pretioque minisque* – mixing threats with imprecations). The subterfuge of Sextus in entering the house as a guest when he was really an enemy is punned by Ovid's phrase *hostis, ut hospes*, thus playing on the words for 'guest' and 'enemy': in Livy it was *hostis pro hospite*. One cannot help thinking that Ovid composed his poem with a copy of Livy at his elbow: or else that both Ovid and Livy are echoing some common source that is now lost to us.

The residual moral of the story has, of course, a nationalistic tincture: beastly Etruscan tyrants, decent Roman gentlemen. But what was the source of the story? Some scholars believe that the Livian account of the Tarquins is indebted to a trilogy of *fabulae praetextae*: that all Livy does is to turn 'historical tragedy' into 'tragical history'. One theory is that these stories had been devised by a Republican fabulist, Fabius Pictor, a Roman who wrote in Greek and coloured his annals with plenty of Hellenic fiction. Livy venerates Fabius as his most ancient source (*scriptorum longe antiquissimus*), but modern views of Fabius condemn his work (of which we possess nothing but fragmentary mention) variously as 'deceit', 'fabrication' and 'rubbish'.

An alternative theory was popularized by Lord Macaulay in the last century. Macaulay, noting that 'the early history of Rome is indeed far more poetical than anything else in Latin literature', took up the idea, already developed by several Continental scholars, that stories such as that of Lucretia derived from ballads. Macaulay set himself to reconstructing the putative ballads that had been the entertainment of early Rome, imbuing them with all the 'passions and prejudices' of their age; hence the *Lays of Ancient Rome*, and hence the best-known Etruscan in Victorian England, Lars Porsenna of Clusium (Chiusi), who swore by the Nine Gods. The ballad of Horatius holding the bridge against Etruscan invasion is a highly successful piece of verse: it captures all the cockiness of xenophobic propaganda (*What noble Lucumo comes next/To taste our Roman cheer?*) and in places even achieves the authentic, regular thud of epic:

> Horatius smote down Aruns:
> Lartius laid Ocnus low:
> Right to the heart of Lausulus
> Horatius sent a blow.

A formidable Classical scholar, Macaulay claimed to have reproduced the original 'Saturnian' metre in which these ballads were cast. He did not, however, believe that such songs were circulating in Livy's time: his idea was that the ballads had at some stage been written into chronicle form and that such chronicles had then been consulted by historians of Livy's ilk.

Livy, as we have seen, was not without suspicion for some of his source material, but he would have had to use it regardless. Not all of his readers take his caution seriously, though. Machiavelli, for instance, took Livy's first ten books as the historical truth. In his book, *Early Rome and the Etruscans* (1976), the late R. M. Ogilvie cited Livy as a 'primary source' for the history of Etruria. We can appreciate the manner in which poetic history (or even historical poetry) gains its footholds in the consciousness. Tennyson knew full well that more than 600 men took part in the Charge of the Light Brigade, and we know (thanks to the survival of one of his wife's letters) that his reasons for settling on that figure were good poetic ones – principally, to suit his metre. This was dangerous of him, as he himself confesses: *The song that nerves a nation's heart/Is in itself a deed.* When this is coupled with the Roman conceptions of what history was (for Quintilian, *historia* is virtually poetry – *proxime poetis* – and should be regarded as a sort of prose poem – *quodam modo carmen solutum*), we believe that there are very good reasons for treating the Roman literary testimony as worthless for the proper history of Etruscan Italy.

Archaeology as history: the purpose of *Etruscan Italy*

Recognizing the deep faults of myth within the Roman history of pre-Roman Italy is not controversial. In 1855 Sir G. C. Lewis produced two tomes entitled *An Inquiry into the Credibility of Early Roman History*: his is a deliberative and generally just attempt to winnow truth from fiction in the Roman historians. Many other ancient historians would prefer this sort of enterprise: to accept Livy as flawed, but give him the benefit of the doubt wherever necessary.

In this book, we have preferred to eschew this compromise. *Etruscan Italy* seeks to present archaeological history, by which we mean a history based entirely and exclusively upon the tangible

results of archaeology. In itself, this is not original: David Randall-MacIver, in his last lecture ('Who were the Etruscans?', delivered in New York in 1942), affirmed a lifetime's commitment when he concluded that the sole source of truth for knowing about the Etruscans was archaeology, 'on which alone any valid arguments can be based'. Despite this, no archaeologist has yet tackled Etruria without backward glances to the literary sources. The two types of evidence, literary and archaeological, are usually juggled. To jettison the literary sources completely has always seemed rash. It may be. We are aware that the trowel has no monopoly on the truth. Archaeology, setting out to demythologize, may create new myths of its own: it leaves much to interpretation, as does history from written records, and interpretations are confined by limitations too numerous to mention.

The history to which archaeology gives rise is not perhaps what some will consider to be the stuff of history. In this book we chronicle no battles at sea or on land; we describe no campaigns, chart no political careers. Where we have no Thermopylae or Waterloo, we do try to describe the modes by which warfare was generally conducted between states and cities. Where no Gladstone or Garibaldi strides across the page, we give some idea of how individuals within a certain social structure conducted the essentials of life: feeding themselves, procreating, putting roofs over their heads, burying their dead. We attempt to map out the patterns of human existence within a landscape and to put our fingers on what was the actual fabric of existence in Etruscan Italy over the historical period of 1200–400 BC.

'Where archaeology begins, art ceases.' Oscar Wilde's dictum proscribes our work in another way. The reader of this book will find no aesthetic excursus upon the delights or horrors of Etruscan art. Etruscan archaeology has been dominated by objects whose value as works of art has clouded their contribution to the understanding of Etruscan history; indeed, the search – both legal and illegal – for art treasures has ruined most Etruscan archaeological sites. The tomb-robbers of today (*clandestini* or *tombaroli*) persist in blighting well-conducted excavations, primarily because the rewards from the art market are absurdly high.

One further caveat: those who look here for an exposition of the Etruscan language will be disappointed. The Etruscan language has already been competently dealt with by others. With the aid of a vocabulary, anyone can read Etruscan, but Etruscan writing, in so far as it survives at all, is too programmed to yield much historical information. It is programmed both in terms of length, with certain phrases repeated *ad nauseam* in various contexts, and in social terms. Etruscan inscriptions are a study in social relations between certain members of society within carefully defined conventions. The significant variable is an individual's name. What concerns us here, then, is not so much linguistics as literacy: 'the domestication of the Etruscan mind'.

By denoting archaeology as the basis for this history we are not referring to a single method or science. The field of Etruscan Italy is one that plainly demonstrates what has come to be characterized as 'the Great Divide' in archaeological research: a divide that broadly separates the classical archaeologist and the prehistorian. The prime movers here were the prehistorians, who during the 1960s and 1970s accomplished a proper recasting of their subject and left the classical archaeologists to traditional concerns: monumental remains, typologies of artefacts, museum-based studies. Plenty of scope for this sort of traditional activity survives in Etruria, and it is not really surprising that those who term themselves 'Etruscologists' stay with the period rich in artefacts and art treasures, from *c.* 750 BC onwards. Prior to that it is a nightmare of coarse pottery and piles of bones. Conversely, the prehistorians rarely dare to take their theoretical models into the historical period (roughly speaking from 700 BC onwards) probably because models over-simplify matters and historical societies are always complex. Readers who wish to pursue the polemics of this division (the 'Great Divide' which seems a pompous way of describing it!) are referred to the bibliographical guidance at the end of the book. We ought, however, to indicate how it has affected Etruscan studies.

The first division, obviously, is chronological. The axis between prehistory and history is occupied by a period (whose focal date may be given as *c.* 900 BC) termed 'Villanovan' (after the settlement of Villanova, near Bologna, which proved eponymous to a certain class of Iron-Age material): this has become a sort of no-man's land, with prehistorians reluctant to pursue their quarry beyond 900 BC and classical archaeologists equally reluctant to go back into these dark ages. As we shall show, the second millennium BC contains the roots of many of the important social, cultural and political changes of *c.* 900 BC; and the decision to limit ourselves chronologically to the span 1200–400 BC forces us to address precisely the problem of the transition from prehistory to history.

A further division is evident in the subject-matter tackled by classicists and prehistorians respectively. Prehistorians have tended to look at the material of everyday life, the life of the common man. Technology, agriculture and settlement distribution have been major concerns. The classical archaeologists might be seen to be more concerned with the immaterial aspects of existence (or the material existence of an élite portion of society). Their dating procedures revolve around detailed typologies of artefacts, usually tied to the relative chronology already established for the Graeco-Roman world. Radio-carbon dating has so far failed to challenge the sophistication of the 'historical' chronology, but it is worth pointing out that there is nothing essentially unscientific in the methods of classical archaeology (identifying a vase-painter is very much like identifying a certain pollen). It is more a case of wanting to know different things.

Prehistoric research is based on scientific and often interdisciplinary collaboration. The investigation of a landscape calls for a wide range of techniques and expertise. Methods have been developed for gathering representative samples of material in order to comprehend the development of a region. Environmental studies of pollen grains, carbonized seeds and animal bones permit a more systematic understanding of the physical context in which 'cultures' grow. These are accompanied by attempts to reconstruct the human environment, the relationship of individual sites and activities across a given region. By contrast, classical archaeologists take a very selective sample and tend to focus their efforts upon funerary remains or ritual centres: in short, anywhere where the chances of finding *objets d'art* look promising. Very few Etruscan cities have been excavated, and such excavations that have been done at city sites have often been marred by the puppy-like quest for vases and statuary (Marzabotto is a good case of this – at least under certain excavators). At its best, classical archaeology, prosecuted legally, fills museum cabinets (prosecuted illegally, it stocks the auction-houses of London and Switzerland): at its worst, it achieves nothing but object-lessons, and we can sympathize with Lawrence. 'Who wants object-lessons about vanished races? ... Museums, museums, museums, object-lessons rigged out to illustrate the unsound theories of archaeologists... Why must all experience be systematised? Why must even the vanished Etruscans be reduced to a system?' (*Etruscan Places*, Penguin ed., 1950, p. 167).

It is not our wish to make a system of Etruscan Italy; at the same time we shall try to avoid committing Lawrence's mistake of idealization, of converting the Etruscans into proto-hippies, gods-of-the-abdomen dreamers, full of music and enlightenment. It is useless to suppose that the fictions of both Lawrence and Livy will cease to gain popular credence by virtue of this book, but we ourselves are laying no claim to the absolute truth: we are just seeking a nearer approximation to it.

The format of *Etruscan Italy*

The approach taken in this book is thematic but not comprehensive. It is not a handbook to the Etruscans but a guide, at times controversial, to some of the current themes of research. Chapter I prepares the geographical and prehistoric context of the Etruscan story into which the human use of territory is set in Chapter II. This chapter concentrates on the distribution and form of settlements, one of the new areas of Etruscan research. Chapters III and IV develop the theme of production within and distribution between these settlements, areas of research where, although much remains to be done, much has been achieved recently as interests shift from the art historical pre-occupations of the past. Chapters V, VI and VII are more selective since they represent new perceptions of older fields

of research. Language is treated not as a linguistic problem but in the guise of the innovation of literacy. Ritual is not perceived as *religio etrusca* but is assessed in its three principal contexts: cities, cemeteries and sanctuaries. Warfare is considered as a theme that is revealing of many other aspects of Etruscan society. Finally, Chapter VIII draws on burial (the approach of the prehistorian) and iconographic symbol (the approach of the classicist) in a common attempt to investigate the distinctive hierarchical structure of Etruscan society.

Since *Etruscan Italy* does not set out to replace preceding works on the Etruscans it is worth reviewing the scene that has already been set by one important volume translated into English, *The Etruscans* by Massimo Pallottino. This work was divided into three sections: the historical position of the Etruscans, aspects of their civilization and the Etruscan language. *Etruscan Italy* reviews the first section (at the end of this chapter), develops the second, exploring the new thematic lines of research outlined above, and ignores the third except under the more interesting guise of literacy. Many of the archaeological controversies considered fundamental by Pallottino are now resolved in favour of his solution. The question of origins is not the same burning issue. The misconception of the language as mysterious and indecipherable has been long abandoned.

Where does Etruscan Italy lie historically and geographically? Today there is little controversy, in contrast to the time when Pallottino first wrote in 1944, that the Etruscans were an indigenous people in Central Italy. They developed from a local Bronze-Age population (from at least 1200 BC), at times in intense interaction with outside groups, but not directly dependent on those external groups for their own development. At the height of their power in the sixth and fifth centuries BC, the Etruscans were a major Mediterranean force, although generally fragmented into a number of individual city states. They expanded outside their principal area (bounded by the Tiber to the south and east and the Arno to the north) into Campania to the south and the Po valley to the north. It should be said that since the following account of Etruscan Italy is thematic it will often deal with some of these areas only in passing (especially

Campania). Culturally and politically, the Etruscans were a highly-developed example of the changes also current amongst neighbouring groups, such as the Picenes and Umbrians to the east, the Veneti to the north and the Sabines and Volsci to the south east. One group, the Romans, surpassed the Etruscans in political development and became their masters.

I
PHYSICAL ENVIRONMENT AND PREHISTORIC BACKGROUND

'Poets make the best topographers' (W. G. Hoskins). If that were a fact, it would justify some measure of romanticism in this account of Etruscan Italy as a setting for human action, for the landscape remains a dramatic one even despite modern efforts to pollute and degrade it utterly. Italian contains a useful word for describing Etruscan places: *suggestivo*, 'suggestive', naturally romantic and invested with a particular spirituality.

We, however, will keep our feet on the ground; or rather, we shall take not the poet's view but the view of a kestrel or an aircraftman, looking down upon the physical cradle of what we see retrospectively as Etruscan culture. And our vision will stray over time as well as space, noting the divers efforts towards control of the environment made by those who inhabited it. Broadly the change in prehistory is this: at the beginning of the fifth millennium BC, human settlements were located predominantly so as to exploit the local resources of the physical environment, but by 1200 BC the physical environment was replaced by the socio-political environment as the dominant force, and by 400 BC a fundamentally political landscape had been formed, within whose structure people had developed the technology to control the physical environment in a radical manner.

As it is described here, Etruscan Italy is not consonant with central Italy. The area covered is equivalent to the modern regions of northern Lazio and Tuscany, with contingent mention of Umbria, Campania, Emilia and the Veneto. We do not cover the Marche and the Abruzzo for these are both culturally and geographically distinct, even though they form part of many definitions of 'Central Italy' (fig. 2c).

The structure of the landscape

The characteristics of the landscape of central Italy have changed but they have not changed uniformly. It may be envisaged in the following way: as a rocky 'skeleton', which is the structural geology and which remains relatively stable over the human time-scale that we are considering (even though it is subject to earthquakes and would be considered young in geological terms); a skeleton whose flesh is the sediment that accumulates and whose clothing is the vegetation. This is a much used metaphor, but one that works well for Mediterranean lands. Whereas the body is relatively stable, the flesh and clothing are much less so. The cover of sediment and vegetation here has been greatly affected by climate and human action. Not so much so, however, that it defies an assessment of its structure. We have divided it up into six areas.

(i) **The coastal plains.** The Tyrrhenian coastline of Etruria runs approximately 560 km (350 miles). Those motorists adventurous enough to drive down to Rome from the South of France along the course of the Via Aurelia will appreciate the nature of this coastline: a sequence of sweeping bays, both small and large, punctuated by rocky headlands and promontories. These headlands and promon-

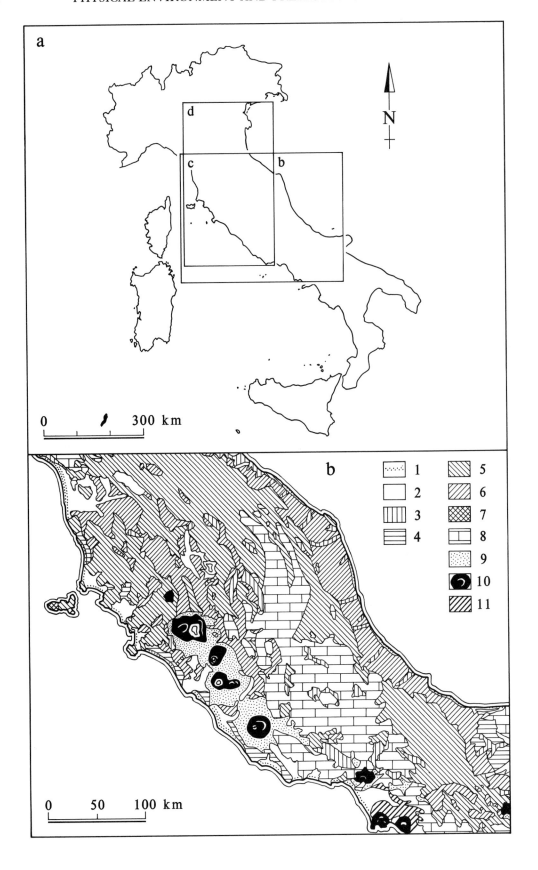

2 *Map of Etruscan Italy:* **a** ***The modern geography of Italy showing the breakdown of separate maps;*** **b** ***physiographic divisions.*** **1** *Littoral sands or shingle.* **2** *Coastal alluvial plains.* **3** *Alluvial plains with terraces and dejection cones.* **4** *Marine terraces.* **5** *Conglomerates, sandstones and clays.* **6** *Pliocene plateau and basins.* **7** *Crystalline rocks.* **8** *Limestone rocks and plateaux.* **9** *Incised tufa plains.* **10** *Volcanic cones.* **11** *Plains of volcanic accumulation;* **c** ***Main geographical areas mentioned in text*** *– this is also the area covered by most distribution maps in the book;* **d** ***The Po Valley*** *– this is the area covered by fig. 13b.*

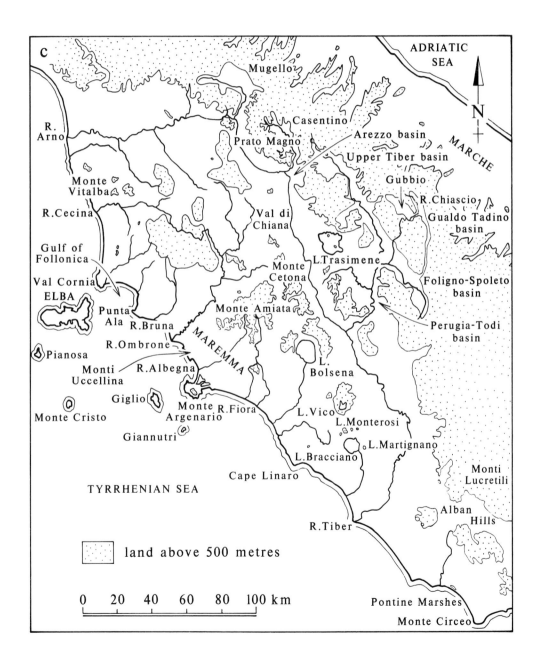

tories have remained relatively unchanged over the last 3000 years, but the shore itself remains highly unstable. The modern effects of this instability may be seen at decayed resorts such as Marina di Pisa, where tons and tons of concrete have been dumped offshore in an attempt to keep the sea from swallowing the town. The ancient changes can sometimes be traced archaeologically. It is clear, for example, that the area north of the Arno delta (north, therefore, of places like Marina di Pisa) was quite different in Etruscan times. Geomorphological and archaeological evidence suggests that the coast around the delta would have been at least 5 km (3 miles) further inland in the Etruscan

3 *Map of the changing coastline around archaic Massarosa and modern Pisa (after Mazzanti and Pasquinucci 1983).*

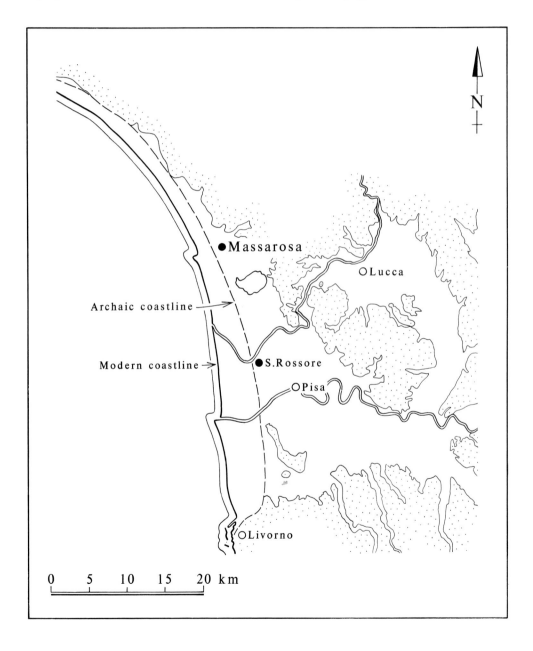

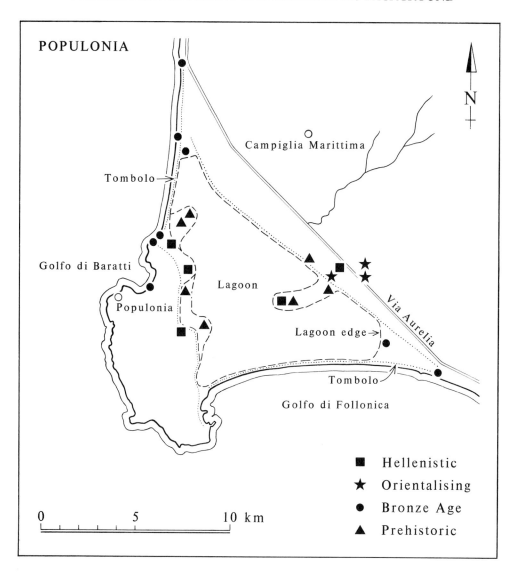

POPULONIA

Campiglia Marittima

Tombolo →

Golfo di Baratti

Lagoon

Populonia

Lagoon edge →

Via Aurelia

Tombolo →

Golfo di Follonica

■ Hellenistic
★ Orientalising
● Bronze Age
▲ Prehistoric

0   5   10 km

4 *Map of changing coastline around ancient Populonia (after Fedeli 1983).*

period. The archaic site of Massarosa was placed on piles in what must have once been a seasonally waterlogged site, now 3–4 km (2–2½ miles) inland.

More evidence of this comes from the modern plain adjacent to the Etruscan city of Populonia: this plain was lagoonal in Etruscan times and its extent can be shown by the succession of archae-ological sites on the sand bars and lagoon edges (fig. 4). During the Neolithic period there were scattered activities amongst the lagoons; in the Bronze Age, there was settlement along the sand bars protecting the lagoons. By the seventh century BC sites encircled the probable location of the lagoons. It is evident from maps dating to the fif-teenth century that considerable portions of this plain were still lagoonal then; drainage did not in fact take place until the nineteenth century. The

5 *The Orbetello delta seen from Cosa by Samuel Ainsley* (British Museum).

implications for the centre of Populonia are that access to the city would have been along an extensive sand bar, which in turn would have served as a simple port area for shipping. One further area of survey is important for this analysis: the Albegna valley. The Albegna runs into the sea just to the north of the *tombolo* formations flanking Monte Argentario – which still protects an inland lagoonal area today (Orbetello: fig. 5). Settlements appear to be absent in the area of the valley bottom, but along the sand bars settlement is intensive from the Bronze Age onwards.

The Albegna valley forms an important natural break between north and south Etruria, a division that came to be exploited politically by the settlement organization of the seventh century BC. The northern coastline is a complex pattern of erosion and deposition of sediment, which have changed the area so much that it is difficult to establish more than localized patterns of change. South of Monte Argentario, however, the coastal strip is more stable. It is characterized by Plio-Pleistocene beach levels containing evidence of earlier Palaeolithic settlement; and in due time it became the area favoured for the *emporia*, or trading stations, such as Graviscal and Pyrgi. On the wider stretches of these bars, shallow draught shipping could have been readily beached, and there was space for the construction of substantial settlements. Subsequent encroachment has been slight: on the beach at Ladispoli one can still make out the remains of jetty structures once associated with Alsium, the nearest port that served Cerveteri.

An important structural feature of this coastal landscape is Cape Linaro: here the coast is more rocky, bounded by cliffs. The Cape forms the westerly extension of a ring of hills that runs inland, again furnishing a political boundary for the Etruscan city-states; this hill country also proved a significant source of mineral resources (fig. 6).

The last prominent feature of this coastline is the Tiber delta, which became a source of political friction from the Orientalizing period (750–580 BC) partly fuelled by the salt resources located near key sites such as Ficana. Further south, the Pontine marshes were not effectively drained until the time of Mussolini but this drainage programme was archaeologically instructive, since sub-surface deposits revealed considerable quantities of Palaeolithic material, which have not been found subsequently in similar quantities on the modern drained land surface. This suggests that there has been a considerable build-up of sediment over a long period of time.

The lagoonal conditions along the Tyrrhenian coast are typical of the early stages of coastal evolution for many other areas of the central Mediterranean. Sediment has been deposited vertically and horizontally in a most measurable form since the Roman period, but clearly the process was active well before then. Reconstructing the coastline is not easy and is complicated by the notion put forward by some authorities that the level of the Mediterranean was 1 m (3 ft 3 in.) lower in the Etruscan period than today. As a general rule, the beach areas have been stabilized only in modern times, and so when we speak of certain 'coastal' Etruscan centres, such as Cerveteri and Tarquina, we are referring to the more stable and elevated landforms immediately inland on which such cities were sited.

The lagoons were favourable to particular types of economic exploitation, of course: namely, fishing and animal grazing. Such activities continued certainly into the first millennium BC and probably beyond: but by the sixth century BC political pressure led the local populations to be less directly associated, except perhaps cyclically, with lagoonal areas.

A number of islands lie off the Tyrrhenian coast, of which Elba deserves special mention. It lies about 10 km (6 miles) offshore, within easy sight of

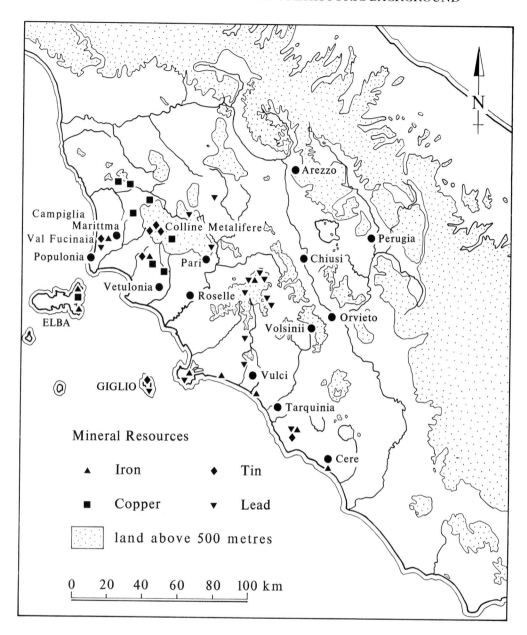

6 *Location of Mineral Resources (after Sestini 1983).*

the mainland, and is composed of a richly mixed geological structure which includes schists, diorites and limestones. The tectonic confusion made a great variety of minerals accessible in Etruscan times (fig. 6). Other islands of the northern Tuscan archipelago are smaller (Gorgona, Capraia, Pianosa, Montecristo, Giglio and Giannutri): they contain less than Elba in the way of resources but are well-placed strategically for communications. The area further south, from Monte Circeo to Campania, boasts further islands: one of these, Ischia, will impinge upon our archaeological history of Etruria not because it is Etruscan, but because it carries the fair claim to be the pioneer zone of Greek colonization in the western Mediterranean.

(ii) **The Maremma and the Tuscan upland.** Tuscany, like Gaul, may be divided into three parts: the Maremma/western highlands, the Siena trough and the Chianti. These are the three principal components of the Tuscan upland, an area of variable geological formation and height. The Maremma and western highlands fringe the coast and divide up the coastal plains described above. An account of travelling in the Maremma in 1909 describes its dangers then as those associated with marshland (M. L. Cameron, *Old Etruria and Modern Tuscany*, p. 212): predominantly the infestation of malaria (*mal-aria*, 'bad air'), which was still lingering when D. H. Lawrence visited Vulci in 1927. The water-logging of the Maremma is, however, a post-Etruscan phenomenon, and there is no real evidence that malaria was a factor in the decline of centres like Vulci. Today it is a fertile expanse of grain fields and olive groves, although closer to the coast, near Grosseto, herds of water buffalo may still be sighted: their milk is prized for the *mozzarella* cheese.

The mountains are principally composed of Tertiary sandstones penetrated by some harder, older rocks; and the northern portion is mostly of a lower altitude (below 300 m (1000 ft) except near Monte Vitalba) than the southern (reaching over 1000 m

(3200 ft) towards its most northerly sector). Many of these upland areas would have been unsuitable for much agricultural activity in the first millennium BC, although they were not high enough to act as substantial barriers to communication. Some contain mineral resources, which are thought to have been exploited from at least the late Bronze Age (fig. 6).

The Siena trough (fig. 7) is occupied by much softer Pliocene rocks that under modern cultivation have become susceptible to erosion. The trough allowed relatively easy communication along its course but its agricultural suitability is variable, depending upon surface deposit. The compact clays would have been generally unfavourable to early agriculture and particularly subject to erosion, while the coarser sands were more readily cultivated, if less fertile. To the north, the Chianti area marks a rise in altitude, although rarely exceeding 1000 m (3300 ft). The parent rock here is largely sandstone, with some peaks, such as Monte Cetona to the south, emerging in limestone. The terrain is not easy to cultivate without making the investment in terracing, which dominates the present-day appearance of the area, and settlement was probably not sufficiently intensive for this to be undertaken before the late Etruscan period. Much of the area would have remained under forest.

The southern Tuscan upland meets the north-

7 *The Siena Trough.*

erly extension of volcanic activity. It is a zone with some mineral resources (fig. 6) but it must have been rugged and inaccessible during the first millennium BC. Monte Amiata at the centre rises to 1700 m (5500 ft): it is still densely wooded, and the forest cover may be presumed to have been still more extensive in pre-Roman times.

The Tuscan upland area as a whole lay between the more scrupulously exploited zones of the coast and the inland tectonic valleys. Volterra and Monterriggioni – the only Etruscan centres of importance and long duration – were placed at the head of communication channels facilitated by rivers cutting in from the coast. Otherwise the area may be seen as an intermediate geographical space of variable fertility and availability of resources, serving as a buffer area between larger centres (see Chapter II).

(iii) **The inland tectonic valleys.** The interior of Etruscan Italy is dominated by a series of roughly parallel drained lake basins. A number of these valleys took on political significance in Etruscan times; many have complex drainage patterns that have altered considerably over time, most recently as a result of human tampering. They are usually flanked to one side by a prominent escarpment

8 *The Mugello.*

fault, which provokes asymmetrical drainage and both alluvial and colluvial deposits. Many of the valleys contain remnants of Plio-Pleistocene deposits that were too heavy for early agriculture. Their agricultural potential is strongly affected by their verticality: some may offer both lowland arable scope and upland pastures and woodlands, but fertility varies very much according to local factors, especially the proportion of heavy, clay-based (and generally Pleistocene) soils to the lighter soils of more recent formation. Hence the political systems that evolved around these valley networks would have been based upon not only valleys as channels of communication but also valleys as mixed agricultural resources – resources that would have been greatly limited by the increasing altitude of even the valley bottoms as one moves east into the Apennines.

Moving from north to south, and then from east to west, ten major basins can be identified: the Mugello, the Arno plain, the Valdarno connecting with the Casentino (the upper Arno) to the north, the Val di Chiana, the upper Tiber, the Perugia-Todi, Foligno-Spoleto, Gubbio and Gualdo Tadino basins. There are further smaller basins in southern Umbria (which as a region may justly claim itself to be the 'green heart of Italy'). The basins to the extreme north and east (Mugello, Casentino, Gubbio and Gualdo Tadino) are placed

within the Apennines themselves, but only the Casentino is a properly closed valley, with one restricted entrance from the south. In fact the Casentino is so isolated as an upland valley that in the medieval period it was favoured as a place of refuge by monastic orders. By contrast the Mugello formed an important communication route (fig. 8) through the Apennines towards Marzabotto and Bologna. The Valdarno, which effectively connects the two preceding basins, opens out from a narrow gorge at the point of confluence with the River Sieve into a wider valley bordered by gentle Pliocene hills. This is an area that today has a fairly dense rural population, but the heavy Pliocene soils would not have suited early agriculture. The valley proceeds south-east, bounded to the north by the high pastures of the Pratomagno and to the south by the Chianti uplands. It passes a small gorge and almost immediately enters the well-defined basin of Arezzo. This basin is well circumscribed by hills and provides an important centre of communications, not only from the Valdarno, but north into the Casentino, east into the upper Tiber, and south into the Val di Chiana.

The Val di Chiana is a relatively flat and wide plain stretching to the south, down to Chiusi and Lake Trasimene. As a valley it appears to offer obvious agricultural resources and is today claimed as the source of the best meat in Italy, at least by Tuscans. Conditions during the first millennium BC are difficult to reconstruct, given the considerable changes in drainage even within the historic period. After its lacustrine phase, the basin was once drained by the Tiber to the south, but this system was upset by a combination of tectonic, alluvial and human action, which altered the drainage patterns. In the post-Roman period the valley became depopulated and was effectively drained only by Fossombrone in the late eighteenth century. However, it was probably fertile in Etruscan times, if prone to waterlogging (as mentioned by Strabo in his *Geography*, V, 2, 9). At the southern end of the Val di Chiana the limestone peak of Monte Cetona provided an upland retreat for settlement, withdrawn from the valley bottom and yet with good access to both upland pasture and more fertile terrain. Intermediate positions – on the boundary of hill and mountain country of Pliocene and earlier

date encircling the former lake basin – were also choice settlement zones; there was also occupation of the interfluves of the Pleistocene valley bottom, allowing access to some lighter sandier soils and some lowland grazing, conditioned by seasonal flooding.

The Tiber has retained the modern catchment of the most southerly portion of the Val di Chiana. In its upper course, the river and its tributaries the Chiascio and the Topino also drain the remaining intermontane basins of north-east Umbria. This is the birthplace of the poet Propertius (*c.* 50 BC), saluted by him as 'rich in crops, a land of generous fields': in his vision, fields nourished by the dust of his Etruscan forefathers. Two broad basins stretch south from Perugia towards Todi and Spoleto. The potential conditions for economic development in these basins are broadly similar to those of the Val di Chiana except in one essential respect: they lie a further 50 km (31 miles) east and were marginalized in the early political development of Etruscan Italy. Both basins possess extensive alluvial plains; in the case of the Todi basin, this is without the drainage problems of the Val di Chiana. The sides of the Todi basin are flanked by Plio-Pleistocene deposits, as is the western side of the Foligno-Todi basin, but these sand-clay conglomerates were less suitable for early cultivation and were covered in scrub as recently as the 1940s. As for the other basins of Umbria, the sandstone marl formations that provide the underlying body of relief are locally broken by prominent limestone peaks.

A continuous line of limestone peaks forms the eastern flank of the Umbrian basins, interrupted only by several stream-induced passes and occasionally by upland plateaux, most notably that of Colfiorito. This limestone chain overlooks a major communication route through the Apennines, a route that was followed when the Romans created the Via Flaminia. One basin – that of Gualdo Tadino – runs parallel to this route; the last basin, Gubbio, is reached either by this route from the east or from the Upper Tiber to the west.

(iv) **The volcanic landscape of southern Etruria.** The volcanic area of central Italy constitutes the largest single expanse of volcanically-formed rock in continental Europe. It involves a complex sequence, of which only the more recent activity needs to concern us here. The area can be taken as three volcanic provinces: the Tuscan (which lies south of the Tuscan upland, around Monte Amiata), the Roman and the Campanian. The northerly Tuscan is earlier in date – between nine and one million years ago – and represents a phase of only minor volcanism. A significant change took place around one million years ago in the chemical composition of the volcanic activity, and two new provinces – the Roman and the Campanian – replaced the first. The Roman province subdivides into four districts: from north to south, the Vulsinii (Bolsena), Vico, Sabatini and Alban complexes. Each of these has, at its centre, one or more crater lakes. The Sabatini district, for example, is made up of a grouping of 20 to 30 craters of which three would have been filled with water in the first millennium BC: Bracciano, Martignano and Baccano (immediately to the east of Martignano). The date of the cessation of volcanic activity is difficult to fix in the Roman province, but appears to be in the order of 40,000 years ago. The importance of the volcanism for us is in terms of its effect on the evolution of the landscape and the provision of resources: there is no Etruscan Pompeii.

The major processes after the deposition of the last major ash flow tuffs were those of fluvial erosion and accumulation. In the Sabatini district the east-west streams had a gentle effect upon the landscape, while the north-south streams cut deeply into the volcanic strata. The erosion revealed a succession of permeable and impermeable deposits that produced numerous springs and, along the north-south axis, deep canyons of approximately 100 m (330 ft) deep, which divided the terrain. This accounts for the many spectacular, mesa-like cliff-edge plateaux in the landscape that offered excellent sites for isolated and defensible settlement. These began in the Bronze Age (1200–900 BC) and flourished in the Archaic period (580–400 BC), when the cliffs cut by watercourses were incorporated into systems of man-made walls. A good example is San Giovenale, occupied in the late Bronze Age and Archaic periods (fig. 87, Chapter VII). In certain areas, the preceding parent rock comes to the surface from under the more recent volcanic deposits. The coastal area is backed by Pliocene clays, marl and sandstone and, to the south of Civitavecchia, by harder sandstones: these represent a continuation of the type of geology found further north, making similar constraints upon settlement and exploitation.

The rapid succession of recent geological and geomorphological activity made available a series of resources. The volcanic tuffs are more or less compact, suiting both intensive and less intensive agriculture; they will be frequently encountered in Etruscan sculpture and construction, being easily cut and quarried. 'Tufa' is the generic name for such stone, but finer distinctions will also be found, such as 'nenfro', or 'peperino'. It is still used for much rustic building, although travertines (especially quarried around the Tivoli area) are preferred for most city purposes. The softness of tufa may be gauged by the depth of wheel-ruts found where it has been used as a road surface. Other important raw materials dwell at the bottom of the stratified deposits. Hence the Pliocene clays exposed in the river beds were used for house floors, pottery and tiles; in addition the timber from the large tracts of forest would have been valuable for shipbuilding. Some of these areas of forest were notoriously dense: the Ciminian woodlands, just north of Lake Vico, are described as *invia atque horrenda* in the Roman histories, 'impenetrable and awesome', and they still command respect from anyone wanting to walk them, even though the present forest is not the forest of Livy's time. And, of course, the lakes themselves: Lake Vico is still relatively unspoilt, and may look now

9 *Lake Vico* (British School at Rome).

much as it did in Etruscan times (fig. 9); Bracciano and Bolsena are less intact. There are still many springs, some developed into spa-centres (e.g. Saturnia), others simply places where thirst is sweetly quenched by naturally refrigerated mineral water.

Two further areas belong to the geographical and historical definition of Etruscan Italy if only tangentially:

(v) **The Po valley.** This is tedious terrain to drive through today: low-lying, industrialized, often hazy. It is bounded to the south by the Apennines, and only a few passes, particularly through the Mugello, allowed access to the rest of Etruscan Italy. Otherwise communication routes were via the seaboard, a highly important factor in the development of Etruscan settlements, such as Spina, on the Adriatic coast. The Po valley was always an area of potentially high agricultural production but was also subject to problems of drainage: to the north, the Venetian tract was, as might be expected, very swampy and lagoonal and has suffered major changes of coastline since Etruscan times; to the south, the Emilian area has a narrow high plain close to the Apennines created by the seasonal flooding of the Apennine rivers.

(vi) **Campania.** Campania is a geographical area centred around the gulf of Naples. Its northern half contains tectonic valleys similar to those of more northerly central Italy. In the southern half the Apennines rise directly from the Campanian plain. A great diversity of environments exists within the region because of the great range of parent rocks – limestone, volcanic ash, lava and alluvium; from these derive some highly fertile volcanic-based soils (particularly around Mount Vesuvius and the Campi Flegrei) as well as some less manageable waterlogged deposits.

Climate

A major factor that distinguishes the different areas of Etruscan Italy is the climate and modern patterns give a guide to the relative conditions. The coast, buffered by the Mediterranean Sea, would have had a typical Mediterranean climate with dry, even arid summers, especially in July and August, and mild, damp winters. Relief and altitude would, however, have brought considerable variation to the area. Annual rainfall in central Italy can vary from as little as 600 mm (24 in.) on the coast to as high as 1500 mm (60 in.) in the mountains, although the contrast is reduced by the location of the central Apennines at some distance from the Tyrrhenian Sea. A further contrast is that more of this rain falls in the spring on the coast and in the autumn in the inland areas. Temperature is also strongly influenced by altitude; more than 15 days of snow per year can be expected in the mountains, whereas snow is relatively rare on the coast. These differences profoundly affect the growing period for agricultural production and limit the types of crop and natural vegetation that can be grown. These differences also placed certain constraints on the degree of economic development that was possible in the societies we are describing.

Climatic change or the influence of man?

Climatic change has not been considerable since the first millennium BC and many vegetational changes were probably induced by human activity, although some general climatic changes are recorded for the last centuries of the second millennium BC. Lake levels in the mountain valleys appear to have fallen, suggesting either increased mean temperatures or decreased rainfall or both. This may have created some additional stress in an economy whose actions were already contributing to the degrading landscape. Pollen cores allow us some insight into some of the more graded changes.

There are now two regions covered by detailed pollen information: the volcanic landscape (Baccano and Monterosi) and the inland tectonic valleys. The pollen cores in the volcanic landscape suggest that human impact was significant only from the Roman period when the mixed oak forest was cleared and rates of sedimentation in the lake increased (from erosion products). It should, however, be kept in mind that these volcanic lakes were closed systems marginal to the major centres of agricultural production. The information from the southern limestone tectonic valleys of central Italy suggests the presence of a mixed oak forest punctuated by a series of agricultural enterprises. Some of the most fertile (in part aeolian) soils were probably eroded away during this first agricultural activity and never recovered. The problem became worse in the late Bronze Age when this vegetation was extensively cleared for the first time and severe widespread erosion was induced. This most probably led to a temporary abandonment of certain sections of the landscape. *Macchia* (scrub) would have taken hold until technologies such as drainage and terracing were sufficiently widespread to counteract the problems of man's making.

10 *Neolithic site at S. Marco (Gubbio) under excavation.*

The Prehistoric Background

The outstanding characteristic of the early economic, social and political formation of central Italy is how undeveloped the area was until the later Bronze Age. In earlier millennia there was little sign of the complexity of later social and political development. This relative immaturity compared with other areas of Italy and the Mediterranean may be of some importance in explaining later developments. Firstly, central Italy was an area with a potential for economic development that had been little degraded by human action at the middle of the second millennium. Secondly, central Italy had not been subject to the cycles of rise and fall of social and economic complexity that affected other parts of the peninsula. The steady development of economy and society in central Italy as well as its strategic position in the Mediterranean were the foundation for the subsequent outstripping of other areas in economic and political complexity.

The same thematic considerations of prehistoric Etruscan Italy will be surveyed in the order adopted for the Etruscan part of the book (Chapters II–VII): hence, settlement, subsistence and technology, trade and exchange, cultural change, ritual, warfare and social organization.

(i) **Settlement.** There was a general expansion of settlement over the recent prehistoric period to 1300 BC. The earliest Neolithic settlements (*c.* 4000 BC) were located only in lowland areas (fig. 10) and generally on the lighter well-drained soils. There followed a gradual expansion into areas of higher altitude by the later Neolithic period (*c.* 2800 BC). By the Chalcolithic period and early Bronze Age, a wide range of locations were occupied. This trend developed into the upland and lowland coverage of the landscape by the middle Bronze Age. Throughout this period there was little sign of differences in the size or importance of sites. Settlements were exclusively made up of simple communities with no evidence of complex house building or of fortification.

(ii) **Subsistence and technology.** The earliest agriculture practised in central Italy comprised small horticultural clearings, some larger and fairly sophisticated agricultural communities and, at a slightly later stage, more pastoral communities. At the site of Pienza in Tuscany, a wide range of domesticated animals (sheep/goats, cattle and pigs) and plants (emmer – a species of wheat – bread wheat and barley) were present, and husbandry practices do not appear to have been strikingly different from those of more recent times. In the more marginal valley of Gubbio, the site of San Marco was probably placed in a small clearing in oak woodland for the cultivation of grain and the grazing of domestic animals, but part of the economy was also devoted to the hunting of deer and the collection of nuts and fruits, including grapes. By the later Neolithic period more pastoral communities were also present, as represented by the site of Norcia in Umbria.

These mixed economies continued into the Chalcolithic period and intensified in the middle Bronze Age. By the middle Bronze Age there were stable mixed farming lowland sites, such as Luni sul Mig-

none, that formed the fixed point in a wider seasonal system. The summer seasonal sites were not only placed at high altitude but also had their bone refuse dominated by sheep and goat, for example Grotta a Male at 950 m (3100 ft). Winter seasonal sites may have been placed in coastal positions. From this stage there are indications that a more diverse use of animals was achieved by, for example, fully exploiting milk as a stored food.

Flint and bone technologies remained important throughout the period before 1700 BC and were even significant up to the latest Bronze Age (*c.* 1200 BC) when bronze was fully established as a raw material. In the early and middle Bronze Age, metal items were relatively rare and restricted in range. A few types of pins, daggers and flat axes dominated the early Bronze Age. Rare concentrations of metal finds have traditionally been given a cultural definition unique to the area in which they were found, for example at Montemerano. In the middle Bronze Age, there was little notable increase in either diversity of forms or quantity of material. Axes, daggers, points and some early fibulae are the most numerous items. Metal was probably a scarce and prized resource that was constantly reworked. Pottery production appears to have involved more sophistication. Although central Italy was only peripherally involved in the use of painted wares in the Neolithic period, the flasked vessels of the Chalcolithic period and the Apennine pottery of the middle Bronze Age show considerable craftsmanship (fig. 11).

(iii) **Trade and exchange.** The trade typical of this period is generally denoted exchange since it probably took the form of reciprocal contacts between neighbouring groups. Elsewhere in the central Mediterranean, exchange may have been controlled by competitive leaders of communities who had more ready access to resources or external contacts. This applied much less to Central Italy where underdevelopment in economy, society and exchange went hand in hand. Some resources (clay and flint) would have been available at a local level, since they could be collected from river beds, which were generally rich in reworked Plio-Pleistocene sediments. Other resources (crystalline and igneous stone for axes, obsidian – a distinctive vol-

11 *Gaudo pottery* (British Museum).

canic glass – ochre, amber and metals) were much more restricted in their distribution, and access was only possible through exchange. The sources and the stages in production and for certain of these products can be readily established. Research has been carried out most successfully for obsidian and for some of the earlier metalwork. Little other exchange has left any archaeological trace and can only be surmised to have taken place in conjunction with the trade that has left its mark.

The studies carried out on obsidian illustrate the complexity of the exchange of the period 5000–2800 BC, although characteristically the complexity barely touches the central Italian area. There were many competing sources of this raw material, which had to be brought across the sea, mainly from Lipari, north of Sicily, Palmarola off the Tyrrhenian coast and, to a lesser extent, from Monte Arci on Sardinia. The high-quality Lipari obsidian covered the largest distance. The obsidian that reached central Italy was at the end of a long line of distribution involving many individual transactions. In central Italy it formed only a very small percentage of the stone tool assemblages and has been found only very rarely in the inland tectonic valleys. It is probable that the little obsidian that did reach central Italy was associated with a certain prestige in common with the polished stone axes and fine painted pottery (of Ripoli/Serra d'Alto type) of the same period. The exchange of these items may have served to maintain the social contacts for exchanging items that are not preserved in the archaeological record.

Chalcolithic society was set in a prestige exchange network (see below) centred on fine flint-work and shells. In contrast to this the distribution of metal is illustrative of the more restricted exchange networks of the period before the late Bronze Age (2800–1300 BC). Metal resources were available fairly locally in central Italy and were initially not exploited intensively. Metals are difficult to source. Metal is a commodity that can be re-used and the signature of its original production centre lost or confused. From the work that has been carried out production appears to have been highly localized since the proportion of tin in the bronzework varied considerably. In the succeeding period from 1500–1300 BC only the finest pieces of Apennine pottery might have been exchanged. Although most of central Italy had a common pottery style, it appears to have been little involved in the wider exchange contacts of the Mediterranean.

(iv) **Cultural change.** Cultural change (as defined for our purposes in Chapter V) is measured almost exclusively in terms of different pottery styles. One can only speculate, for instance, on the linguistic groupings involved, even if it might be attractive to see the Etruscans as successors to a residual Mesolithic group speaking a non-Indo-European language. Early Neolithic groups used impressedware pottery and vessels of the 'Sasso Fiorano' type. Painted pottery was generally rare, although some imitations of fine red slipped 'Diana' vessels from the later Neolithic period, have been found. Fine burnished flasks and copper daggers were characteristic of the grave goods of the Chalcolithic period and were strongly linked to status within society (see below). The early Bronze Age is particularly hard to define in central Italy and involves slight changes in typology normally defined as the proto-Apennine but successfully identified only in southern central Italy. From this period distinctive handles and carinated cups become an important characteristic of fine vessels, which continued in many forms into the Archaic period. Prehistoric society, by definition, lacked writing but can, nevertheless, be assumed to have been rich in irretrievable mythology.

The evidence for contacts abroad is much sought by those scholars bent on proving that the 'civilization' of Italy was effectively its Hellenization: but so far the traces of Mycenaean activity in central Italy are extremely tenuous (see further below

in Chapter III). This contrasts substantially with the considerable contact of Mycenaean groups with eastern Sicily, the Lipari islands and southern Italy as far north as Vivara, on the coast near Naples. Explorers from the Levantine coast seem to have been more interested in Sardinia, and most lateBronze-Age developments in proto-Etruscan or 'Villanovan' Italy can be put down to indigenous factors.

(v) **Ritual.** The deposition of exotic objects in caves remained a constant theme of the nonfunerary ritual of later-prehistoric central Italy. A good case is the Grotta Lattaia on Monte Cetona in which various types of exotic painted pottery (including Serra d'Alto and Diana) have been found. The Grotta Lattaia was one of a complex of ritual caves on Monte Cetona that continued in use during the Bronze Age. In particular, large pottery storage vessels filled with grain and other produce were placed in the caves of Belverde as part of a long lasting agricultural ritual that continued for about 1500 years from the Chalcolithic period to the late Bronze Age. Another important case from the Bronze Age is that of Grotta Misa in the Val di Fiora where there was evidence of a periodical ritual involving fire and agricultural produce. Other similar deposits are known for the Bronze Age from Umbria and Lazio. It is interesting that some of these were re-used during the Archaic period.

Evidence for funerary ritual is remarkably scarce for the Neolithic period and when such items are found they form part of more general ritual deposits, such as the Grotta dell'Orso. Only the Chalcolithic period has good evidence for rich burials in organized cemeteries (fig. 12), but these are best considered in the context of social organization (see below). The first part of the Bronze Age has a similar lack of burial evidence until the introduction of cremation burials in well-defined cemeteries in the Latest Bronze Age (c. 1200 BC)

(vi) **Warfare.** Warfare is probably a misnomer for the prehistoric period: 'raiding' is a much more apposite description of the type of conflict that is undertaken by small-scale societies. The technology of warfare at this time was undeveloped.

12 *A Rinaldone tomb under excavation. (Authors' photo: reproduced by kind permission of Nuccia Negroni Catacchio).*

Before 2800 BC, flint and wooden weapons were used; after 2800 BC, weaponry was one of the first types of tool to appear in the new material of bronze. The warfare of the late Bronze Age falls into this same category of raiding, so our main treatment of warfare (Chapter VII) begins *c.* 900 BC.

(vii) **Social organization.** For most of the period before 1300 BC, 'egalitarian' would be the best description of the simple agricultural societies of central Italy, although this term probably carries a number of misleading connotations and masks considerable variation in levels of complexity. The main type of burial in central Italian in the second millennium BC (Rinaldone) was collective: that is, a number of corpses were placed together. In some cases, there was no substantial delay in burial, unlike further north, and individuals were placed with a large number of prestigious flint daggers. There were no major distinctions in wealth between graves; proper social ranking, although claimed for this early date, is difficult to substantiate.

In the next chapter we can begin to unravel the threads of social and political change in Etruscan Italy.

II
SETTLEMENT AND TERRITORY

The Etruscan landscape is easily romanticized: ruins on a plateau; a gorge whose face is pocked with tomb-facades; boys switching cattle through what was once a city shimmering with paintwork and riches. The Roman poets found the transition of Etruscan cities into barnyards a poignant exemplum of the world's ephemerality. Archaeologists, as we noted in our Introduction, have assisted the romantic image by eschewing the excavation of the cities in favour of the tombs: but as the tomb-supply dries up, or as archaeologists become more scrupulous, the cities are beginning to be explored more accurately. As we write, there are two major projects in hand for the excavation of Tarquinia and Cerveteri.

Tarquinia and Cerveteri were two major centres of power, but of course the story of Etruscan settlement does not end with such centres (fig. 13). The land between the cities was also inhabited, and to trace that habitation it has been necessary to develop techniques of field survey that will tell us more or less how many intermediate settlements and farmsteads occupied a certain territory. This sort of research, sometimes derided as 'Boy Scout archaeology' (the British are keen practitioners), has the advantage of being cheap; and although the scope for it within Etruscan Italy remains large, some good results have already been achieved.

We feel able to present a tentative guide to the human geography of pre-Etruscan and Etruscan Italy in four broad chronological stages: the late Bronze Age (c. 1300–900 BC), the Villanovan period (c. 900–750 BC), the Orientalizing period (c. 750–580 BC) and the Archaic/Classical period (c. 580–400 BC). In particular we can establish where and in what sort of density human pop-

13 Ancient and modern sites mentioned in the text.
a Etruria (opposite): 1 Comeana. 2 Quinto Fiorentino. 3 Fiesole. 4 Florence. 5 Monte Falterona. 6 Verucchio. 7 Castellina. 8 Castelnuovo di Berardenga. 9 Arezzo. 10 Volterra. 11 Casal Marittimo. 12 Siena. 13 Murlo (Poggio Civitate). 14 Asciano. 15 Brolio. 16 Cortona. 17 Pianello di Genga. 18 Populonia. 19 Pienza. 20 Montepulciano. 21 Castelluccio di Pienza. 22 Sarteano. 23 Chiusi. 24 Perugia. 25 Colfiorito. 26 Scarlino. 27 Vetulonia. 28 Grosseto. 29 Roselle. 30 Orvieto. 31 Norcia. 32 Monteleone di Spoleto. 33 Talamone 34 Doganella. 35 Magliano. 36 Marsigliana d'Albegna. 37 Poggio Buco 38 Scarceta. 39 Sovana. 40 Pitigliano. 41 Sorgenti della Nova. 42 Castro. 43 Bisenzio. 44 Gran Carro. 45 Piediluco. 46 Grotta a Male. 47 Orbetello. 48 Cosa. 49 Vulci. 50 Regisvilla. 51 Tuscania. 52 Musarna. 53 Castel d'Asso. 54 Viterbo. 55 Acquarossa. 56 Gravisca. 57 Tarquinia. 58 Torrionaccio. 59 Norchia. 60 Luni sul Mignone. 61 S. Giovenale. 62 Blera. 63 Civita Castellana. 64 Monte Rovello. 65 Rota. 66 Civitavecchia. 67 Stigliano. 68 Monterano. 69 Pyrgi. 70 Alsium. 71 Cerveteri. 72 Veii. 73 Fucine. 74 Ficana. 75 Praeneste (Palestrina) 76 Lavinium. 77 Velletri. 78 Cisterna. 79 Satricum.

ulations were gathered and with what degree of formality these populations were structured. At a second level we can interpret these patterns in organizational terms in order to explain why Etruscan settlement was so arranged: human settlement often holds important clues about how society and politics were organized (see also Chapter VIII).

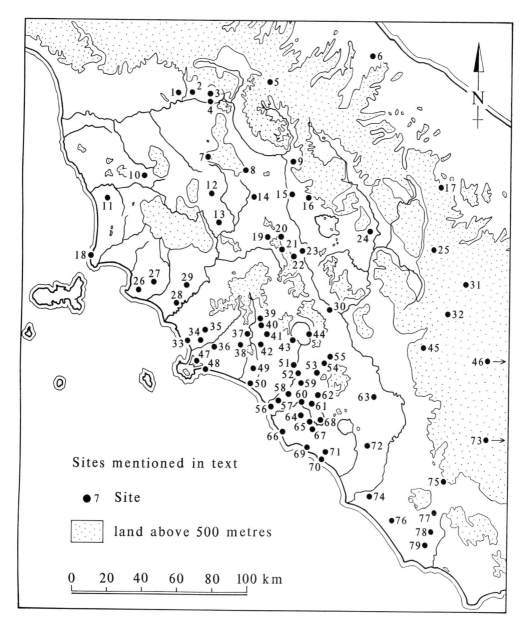

Sites mentioned in text

• 7   Site

land above 500 metres

0   20   40   60   80   100 km

a

Late Bronze Age settlements, 1300–900 BC

As outlined in the Chapter I, the story of Etruscan Italy has to be taken back into the later Bronze Age when the relatively quiescent Neolithic society was transformed into a vibrant Bronze Age economy. From about 1300 BC, there were linked changes in settlement and economy: settlements were relo-

cated in zones that offered a greater potential for agricultural and perhaps metallurgical production. Topographically, settlements became divided equally between upland locations (on a hill or on a naturally defended tufa outcrop) and inland lowland positions.

The latest Bronze Age (c. 1200 BC) appears to have been a period of major demographic expansion, reflected in a major increase in the number of

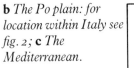

b *The Po plain: for location within Italy see fig. 2;* **c** *The Mediterranean.*

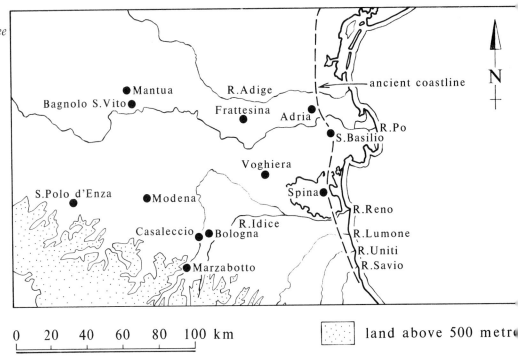

Mantua

Bagnolo S.Vito

R.Adige

Frattesina

Adria

ancient coastline

R.Po

S.Basilio

Voghiera

S.Polo d'Enza

Modena

Spina

R.Reno

R.Idice

Casaleccio

Bologna

R.Lumone

R.Uniti

R.Savio

Marzabotto

N

0   20   40   60   80   100 km

land above 500 metre

Istros

Languedoc

Provence
Cap d'Antibes

ADRIATIC SEA

CORSICA

Rome

Dodona

SARDINIA

Palmarola

Naples

Lesbos

Aeolis

Ischia

Broglio

Ephesus

Alicante

M.Arci

Corfu

Smyrna

Thermopylae

Samos

Lipari Is.

Athens

Euboea

Lycia

Ras el Bass

Motya

Olympia

Corinth

Naxos

SICILY

Sparta

Kition

Syracuse

Rhodes

CYPRUS

CRETE

MEDITERRANEAN SEA

N

Naukratis

0   500 km

Tocra

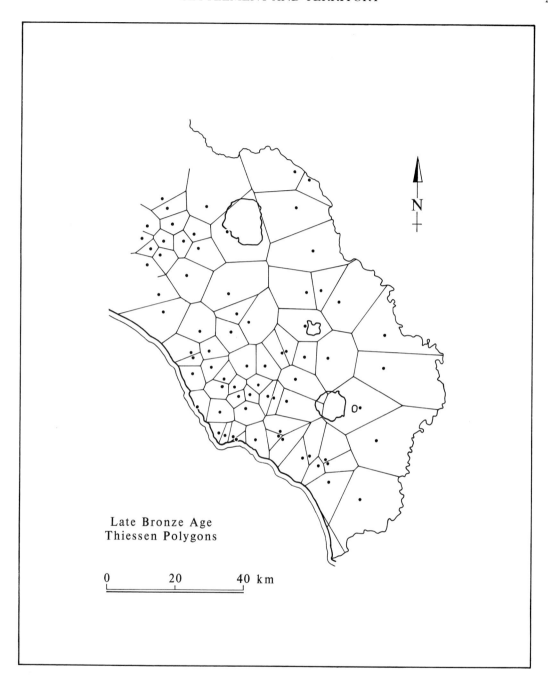

14 *Late Bronze Age Thiessen polygons (after di Gennaro 1982).*

settlements, and this may be an underlying reason for a new crucial factor in settlement location. Settlement was no longer organized predominantly as a response to economic requirements in relation to the local environment but was influenced by underlying socio-political considerations. In other words, settlement was placed in a location not only good for exploiting resources but also considered to be of a suitable social distance from other rival set-

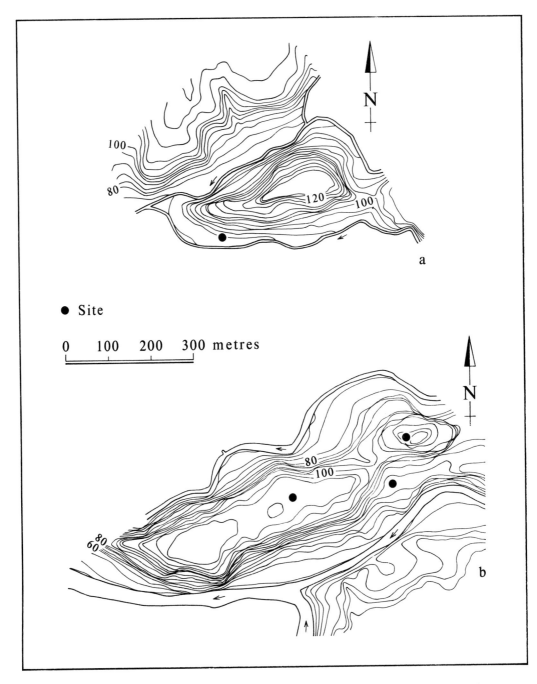

15 *The topography of typical late Bronze Age settlements in South Etruria.* **a** *Torrionaccio (terraced into the side of the hill);* **b** *Luni Sul Mignone (on the summit of the tufa outcrop) (after di Gennaro 1986).*

tlements. Additionally the new settlement organization may have been a response to a degrading environment (see Chapter I) caused by intensive agricultural activity (see Chapter III). Naturally, the solution to these environmental and social requirements varied across pre-Etruscan Italy.

Research has been most intense in South Etruria, between the Tiber to the south and Fiora valley to the north. This work has centred on the examination of tufa outcrops dated by small scatters of material found sometimes on the tufa outcrops themselves and sometimes on the slopes immediately below. A distinctive pattern has emerged revealing that about 65 per cent of known settlements were located on small outcrops of tufa or in upland, similarly defensible, positions. Even allowing for the type of research undertaken, there was clearly a movement towards more defensible upland positions. This suggests the presence of competitive political pressures, characterized perhaps by the intermittent raiding of one group on another to steal resources such as livestock. Not all available defensive positions were occupied; there is evidence that they were sometimes occupied selectively to allow regular spacing between settlements, thus respecting the social distance of one community from another. It has been calculated that each community probably had about 50 sq. km (19 sq. miles) under its control (fig. 14). In addition, over a quarter of these defensible sites appear to have expanded outwards and often downslope from the naturally defined defensive area, creating a localized population nucleus.

This politically motivated pattern of regularly spaced clusters of population was not uniform. There were more dense concentrations of settlement in areas linked to particular resources, such as subsistence and metals, as in the Tolfa hills and the Val di Fiora. In contrast, other areas of south Etruria appear sparsely settled. This view has been substantiated by recent work around the Etruscan city of Tuscania where relatively low numbers of pre-Etruscan sites have been found. Furthermore, undefended settlement locations (cave, lowland, coastal and lakeside), although less intensively investigated, still represent a sizeable proportion (between 30 and 40 per cent) of the total number of known sites.

In spite of these first signs of a politicized landscape in South Etruria, settlements do not appear to have been greatly different in character from one another. The range of settlement size increased overall, but was still concentrated between 1 and 6 ha (2.5 and 15 acres). The average appears to have been about 4.5 ha (11.25 acres), representing a population of perhaps a little over 100 inhabitants. A recent exciting development could change this current pattern drastically, however. Late Bronze Age settlement has been found under the urban occupation of several major Etruscan cities: Orvieto, Tarquinia, Veii and others. These pre-urban settlements may have been of considerably larger size, but so far only limited areas have been investigated.

At present, the internal organization of other villages does not appear to have been very complex (fig. 16). A small village such as Torrionaccio was most probably a string of oval huts terraced into the hillside. A naturally defensible village such as Sorgenti della Nova had small groups of huts cut into the terraced plateau. The building techniques and the internal organization of these settlements were simple. The most characteristic form is an oval house of approximately 11×5 m ($12 \times 5\frac{1}{2}$ yd), cut partly in the rock and held up in part by posts. There is only tentative evidence of any complexity of organization. It has been suggested that some of the structures at Luni sul Mignone, 9×18 m (10×20 yd), and Monte Rovello, 7.65×15.25 m (8×16 yd), were larger and more complex than others, but stratigraphic problems at the first site and lack of extensive excavation at the second make this difficult to assess.

Settlement appears to have been less dense outside South Etruria. Certain areas such as the Chianti, although investigated fairly systematically, seem to lack late-Bronze-Age settlement completely. The effect is partly created by the difficulty in recognizing late-Bronze-Age pottery in some of these areas. The Populonia region is a good example. Only one small village on a low hill (Poggio del Molino) is readily recognizable from pottery types excavated in south Etruria as late Bronze Age. If less rigorous dating standards are accepted, a pattern does emerge in the Populonia/Maremma region: clusters of two or three sites separated by about 25 km ($15\frac{1}{2}$ m) of less densely occupied ground where sites appear to be strung along particular zones of resources. Other clusters of sites have been found further inland. At Monte Cetona an upland limestone escarpment and some slightly lower hillslopes attracted a concentration of indi-

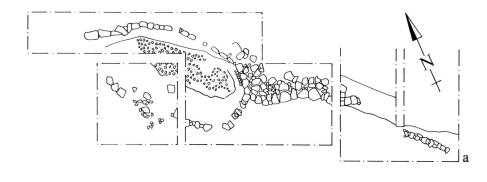

0   5   10 metres

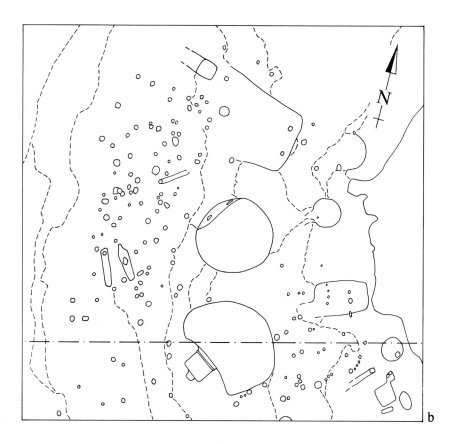

16 *Ground plans of late Bronze Age huts.*
a *Torrionaccio (after Cassano and Manfredini 1978)*
b *Sorgenti della Nova (after Negroni Catacchio 1981).*

vidual settlements. This type of settlement organization was shared by limestone escarpments further east in Umbria, although this is strictly outside the ambit of later Etruscan Italy. Other upland lakeside concentrations of population around the Piediluco and Fucine basins are also outside the later Etruscan area but they illustrate the varied settlement solutions of late-Bronze-Age society. The settlement systems of the late Bronze Age suggest that although identifiable natural resources still directly attracted population, social and political factors were beginning to draw populations together in co-operating units. These units would in turn have required more complex political organization (Chapter VIII) but would not have placed such pressures on society as in the succeeding Villanovan period.

Villanovan-period settlements,
900–750 BC

At about 900 BC the socio-political motivation for the location of the principal settlements became dominant for the first time throughout Etruscan Italy. Although some authors have continued to emphasize the ecological setting of the principal settlements, it is the regular spacing of these settlements that seems the most evident factor. The new structure of settlement was originally considered to be based on radical transfers of population from the dispersed settlements of the Bronze Age to the newly founded nucleated settlements of the Iron Age. The first excavations and detailed surface studies of these major centres have shown, however, that Bronze-Age settlement was already present at least in a restricted area of almost every Villanovan centre in South Etruria. Some of the Bronze Age settlements were better placed in the landscape. Those that could probably enlarged themselves by incorporating people from less well placed settlements. The later changes in the Villanovan Iron Age were still radical and, indeed, had a

profound effect on all later settlement organization; however, they are more explicable in terms of a relatively gradual process, where certain settlements managed to monopolize political power and draw in the population. This mobilization and incorporation of external populations appears to have had an effect also on areas strictly outside later Etruscan Italy: areas such as Piediluco in southern Umbria and the Monti Lucretili in eastern Lazio appear to have been effectively abandoned. This in part allows us to explain the greatly increased surface area of settlement occupied in the Villanovan period within the South Etruria area. Other possible reasons are an increased population and an initial low density of occupation within each settlement area (see below).

The human landscape of South Etruria was undeniably revolutionized. For the first time there was a planned landscape organized in a way that expressed the social distinctions between communities in terms of physical distance. Settlements occupied large plateaux of mainly between 85 and 150 ha (212–375 acres) in extent, containing something like 1000 inhabitants. They were surrounded by their necropoleis (discussed in more detail in Chapter VIII) and controlled, according to some scholars, a hinterland of between 1000 and 2000 sq. km (380–760 sq. miles). Other scholars argue for a gradually developing landscape where large centres would have started by controlling a much smaller area and increased their territorial control only as their political influence increased. In the ninth century BC, few small settlements survived; the examples that did were disproportionately small and located generally in areas peripheral to the major centres.

The measure of the extent of political control from these large centres is a matter of some controversy since it most probably varied over time and there are no historical records to check our conclusions. Some scholars have tended to consider Roman and medieval political boundaries to have their roots in Villanovan and Etruscan times (fig. 17c). This argument can be dismissed since, although some boundaries may be historical, they are by no means inflexible. Further scholars have considered the distribution of specific styles of pot-

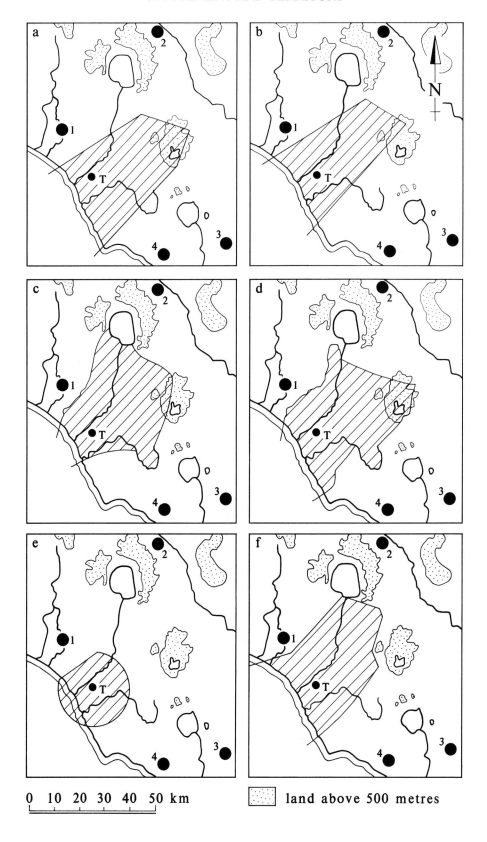

0 10 20 30 40 50 km

land above 500 metres

17 *Modes of measuring territory around Tarquinia.*
a *Thiessen polygon;* **b** *simple weighted Thiessen polygon;* **c** *historical records (after Pallottino 1937);* **d** *Thiessen polygons modified to take account of geographical features;* **e** *XTent mathematical model (undeveloped phase);* **f** *XTent mathematical model (developed phase).* **1** *Vulci;* **2** *Orvieto;* **3** *Veii;* **4** *Cerveteri.*

tery or monumental funerary architecture to be most important. This is also a dangerous procedure since the influence and interaction of a centre can extend much beyond its political control. The continuing debate has led more recent scholars to suggest simple spatial and mathematical solutions (fig. 17), but the problem of such solutions is how to decide the phase of development to which they best apply. In our opinion only one solution (fig. 17e) is suitable for the Villanovan period. The others apply better to a fully developed city state.

The simplest illustrated solution is to place the boundary midway between one centre and its neighbour (fig. 17a). More complex solutions have taken account of either the size and influence of each centre (figs. 17b, e, f) or local geographical boundaries (fig. 17d). Another solution allows the possibility of one centre either being more powerful than its neighbour and incorporating it under its political control or leaving swathes of territory unoccupied (figs. 17e, f). The Villanovan centres probably did not control all the territory between each other but expanded over time as they became more complex politically. This can be confirmed by the recent discovery that colonizing settlements were founded on the probable edge of the political territories of the major settlements after about 100 years of political and economic expansion in the Villanovan period.

Unfortunately, the internal organization of Villanovan period centres is poorly known. Surface

18 *Comparison of Veii in the Villanovan period at two phases of archaeological research.* **a** *1961 (after Ward-Perkins);* **b** *1982 (after Guaitoli).*

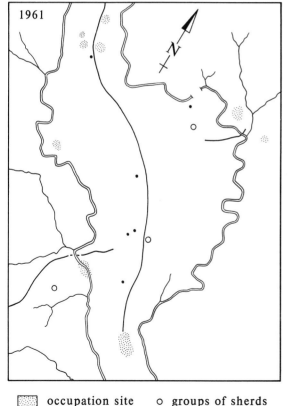
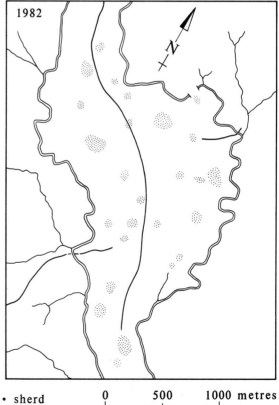

▨ occupation site ○ groups of sherds • sherd

0   500   1000 metres

field surveys have produced conflicting results (fig. 18). Work at Veii in 1961 revealed a number of discrete limited scatters of occupation on the large pla-

19 *Distinctive location of the Iron Age (Villanovan) site of Gran Carro in modern Lake Bolsena (after Tamburini 1986).* **a** *detailed location.*

teau. This suggested the explanation that the original Bronze-Age groups that contributed to the population of the new centre retained a certain individual identity. The identification of separate cemeteries encircling the settlement appeared to support this point of view. More recent work in 1982 recovered a more continuous pattern of settle-

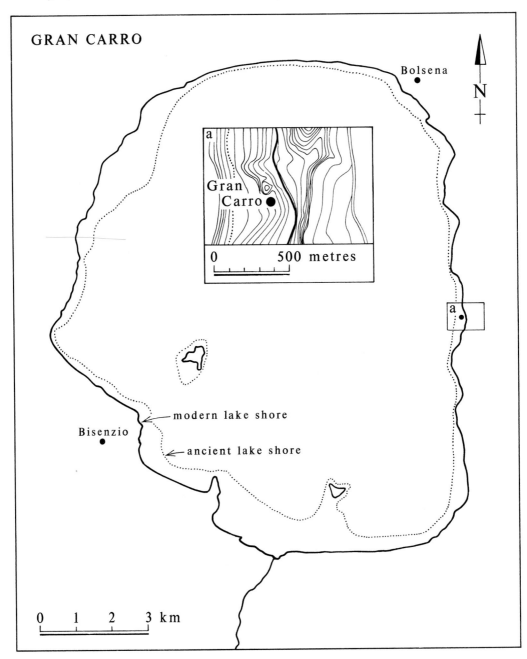

ment that has been interpreted as evidence of a fully unified community from the first occupation of the plateau. These two points of view are not necessarily mutually exclusive. There must have been stages by which the incoming Bronze Age populations were incorporated within the communities that occupied the new centres.

20 *The Villanovan period hut structures at Tarquinia (after Linington 1982).*

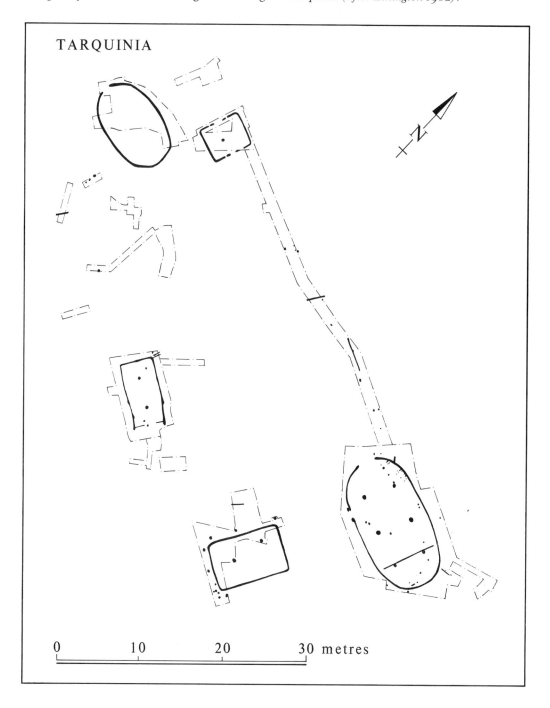

TARQUINIA

0   10   20   30 metres

Only open area excavation can enable these alternatives to be examined. Unfortunately, most of the major centres are covered by the monumental remains of the Hellenistic, Archaic and even medieval and modern periods, and only a few narrow trenches have penetrated below the latest occupation levels in the recent excavations of Tarquinia and Cerveteri between the walls of these later levels, sometimes by mistake. Two settlements have been investigated partly in their own right (the lakeside site of Gran Carro on Lake Bolsena and a small part of Tarquinia) and there is some promise of exciting information from the current excavations at Tarquinia and Cerveteri. Gran Carro, in common with a number of other local contemporary settlements, was preserved beneath the rising waters of the lake in a former volcanic crater. It included the excellent preservation of organic remains discussed in Chapter III, but has lacked systematic study. From the available information, it appears that a small village of about 1 ha (2.5 acres) in size constructed largely of wood was placed on the lake shore (fig. 19). The site is also significant since it provides some information on a small Villanovan-period centre located at some distance from the major centres of population of its time, but this must be regarded as exceptional because of its unusual location on the edge of a volcanic lake.

The work at Tarquinia has been more systematic and as such can be taken as a rare and perhaps representative sample of a large Villanovan-period centre (fig. 20). In the course of test excavation following resistivity survey of the necropolis area, substantial traces of 11 and indications of at least a further 14 Villanovan-period hut foundations were found under the tumuli of sixth-century tombs. Four of these were oval and where reconstructable were of large dimensions (12–16 m × 7–8 m or 13–17$\frac{1}{2}$ yd × 7$\frac{1}{2}$–8$\frac{1}{2}$ yd) supported by four posts. Another seven were rectangular and ranged quite considerably in size and form. The nature of the work and the state of survival did not allow an open area excavation and therefore only slight information on the layout and functional division of the settlement was obtained. The few artefacts that were found were sufficient to confirm the date of the structures and their use for cooking and stor-

21 *The development of Tarquinia in its early phases: the late Bronze Age and the Iron Age (Villanovan).*

age. The evidence was also enough to prove the occupation of an extensive adjacent area of approximately 2 ha (5 acres), at a relatively low density (only half the trenches investigating the tombs found earlier material). It showed that, in the case of Tarquinia, two adjoining volcanic plateaux were occupied at points at least 4 km (2.5 miles) from each other and that these plateaux were not occupied in their entirety, thus forming a dispersed agglomeration of population (fig. 21). Both surface survey (at Veii) and excavation (at Tarquinia) suggest that small clusters of settlement were arranged as distinct but probably co-operating communities across the naturally defined area of the plateaux. At Tarquinia it appears that each of these communities had some larger oval buildings around which smaller square buildings were grouped. This can allow us to infer patterns of increasing differentiation and organization in society of the Villanovan period, although the functional explanation, whereby the oval huts were used for cattle and the rectangular huts for sleeping, is equally possible. The large groupings of population put strains on Bronze-Age society that had to be resolved by the development of new social and political structures.

The pattern of South Etruria was not repeated uniformly elsewhere. The development of northern and eastern Etruria was different in timing and process. A Villanovan-period phase has not been found in some of the later cities (Arezzo) and socio-economic development (reflected in settlement organization) was much slower to develop. Chiusi at the boundary of North and South Etruria formed a somewhat special case. There was a shift in settlement at about 900 BC from the high ground of Monte Cetona occupied in the Bronze Age but this was not uniquely towards the centre of Chiusi. Chiusi was the largest centre but was almost rivalled in size by a ring of smaller contemporary settlements at Sarteano, Castelluccio di Pienza and Montepulciano. This settlement pattern suggests a less centrally organized society and also the basis for a more complex political organization if Chiusi was to control the other local settlements only slightly smaller than herself.

TARQUINIA

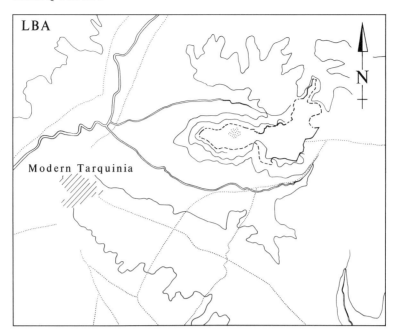

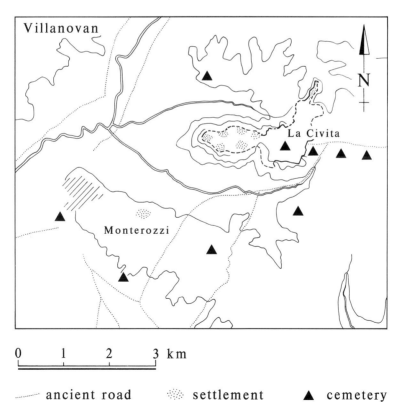

Settlement characterized by its association with 'Villanovan'-type cemeteries also extended south to Campania and north of the Apennines. Only a brief reference can be made here since a full treatment would require a complete analysis of the settlements of north and south Italy beyond the scope of this book. Recent work in Campania, particularly at Pontecagnano and Capua, has concentrated on cemeteries, but the results are sufficient to indicate the increasing wealth of the settlements that have yet to be studied in detail.

Settlement research has, however, been more detailed north of the Apennines. Work has concentrated on two areas: Bologna and Verucchio. The settlements around Bologna developed into a set of large and flourishing communities, whereas the isolated development at Verucchio appears to have had less socio-political importance. A loose nucleation of villages, characterized by cemeteries, has been identified in the area of modern Bologna (initially to the east), from the ninth century BC. In the course of the eighth century BC, these villages became concentrated in a position between the Rivers Ravone and Aposa, the location of the Etruscan city of Felsina (Bologna). From the middle of the eighth century this centre expanded considerably with a major impact on its hinterland, in particular the valleys of the Apennines to the south. At Verucchio, in common with Fermo further south, a small isolated group of settlements developed in the ninth century in a manner distinctive for their associated cremation burial practices. Whereas Fermo rapidly became assimilated in the later-Iron-Age cultural groups of the Marche, Verucchio appears to have continued into the sixth century as a distinctive type of settlement pattern. In common with the settlements of the Villanovan period at Fermo and in Etruria proper, the settlements at Verucchio developed distinctively on a broad hill top with the cemeteries arranged along its flanks. Similarly, the development of these Iron-Age villages probably owed much to the populations of the latest Bronze Age, already present in the area. The cause of this distinctive development may be linked to the strategic position of the main settlement at Verucchio between north and central Italy, as a commercial centre amongst lesser agricultural settlements.

Orientalizing settlements, 750–580 BC

From about 750 BC there was a revolution in material culture, including the range of imported products (Chapter IV). In our present study, this has the fortunate effect of allowing a finer dating of smaller as well as larger settlements. The period appears to have been a phase of major socio-political development whose threads we will draw together in Chapter VIII. The new material culture was exploited by new social groups, who also left their mark on the organization of settlement. Spatially this involved an extension of territorial power by the major Villanovan-period centres with an impact on three aspects of settlement: the internal organization of the major settlements, the intensified colonization by small (c. 10 ha or 25 acres) and very small (less than 1 ha or 2.5 acres) dispersed settlements and the foundation of short-lived, most probably independent, intermediate-sized settlements on the edge of the expanded territories of the pre-existing centres of the Villanovan period.

The evidence for the internal organization of the major centres is extremely scanty, but the promise has been shown by recent discoveries at Roselle of habitation levels. Substantial evidence of food and weaving debris has been found dating to c. 675 BC in association with structures of the same period. A mudbrick building set within an enclosed area was discovered under later Archaic ritual structures during excavation of the Roman forum of the city. The layout of these seventh-century buildings can be considered one of the first signs of the formally organized demarcation of space within the larger centres of population. It also illustrates the problems of piecing together this information from complex urban stratigraphy where later buildings have robbed and reworked earlier levels. A parallel process can be seen topographically at Tarquinia, where settlement and funerary areas were more formally distinguished. From this period, the Monterozzi area appears to have been restricted to cemetery use, and the La Civita plateau became the main centre of population. We can now recognize the classic model of an Etruscan city surrounded by its cemeteries; this model had only partly formed in the Villanovan period (fig. 21).

In zones under the political control of a major

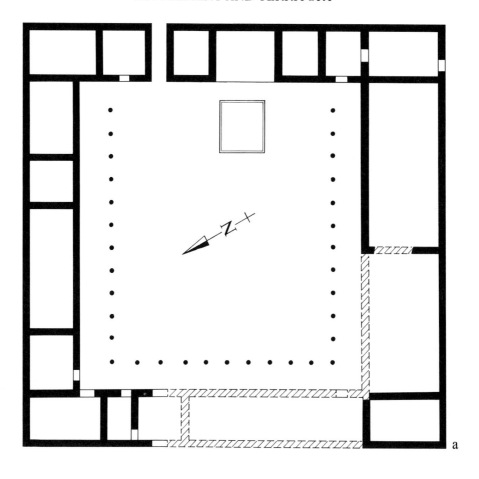

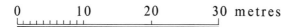

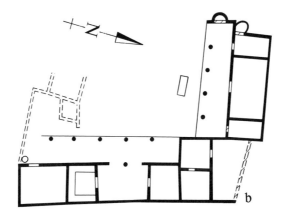

22 *The comparison of colonnaded courtyards from*
a *Murlo and* **b** *Acquarossa (after Prayon 1975).*

centre, there was an increased dispersal of population. Recent survey of the coastal area next to the centres of Populonia, Vetulonia and Roselle has detected small Orientalizing sites in the previously unoccupied intervening area. A further example is the foundation of a group of new moderately-sized settlements (*c.* 10 ha or 25 acres) on the margin of the political territories of major centres such as Vulci (for example, Castro, Poggio Buco and Pitigliano), Tarquinia (for example, Blera, Castel d'Asso and Tuscania) and Cerveteri (for example, Monterano, Stigliano and Rota).

In zones definitely beyond the political control of the major centres (the 'free corridors'), independent settlements of intermediate size (as much as 35 ha or 87.5 acres) were founded. The three primary examples of this development are Acquarossa in South Etruria, Marsiliana d'Albegna on the boundary of North and South Etruria and Murlo in North Etruria. A fourth case is Bisenzio, which survived from the Villanovan period. These are strikingly different types of settlement but they share a significant spatial context: all three are major settlements in their local human landscape and are located on the margins of the major competing local centres. Although the territorial control of all the centres was enlarging over the Villanovan period, there were nevertheless three corridors of resisting territory. The first – and smallest – was in the competitive political landscape of South Etruria, ringed by Orvieto, Vulci, Tarquinia, Cerveteri and Veii, and was occupied by Acquarosa and the Faliscan territory. The second – the largest – was in the more spacious geography of North Etruria, flanked by the large centres of Roselle/Vetulonia, Populonia and Volterra to the west and the smaller centres of Fiesole, Arezzo, Cortona and Chiusi to the east; it was occupied by Murlo. The third was in a natural and human corridor that developed in the Albegna valley between North and South Etruria and was occupied by Marsiliana d'Albegna. These intermediate centres occupied the buffer areas while they were still able to resist the power of their larger neighbours.

From the sixth century, Etruria reached urbanized maturity. The major centres extended their territorial power and brought pressure to bear on the independent centres in the corridors previously beyond their political control. The climax of this was the decline or even the destruction of the centres concerned. Marsiliana d'Albegna was destroyed in *c.* 620 BC; Murlo was destroyed twice, first in 600 BC and finally in 530 BC; and Acquarossa, a stronger, more impressive centre, was eclipsed by her powerful neighbours in about 500 BC. Bisenzio declined over the same period. These larger, politically independent centres were replaced by smaller dependent centres.

The centralization of the authority of the principal cities of Southern Etruria can be seen in the replanning of their internal layout. This replanning often focused on the ritual areas of the city (see Chapter VI), but was never carried out in the rigorous manner prescribed in ritual texts, except in frontier areas. Recent excavation at Tarquinia has shown how, from the seventh century BC onwards, there was a process of monumentalization and successive modification of focal areas of the city. This had already been recorded in earlier excavations at the Piazza d'Armi of Veii, where over a similar period (end of the seventh/beginning of the sixth century) formal rectilinear structures in stone replaced wattle-and-daub curvilinear structures.

The competitive political conditions of the corridor between these principal cities grew extensively over this period. Settlements such as Acquarossa, Murlo and Castelnuovo di Berardenga, before their destruction, responded with elaborate artforms and systematically planned, often ritualized, sectors of the settlement. All three settlements had monumental complexes centred on a colonnaded courtyard (fig. 22) that formed the focus of detailed iconography of authority and power. Even these elaborate measures were not enough to resist the pressure of their powerful neighbours, and the destruction of these settlements heralded the arrival of the Archaic period.

Archaic settlements, 580–400 BC

The human landscape of southern Etruria was dynamic and by no means involved in a steady progress towards political complexity. The ways, means and success of controlling territory fluctuated over time, although, as a general trend, while the political strength of the major cities increased so did the extent of their territorial control. This extended territorial control caused a crisis amongst many of the smaller (less than 10 ha or 25 acres) centres on the boundaries of their territories. In the Vulci area this occurred in the sixth century, for example at Castro. On the margins of the Cerveteri/Tarquinia territory this occurred at the end of the fifth century (Monterano).

Not all the settlements under pressure from the major cities were uniformly destroyed, such as

Tuscania, and recent field surveys may provide some clue as to the different treatment of individual centres. Castro in the seventh century had no known dispersed settlements around it. It appears as perhaps a politically independent microcosm of its powerful neighbour Vulci. Over the course of the sixth century its territory was gradually encroached until the moment of destruction and was replaced by a series of smaller fortified sites. Tuscania, by contrast was surrounded by dispersed settlement in the seventh and sixth centuries and was tolerated by its powerful neighbour, Tarquinia, since it could act in an intermediary role for the control of this dispersed settlement system. In fact in the fourth century it formed part of a

23 *The survey results at the site of La Doganella (after Walker 1985).*

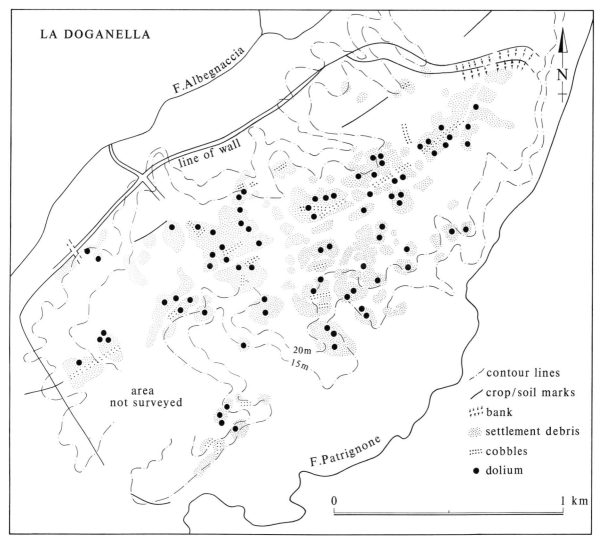

swathe of densely-occupied territory that sat astride the corridor that had formerly been politically independent. Lastly, Monterano formed part of a cluster of dispersed settlements dependent on Cerveteri that appear to have declined together.

A distinctive development of the period was the foundation of ports for the three southern coastal cities that became the formal ritual boundaries between Greek/Phoenician and Etruscan political control. Two of these, Gravisca and Pyrgi, are well known from recent excavations mainly of the ritual areas (see Chapter VI) and a third, Regisvilla, is also under excavation. In settlement terms these are interesting since they represent a modification of the pre-existing settlement pattern as a response to trading contact (see Chapter IV) and were given a ritual dimension to enhance their status on a political frontier between the Etruscan and Greek or Phoenician world. It is interesting to note that the spatial position of Rome may have been very similar: at the ideological boundary between the Etruscan and Latin world.

The important site of La Doganella also probably had a similar mediating role involving commerce on a political boundary, in this case between different cities of north and south Etruria. La Doganella and Magliano were successors to the independent settlement of Marsiliana d'Albegna. Recent detailed survey of the settlement of La Doganella itself permits a fuller treatment, although no standing structures survive (fig. 23). A clear economic and social partition of the settlement can be seen within a walled area of 140 ha (350 acres). The north and west sides of the enclosed area were reserved for storage, cultivation and livestock. A cobbled street with lateral offshoots ran down the centre of the settlement, providing access to rectangular domestic buildings with evidence of storage. Weaving (from loomweights) and metalworking seemed to have been widely dispersed, perhaps at the household level of production, whereas amphorae production appears to have been restricted to the western edge of the settlement as part of a more centralized production system. These distinctions seem to suggest that Doganella was part of a regional production system promoted by Vulci.

South Etruria and beyond

South Etruria was not typical of Etruria as a whole. More northerly areas of Etruria had much less centralized forms of settlement organization. The most clear case is that of Chiusi, where the dispersed settlement system of the Villanovan period was extended. A major difference is probably that the Chiusi area was geared towards subsistence production whereas the southern cities were preoccupied with the control of trade, production and distribution. There is also a clear grading of economic development visible in the settlement organization. The more northerly settlements tend to be smaller and develop later than those of the south and on the coast, and a greater proportion of the population was dispersed in the territory. Important centres such as Perugia and Arezzo developed fully only in the Hellenistic and Roman periods and were on the frontiers of Etruscan expansion in the Archaic period.

The evidence that might differentiate these regional distinctions is difficult to assemble. The smallest Etruscan settlements – the villages and farmsteads and the intensity of land use around them – are not yet well known. Whereas we can make detailed comparisons of the spatial organization of the larger settlements in different regions since they have been almost universally recognized, only a few surveys can be directly compared to provide an understanding of different trends. The territory of Veii appears to have been intensively occupied by small settlements that expanded in number over the Archaic period and were accompanied by technological indicators of intensive agricultural extraction (see Chapter III). At the other extreme, the Chianti area in northern Etruria appears to have had a considerably lower density of occupation with a few scattered settlements. The Albegna valley, the natural corridor between South and North Etruria, appears to have had densities of occupation somewhere in between these two extremes. Only the prime agricultural land was occupied before the Roman period, suggesting a lack of socio-political pressure towards intensification in this buffer area. Political constraints were frequently important, even at this low level of the settlement hierarchy. At Tuscania, small settle-

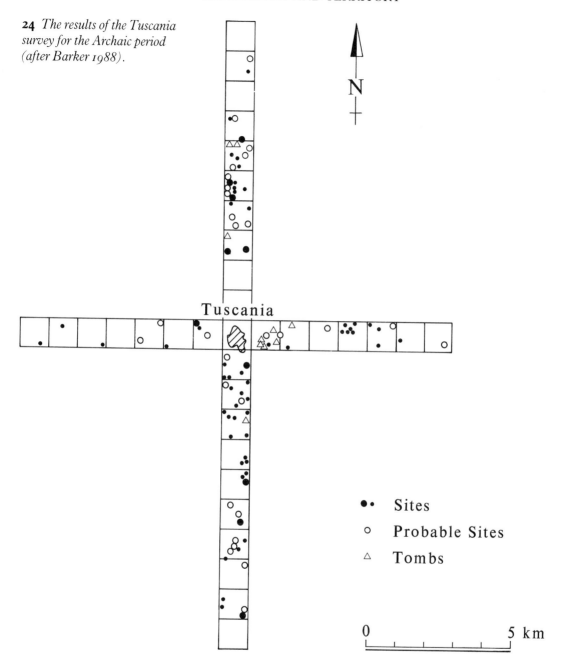

24 *The results of the Tuscania survey for the Archaic period (after Barker 1988).*

Tuscania

●· Sites

○ Probable Sites

△ Tombs

0 ⎣ ⎣ ⎣ ⎣ ⎣ ⎦ 5 km

ments were much more densely distributed in the first 3–7 km (1.8–4.3 miles) around the settlement (fig. 24). Very little work has been directed towards investigating the internal organization of these small settlements, particularly by excavation. Where sites have been excavated they have often proved to be more elaborate than initially

expected. The site of Podere Tartucchino in the Albegna valley is an example of this. A small scatter of archaeological material on the surface of the field concealed a large courtyard structure with evidence for agricultural processing.

The most visible expression of frontier society is located north of the Apennines. The late sixth and fifth centuries were years of profound change when there appears to have been a political expansion of Etruscan power north of the Apennines, affecting a broad area from Verucchio (indirectly) to Spina on the coast to S. Polo d'Enza on the west to Mantua in the north. Some authors have claimed that this formed a unified political expan-

sion centred on Felsina (Bologna), with sites such as Marzabotto, Modena, Spina and Mantua in the second tier and sites such as S. Polo d'Enza, Casa-

25 *The fifth century city of Marzabotto showing functional layout including a detail of a domestic quarter (after Mansuelli 1972).*

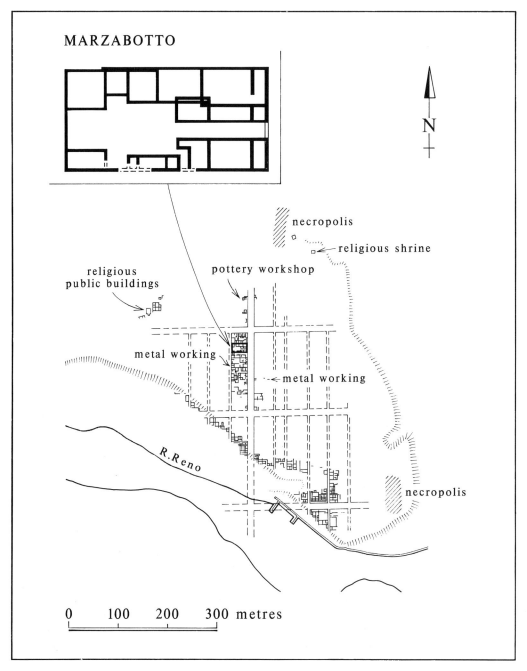

MARZABOTTO

N

necropolis

religious shrine

religious
public buildings

pottery workshop

metal working

metal working

R.Reno

necropolis

0   100   200   300 metres

lecchio, Voghiera and Bagnolo S. Vito in the third tier of the hierarchy. At present it is difficult to confirm the political unity suggested by this picture, but some of the excavated sites do illustrate the processes of settlement formation taking place.

The work at Marzabotto, for instance, illustrates the changes very effectively. Marzabotto has been too frequently proclaimed as a typical representation of the Etruscan city. This it is not. It is nevertheless a very fine illustration of a new town in the spirit of Milton Keynes in Great Britain or Main Street in the United States. The earliest evidence from Marzabotto is from the late sixth century, but this was rapidly replaced by a clear orthogonal plan defined according to ritualized rules (fig. 25). The *cippi* or markers have been identified at the crossroads. The streets were aligned on a grid, and formalized bounded areas were reserved for cemeteries and acropolis. This organization was not purely ritual and also involved the placing of drains and even industrial quarters. Each island block contained seven or eight houses that collectively formed a settlement unit grouped around a central courtyard. A similar process, although of a less idealized formality, seems to have operated at about the same time in the Etruscan landscape generally, working at both a political and a personal level. Some sanctuaries may have marked political boundaries both between Etruscan cities and between the Greek and Etruscan worlds. *Tular* or boundary stones can be seen clearly to demarcate property lines by the late Etruscan period.

Other settlements in the Po valley linked to the Etruscan world had the same regular planning. Spina, one of the two great emporia of the northern Adriatic, was laid out on a grid plan. North of the Po, augering and proton magnetometer survey at Bagnolo San Vito has shown that, in the fifth century, a settlement of about 12–15 ha (30–37.5 acres) was set up, bounded by an earth bank/palisade and at least partly on a regular plan. The plan appears to have been composed of settlement blocks of 120 × 80 m (130 × 87 yd), in part divided by drainage ditches. Excavation revealed evidence of storage and weaving within rectangular wooden post-hole structures. Discoveries at Campo Servirola (S. Polo d'Enza) and Castellarano point to a similar pattern of systematic internal organization.

Something is also beginning to be known of the many smaller settlements of the sixth and fifth centuries that filled in the landscape between the major urban centres of Bologna, Marzabotto and Spina to the south of the Po and Adria and Mantua to the north. S. Basilio near Adria is one of the few to have been excavated, showing simple buildings of wood, wattle and daub. Little evidence has emerged of the internal organization of the settlement, although the fine imported products may demonstrate its role as a small redistribution centre.

It should not be assumed, however, that the planned cities of the Po valley were simply the products of a frontier society on the fringes of Etruscan civilization. The settlement of Musarna in South Etruria shares many of the characteristics of planning. It is again a 'new town' founded in the late-Archaic/late-Hellenistic period on the political frontier of Tarquinia and was probably under Tarquinian jurisdiction. Furthermore, recent survey at Tarquinia appears to have picked up the imposition of a late orthogonal road organization in the city itself. This can probably be linked to the contemporary construction of walls for the city, symbolizing certain ideological changes in society.

Early urban development was more typically organic: in other words it did not take the form of regular planning but developed largely piecemeal. The best information for the early Archaic period comes ironically from the atypical centre of Acquarossa. Here the impression of limited planning *ex novo* and much modification of pre-existing structures is correct, even though the period of occupation was relatively short (200 years or less for most of the building phases). An area of about 1.5 ha (3.75 acres) was excavated on the edge of the naturally-defined plateau where sedimentation had protected the finds more successfully. Zone B is typical of irregular urban development (fig. 26); the curved wall is of an earlier date than the rest of the buildings. Although the buildings are rectangular in form, they are arranged fairly casually. Short-term solutions have been adopted to deal with inconsistencies of the terrain, repairs and new domestic requirements. Even the monumental complex of Zone F has three phases of construction and did not conform to a preconceived plan. Some

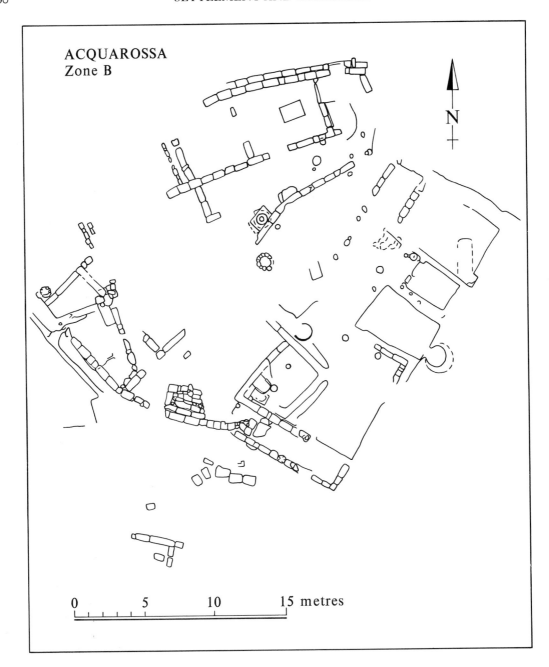

26 *Zone B at Acquarossa (after Viden 1986).*

more densely occupied areas were perhaps organized more regularly (Zone N). These different urban zones most probably reflect different phases and sectors of urban organization. For instance, the more central parts of the city appear to have had the larger centrally planned houses of the richer social classes although most house plans seem to be modifications of the same basic plan: two adjoining rooms entered from one of the long sides and successively improved by the addition of further rooms and a covered sheltered courtyard area. The extensive excavation of different urban sectors has allowed the excavators to make more soundly-based estimates of the density of occupation at 120–210 inhabitants per ha (50–55 per acre) i.e. 4000–7000 people on the 32-ha (79–acre) site. If we can extend this analysis to the largest urban centres we can perhaps estimate a maximum population of about 35,000 people in an Etruscan city.

Settlement organization is a good indicator of the degree of socio-economic development of a particular region. It is so interlinked with the components of human organization that a map of the size and distribution of settlements and the intensity of activity around them can help towards a ready assessment. These are the sorts of contrasts that distinguish Tarquinia from Chiusi and in turn Chiusi from Arezzo.

III
SUBSISTENCE, TECHNOLOGY AND PRODUCTION

Classical authors, followed closely by some classical archaeologists, have given an impression of the Etruscans as an over-indulgent and reprehensibly hedonistic people, prone to corpulence and given to copulating at all hours of day and night. This example of Graeco-Roman xenophobia (see, for example, Diodorus Siculus Bk VIII, 18) is thought to be partially confirmed by the predilection during the fifth century BC for feasting scenes painted on the walls of aristocratic tombs at Tarquinia and elsewhere or even by the later appearance of paunchy figures on sarcophagus covers. In Augustan Rome the jibe *pinguis Etruscus* ('fat Etruscan') could still be made against the roly-poly gourmets who figured in the Roman aristocracy and whose ancestors had been Etruscan. Roman or Etruscan, the picture is distorted: it is silent about the supporting levels of subsistence and production without which no aristocracy could have survived. This image of the opulent Etruscans would not have been possible without a highly organized system of technology and production, but this system was last researched intensively and directly only in the 1920s and has been much neglected until recently. Those who have tried to reconstruct subsistence, technology and production have employed purely indirect indicators. Changes in metal types have been used to understand the economy of earlier periods. Artistic representations, the biased fictions of the classical authors and even eccentric linguistic studies have been extensively used to understand the economy of later periods. Different periods produce different problems, however.

Whereas sites of the latest Bronze Age are now rarely excavated without sampling deposits for faunal and floral remains, reconstruction is least successful for the Villanovan period, the crucial period of social change that lacks settlement excavation. An increased number of settlements of the main Etruscan period have now been excavated, but very few of these have had systematic collections made of bones and seeds. Nevertheless, it is now possible to present new evidence that begins to give us an understanding of the workings of Etruscan subsistence and technology.

The late Bronze Age: increased production

By 1200 BC, there had been a long history of agriculture in central Italy, but production had never been very intensive. From *c.* 1200 BC, or even 1300 BC, the picture completely changes. Agricultural production entered a series of predominantly expansionistic cycles until taken over by the Roman empire. These developments cannot be separated from the studies of settlement and society (see Chapters II and VIII), but here it is possible to report the direct evidence. Two watersheds seem to have been particularly crucial: the development of a sophisticated mixed economy by *c.* 1000 BC and the intensive employment of the classic Mediterranean polyculture (grain, vines and olives) by 600 BC. The crossing of these watersheds had a potentially negative effect on the physical environment, which in turn required technological, economic and social responses. In the late Bronze Age, a diverse and relatively sophisticated mixed economy emerged, although regionally it remained heavily dependent on pastoral activities. A direct indication of this diversity is provided by the study of the refuse of animal bones.

Three major domesticated animals – sheep/goats, pigs and cattle – usually contributed more than any others to the economy. Only a single sample from the site of Sorgenti della Nova indicates a presence of more than 10 per cent of other species. In some respects, this is not a novelty. The importance of the three major domestic species can be matched as early as the Neolithic period. We can, though, identify an increasingly intensive system where plant production is complemented by animal production. By the later Bronze Age animals were exploited not merely for meat but also for less direct products such as milk and manure. Sophisticated artefacts probably designed for making cheese have been found from the middle Bronze Age. Manuring and simple ploughing by oxen may by this stage have allowed the intensification of plant production. This production system is very different from the garden plots close to the settlement, which were most probably characteristic of the Neolithic period.

The main domesticated animals

The importance of these three domestic species requires them to be examined in some detail. The diversity of the subsistence economy is easily illustrated by comparing the number of identified fragments of each species using a pie chart for each site and then summarized together in a triangular diagram (fig. 27).

Certain trends are easily identified and can be contrasted with the few sites that do not conform. The first clear trend is that of a set economic pattern, whilst allowing considerable diversity in the importance of two of the species: sheep/goats and pigs. A second trend is that cattle provide consistently less than 50 per cent of the total bone refuse (although it should be pointed out that the technique of identifying fragments may underestimate

the importance of cattle, depending upon how far they were used as a meat supply rather than beasts of burden or suppliers of milk).

The overall pattern is that sheep/goat is generally the most favoured species (between 35 and 60 per cent), with pig (15–40 per cent) or cow (10–45 per cent) in second place. Sheep and goats could have been used for extensive grazing, pigs for more local browsing near the settlement and cattle for a secondary supportive role for traction, dairy products and leather. There are some exceptions to this general trend. At Sorgenti della Nova 72 per cent of the bones were from domestic pig. These figures are based on the finds from one deposit within the site but they nevertheless suggest a considerable specialization in pig (and therefore predominantly meat) production; this is increased if wild boar is also taken into account (see below). A similar specialization but in sheep/goat prevailed at Torrionaccio and Luni sul Mignone.

The late-Bronze-Age subsistence economy cannot be predicted from the nature of the local environment. Two sites on the fringes of Etruscan Italy illustrate this. Gubbio (Mount Ingino) and Grotta a Male have very different subsistence economies, although both are upland sites above 900 m (3000 ft). Torrionaccio and Sorgenti della Nova in South Etruria are in broadly similar volcanic environments but have markedly different stock-rearing practices. By contrast, S. Giovenale and Gubbio have surprisingly similar economies, although the local environment is radically different. Some of the diversity represented in samples may or may not directly reflect differences in stock rearing (or difficulties encountered by archaeologists in translating numbers of bones into numbers of animals in the economy). Rubbish may have been disposed of in various ways. In some sites the samples are from large middens or rubbish heaps, at Gubbio for example: only Gubbio has a sample with more than a 1000 identified fragments. In others the samples are from domestic areas of the settlement, for example at Torrionaccio. Further diversity may stem from ritual or symbolic factors: the artificial caves of Sorgenti della Nova and the isolated midden of Monte Ingino at Gubbio may be such examples. The high presence of pig in both cases may be an indication of feasting. (In the

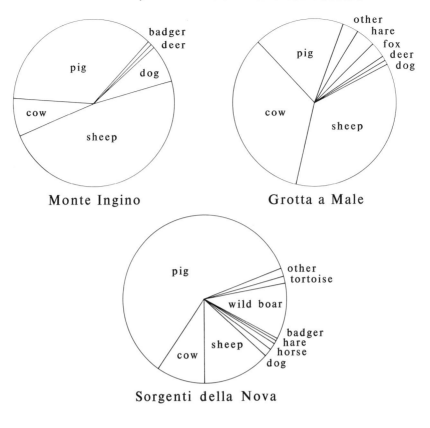

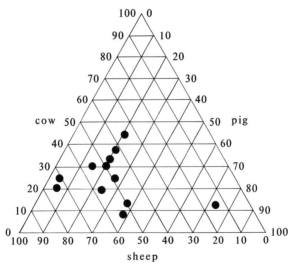

27 *The comparison of late Bronze Age stock rearing economies.* **Above** *pie charts of three distinctive economies from central Italy: Monte Ingino (Gubbio) (an upland midden in Umbria), Grotta a Male (an upland cave in the Abruzzo) and Sorgenti della Nova* *(a lowland defended site in Etruria).* **Below** *all published Bronze Age faunal deposits in central Italy, compared using a triangular (percentage) diagram for the three principal domesticated species.*

Roman world, pork was an 'élite' meat.) Even allowing for these other explanations, it is clear that there were, within broad constraints, a number of alternative strategies for husbandry during the late Bronze Age, including balanced production or specialization in a single species.

Other animals

The species enumerated here form a much lower percentage of the total bone refuse (generally less than 10 per cent). Nevertheless the diversity within this 10 per cent may have been locally significant. Some dogs were present on all but two sites. Sheep dogs may have been employed in the control of flocks, and a particularly high proportion of them (7.6 per cent) has been found in Gubbio, one of the upland sites. The horse is a more controversial domesticate at this period. There is convincing evidence now from Narce, Gubbio, Sorgenti della Nova and Colle dei Cappuccini that horses were already present in small quantities. To this, examples of ass can be added from Luni, Torrionaccio and Sorgenti della Nova. These two animals played a very different economic role. The ass was principally a beast of burden, whereas horses were probably prized by certain restricted social classes as possessions of prestige (see further below and Chapter VII).

Wild animals have been found at every site except Torrionaccio. Deer (roe and red) were the most frequent of these and in one of the Luni samples they comprised 10 per cent of the total. There is some evidence that wild and domesticated versions of the same species played a role in certain stock economies. At Luni (Tre Erici), domesticated cow (43 per cent) was found in association with wild stock (1.5 per cent). Even more strikingly, wild boar (10 per cent +) in addition to domesticated pig made up a high proportion of the animals at Sorgenti della Nova. These may represent hunting activities or deliberate breeding practices where wild stock was introduced to add advantageous characteristics to the domestic stock. Other wild animals are considerably less important and may have accidentally become part of the faunal deposit (badger, fox, dormouse, bat), although the tortoise appears in two riverine contexts

(Narce and Sorgenti della Nova), and hare may represent opportunistic trapping. Fish are present on Monte Ingino, Gubbio, at over 900 m (3000 ft), and, less surprisingly, at Poggio del Molino, Populonia, on the coast; in part, the low recognition of fish in other sites is probably related to sampling procedures (including the lack of fine sieving).

The reduction of wild species may be partly a chronological trend; the later site of Torrionaccio and the later phases of S. Giovenale and Narce have less or, in the case of Torrionaccio, no deer. There is also an environmental factor: upland sites such as Monte Ingino and Grotta a Male have relatively high proportions of wild fauna, and indeed herds of deer may still be sighted there.

A more detailed analysis of two sites: Narce and Gubbio

At Narce, a clear stratigraphy analysed with an appropriate archaeological methodology has allowed more concrete, if localized, results. At this site there seems to have been a stable mixed economy with few important fluctuations throughout the period of the late Bronze Age (and indeed into the later periods). In this analysis, the minimum number of individuals has been calculated for the various species; no evidence has been found for a different degree of break-up of bone. If the animals were raised exclusively for meat, cattle would have been the most important, followed by sheep/goats and pigs. Work has also been carried out on the age structure of the animals at the time at death. Most of the sheep/goats were killed in their second or third year; this strategy probably allowed maximum production of both meat and secondary products such as wool and milk. Pigs were also killed mainly in their second or third year of life, presumably for their meat. Cows were killed at an older age and, given their small numbers, were probably valued for their specialized products other than meat (including traction).

The preliminary results of a similar methodological approach at Gubbio can be added to these analyses. It is probable that the midden represents the refuse of periodic feasting rather than the full subsistence economy. Most sheep and pigs were killed at less than two years old; only cattle, present in much smaller quantity, may have kept a more specialized role in providing milk and traction.

Plant foods

Other food refuse is found in the form of carbonized seeds and nuts, which are rarely recovered unless samples of soil are taken and the carbonized remains collected by flotation. This evidence also contributes to the picture of a relatively diversified mixed economy. A similar range of species is present at most sites, but different crops seem to be more important at some sites. At Sorgenti della Nova, broad bean, barley and bread wheat are present. At Narce, emmer is the dominant species, followed by broad bean, pea and other rarer items such as Cornelian cherry. At Torrionaccio, there is a spread of species in the small sample: einkorn, emmer wheat, bread wheat, barley and broad bean. A similar pattern is visible at Luni sul Mignone with the addition of vetch. The evidence from Gubbio suggests greater flexibility and a rather different form of exploitation; although emmer is present with barley, the presence of pea and spelt suggest a localized upland adaptation.

Other indicators of the human impact on the environment

In a few favoured locations of Central Italy the same exceptional preservation conditions of the sub-Alpine Bronze-Age villages of northern Italy are encountered. As in northern Italy, settlement structures and associated debris have been preserved in waterlogged conditions. Submerged on the edge of some of the volcanic lakes of South Etruria wooden structures of this period have been found that give some idea of the vegetational resources exploited. A further potential indicator of environmental conditions is pollen since, under certain conditions, ancient pollen survives and can be identified as belonging to a specific species. Only a few pollen studies are available from the volcanic lakes of South Etruria and these seem to show limited effects of cultivation on the micro-environments of the volcanic craters from which the pollen mainly derives. The work carried out in the Gubbio valley attests the intensification of land use during the late Bronze Age and a correspondingly more diverse and intensive production of food.

Subsistence in the ninth and eighth centuries BC

For the early Iron Age (ninth and eighth centuries BC), direct subsistence evidence is less available; this is not unconnected with the rarity of settlement excavation. At Narce, the animal sample appears to indicate relative continuity in the stock economy, marked only by a slight fall in the proportion of cow. The limited macrobotanical evidence from Gubbio around 760 BC suggests intensification by specialization in club/bread wheat. The most spectacular, but highly exceptional, evidence comes from Gran Carro, a well-preserved lakeside site in southern Etruria. In the local waterlogged conditions of this very distinctive ecosystem, cultivated grapes dominate the sample of seeds. This is the earliest known appearance of the cultivated vine in central Italy, although earlier occurrences of wild vine are known from Belverde and the full Mediterranean polyculture (of grain, vine and olive) has been claimed from Brolio in Southern Italy in the final Bronze Age. The Gran Carro sample is otherwise dominated by collected fruits such as cherry, plum and to a lesser extent hazelnut. Some more common agricultural plants, such as emmer and broad bean, are present only in small quantities, perhaps because of the particular conditions of the volcanic lake where agriculture was less important.

Subsistence in the seventh and sixth centuries BC

Subsistence studies of the seventh and sixth centuries are depressingly dependent on indirect evidence and the testimonies of later classical authors. Few palaeobotanical or faunal studies have been undertaken and these have generally received low priority in terms of prompt or detailed publication. A recent lavish publication on Etruscan food had less than one-fifth of its contents devoted to the direct evidence of Etruscan food refuse. Furthermore, many of the excavations are related to exceptional, even ostentatious, consumption in funerary and ritual contexts. This is equally true of the evidence from Archaic Rome. Some faunal and floral evidence is available from tomb and other ritual contexts, but this is neither readily quantifiable nor interpretable strictly in economic terms. We can simply report that einkorn, emmer, barley, beans, peas, pigs, sheep/goats, cattle, deer, fish, tortoises and birds were consumed in the funerary rituals of seventh-century Rome. Some other ritual evidence is also recorded for the consumption/sacrifice of cattle, sheep/goats and pig in the pre-Archaic phases of the sanctuary of S. Omobono in Rome.

Two good collections of bone refuse from the seventh/sixth century (from Tarquinia and the S. Giovenale Spring Building) are most probably from highly distinctive, specialized deposits that almost certainly have a religious origin. Deer may be a token of these non-domestic deposits (perhaps related to the cult of Artemis). In the S. Giovenale Spring Building the proportion of deer reaches 56 per cent. No other site in the late Bronze Age had such a high proportion, and the change makes a particular contrast with the quantity found in earlier phases of the same site (less than 5 per cent). The quantity of deer found in the Tarquinia sample is somewhat less (21 per cent), but whereas S. Giovenale was probably still in a largely wooded environment, Tarquinia was by this time a fairly urbanized centre with a highly agricultural territory. Tortoises also appear to have been an important component of the rituals conducted in these centres. The prominence of these ritual deposits suggests that a more systematic sampling procedure needs to be carried out in most urban excavations. We do not have a proper cross-section of refuse deposits, and most collections of plants and seeds are too small to be significant. A further bias is that sacred bones were probably carefully preserved in sacred deposits whereas domestic bones were most probably less delicately cared for and even redistributed as manure on the fields around the settlements.

Despite the inadequacies of our evidence, it remains clear that in the changed economic and political context of Archaic Etruria there is a greatly increased complexity in subsistence production. For the first time, at Acquarossa, cattle appear to be more important than sheep/goats or pigs. From one well documented – and apparently domestic – Etruscan sample of this period at S. Giovenale, pigs and sheep/goats are the most important followed by cattle and deer. At the contemporary rubbish deposit at Narce, there is continuity from the Bronze Age; sheep and goat remain the most important animals, followed by a relatively equal importance of cattle and pigs. A small farm of the sixth century BC recently excavated near Tuscania has yielded signs of specialized wool production. The evidence from Murlo suggests a further variant where cattle and pigs are most important with only a secondary exploitation of sheep/goats. Another interesting dimension is that aristocratic hunting (on the basis of wild boar, deer and wild goat) often appears to have been widely practised in these communities.

The unspeakable are here in pursuit of the highly edible; and it is worth pointing out that the wild boar, or *cinghiale*, is to this day much prized by the alarming number of Italian men in possession of shotguns. Modern hunting is not the preserve of the rich and there is so far little evidence of difference in diet between social groups within the Etruscan communities, since the vast majority of the reported samples are by-products of the excavation of elaborate rather than humble structures. The iconography of Etruscan hunting, however – as evident from painted vases and tombs, for example the *Tomba del Cacciatore* at Tarquinia – suggests that it was conducted by cavaliers, with retainers running along on foot.

The intensive employment of Mediterranean polyculture has to be inferred largely indirectly (fig. 28). Grain was used intensively from at least the end of the second millennium BC after the widespread introduction of bread wheats as well as the less developed einkorn and emmer. The wild vine has been noted in a number of Bronze-Age sites such as Scarceta and Belverde, and the cultivated vine appears to have present in some quantities at least from the ninth century in Etruscan Italy. The olive is known from north and south Italy in the Neolithic and Bronze Age, but it cannot be conclusively proved to have been cultivated on a major scale in central Italy until the seventh century. Evi-

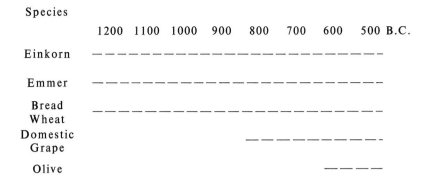

Species	1200	1100	1000	900	800	700	600	500 B.C.
Einkorn	————————————————————————
Emmer	————————————————————————
Bread Wheat	————————————————————————
Domestic Grape					——————————
Olive						————

28 *The probable dates for the introduction of intensive production for five principal cultivated crops (einkorn, emmer, bread wheat, the domestic grape and the olive).*

dence of extensive transport of storage of olives has been found in a shipwreck off the island of Giglio dating from *c.* 600 BC, and smaller vessels may have been used even earlier in the seventh century. A bronze vessel containing olives has also been found in the Tomb of the Olives at Cerveteri (dating from 575–550 BC).

Some limited reported evidence from Acquarossa in the sixth century suggests a developed Mediterranean polyculture system, based on the production and consumption of wine, oil, barley, emmer, oats, beans, vetch and peas. Podere Tartuchino, a small Etruscan farmhouse of the sixth century from the Albegna valley, has produced intriguing initial evidence from a different scale of settlement; grape pips, cereals and ecologically specific weeds suggest that our models of production can soon be much more sophisticated as a result of detailed knowledge at the farmstead level. The Mediterranean polyculture system also has to be considered in its social context. In the eighth and seventh centuries, wine and oil were probably restricted in their availability for consumption. Drinking vessels found in élite graves reinforce this impression. Similarly the prominence of large, often imported, storage amphorae in 'chiefly' graves suggests a prestige value for the consumption of olive oil. This pattern was certainly transformed in the course of the sixth century since later floral evidence suggests a wide availability of the products of this typical Mediterranean system.

The horse, although presumably dissociated from subsistence, was another token of social status, probably because of its importance for the conduct of civil and military protocol. Its presence is insignificant in most faunal assemblages (except possibly at Murlo). We can see from artistic representations, trappings and tomb burials that the horse clearly had a prestige value. The horse appears to have been primarily restricted to northern Italy until the Villanovan period. Horse bits from this period first indicate the prestigious quality of such animals.

It has been suggested that a new, more refined breed was introduced as part of the Orientalizing trade network of the late eighth and early seventh centuries, but this zoological question cannot at present be satisfactorily resolved. It is clear that from this period onwards, horses (and sometimes their associated chariots or wagons) were deposited in 'chiefly' tombs in locations as widely spaced as Populonia, Vulci, Vetulonia, Cerveteri, Marsiliana, Sovana and Monteleone di Spoleto. The horse was a prized part of the élite ideology of the emerging cities of Etruria and Umbria, essential to the status of a cavalier or 'horse-taming' class.

Bagnolo S. Vito, a newly-explored and important site near Mantua, has provided some detailed evidence of subsistence production from a 'frontier' society in the Po valley. The molluscan assemblages confirm the damp, freshwater, but changeable, environment. In this environment pigs appear to have played the dominant role, followed by much lower frequencies of sheep/goats and cattle. Some wild animals were hunted, such as deer and wild birds, but these were of relatively little importance. The ages at death of these species have been interpreted in terms of specialized meat production from pigs, wool and milk production from sheep/goat, and milk production from cows. It is even suggested that pig production involved a sophisticated rearing operation that created a surplus over and above the needs of the settlement and thus created a potential for exchange. Plant foods seem to have followed a similarly distinctive pattern. Legumes appear to have been much more important than cereals, so that einkorn, emmer, bread wheat and barley, although present, were considerably outnumbered by large quantities of beans (particularly in one possible storage area), lentils and peas. The vine was present in only limited quantities. The overall pattern is of a type of specialization not seen in the central part of Etruscan Italy: an adaptation to the local ecology.

Two late faunal and floral samples of the third century from good domestic contexts at Populonia on the coast, at Blera inland and at a ritual well at Pyrgi, suggest some of the possible developments over the intervening period. The faunal samples show the same emphasis on the principal three domesticated species, cattle, sheep and pigs, but there are also signs of the maturity of a mixed Mediterranean farming economy. At Blera, olive stones and grape pips occur in some quantity in a well deposit, suggesting a considerable intensification of these easily recognizable Mediterranean products. There is, furthermore, evidence that the chicken was now part of the farmyard economy as well as other birds. At Populonia, pig was the most important of the domesticated species. The contribution of wild animals appears to have been negligible and where present to have been dominated by small game (such as fox, hare and birds) and roe deer, which prefer more open terrain. All the indications are that the open farmed landscape known in the Roman period was already highly developed. The relative importance of meat in the diet has to be derived from separate sources. Analyses of the proportion of strontium in human skeletal remains suggest a gradual increase in the vegetable component of the Etruscan diet between the Archaic and Hellenistic periods. Ritual consumption appears to have continued much as before. Important evidence is beginning to come from the excavations of the sanctuary of Pyrgi, where, within a pit near the altar of Area C, a good collection of sacrificed bulls or cows, pigs and other wild and domesticated animals was found dating to the third century BC.

Intensified use of land and sea

The clearest evidence of intensification in subsistence is derived from indirect technological sources and from the study of settlement. Other changes can perhaps be inferred, although material evidence is difficult to find. By the eleventh century BC, hillside terracing must have been an important skill in order to intensify production on the steep and unstable slopes of many areas of Etruria and Umbria. The late-Bronze-Age site of Torrionaccio was terraced into a hillside, and a high proportion of other contemporary sites in South Etruria were located on hillslopes. Much of this localized terracing was probably abandoned when settlement was radically reorganized in the ninth century BC only to be taken up again more intensively from the seventh century onwards.

By the sixth century BC, hydraulic engineering (particularly drainage) was also clearly employed in the most developed areas of south Etruria. In the territory of Veii, underground channels (cuniculi) to divert streams causing erosion problems were constructed at least before the fourth century BC (fig. 29); in this context, the soft tufa allowed a ready engineering solution. There is no evidence, however, that potentially more serious drainage problems in the inundated coastal areas and lake basins of north Etruria were solved so effectively. These engineering projects can be combined with other evidence to show the intervention of centralized political authority outside the major centres. For instance, it was the Etruscans who constructed the first major roads and bridges in central Italy. These communication routes certainly served as much for the control of the production and distribution of subsistence goods as in the movement of the more precious objects that have survived better and are readily seen in the modern museum.

Some limited evidence is now available for an understanding of marine technology. Enough shipwrecks have been located along the Tyrrhe-

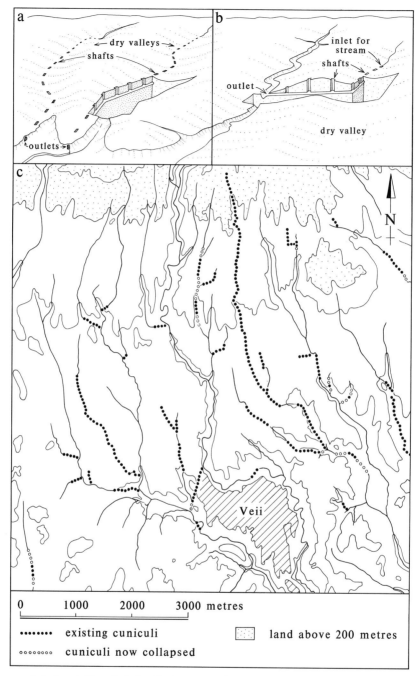

29 *Drainage tunnels in South Etruria (after Judson and Kahane 1963).* **a** *longitudinal tunnels (along valleys);* **b** *transverse tunnels;* **c** *distribution of tunnels.*

nian coastline to provide some demonstration of the nature of Etruscan communication by sea; however, few of these finds have been excavated properly, and only a few details of the constructional techniques have been recorded. The relative importance of marine resources for subsistence has

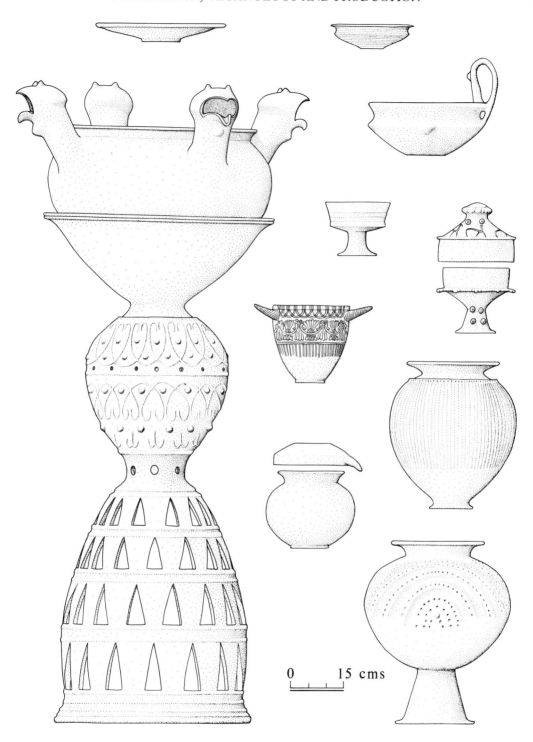

30 *The archaic banqueting service recently discovered at Ficana (after Rathje 1983).*

also been little researched. The presence of fish at Populonia and at other sites indicates the obvious: that, at least in coastal areas, marine resources (as in the Bronze Age) must have played a considerable role in the diet. This is confirmed by the indirect evidence of seafaring and fishing equipment represented in figurines, on pottery vessels and in other figurative form, as reported so readily in most books on Etruscan thalassocracy, i.e. control of the sea.

The technology of eating well – or less well

Pottery is strongly related to eating and drinking, although this is not always clear from the studies that have been carried out in Etruria. These studies

have preferred to follow the lines of attribution, the typology and dating. Whilst the subject of this work has been the most expensive, elaborate cooking and food vessels, these formed only a small part of Etruscan ceramics. Three major assemblages can be distinguished: those for the élite and the ritual occasion, those for everyday cooking and finally those for storage.

The utensils of banqueting are preserved in great quantities. These consist primarily of the luxury containers of bronze and imported pottery in which wine and food were placed. Most of these have been found in tombs and are consequently not typical of everyday use. They also include bronze or iron spits for roasting, fire dogs, on which the spits would have been placed, and large metal cauldrons and tripods. A whole banqueting service discovered in an Archaic house at Ficana in Lazio is probably representative of this type of lifestyle tak-

31 a–i *Etruscan cooking stands (after Scheffer 1981;* **j** *a middle Bronze Age 'milk boiler' (after Barker 1981).*

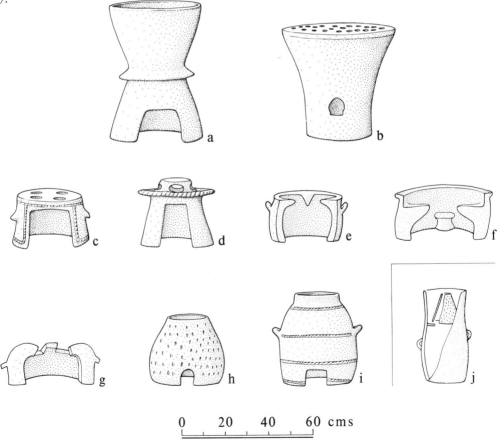

0   20   40   60 cms

ing place at a similar period in Etruria (fig. 30). This service for about 30 people consisted principally of large containers for holding liquid, chalices for drinking and a range of plates.

Everyday cooking has proved to be a less attractive focus of study because it involves coarser, undecorated pottery. Several types of cooking have been distinguished from the study of cooking stands (fig. 31): the long, slow heat of varying intensity over different types of cooking stand, the baking in a small oven and the roasting over an open fire. The technology of long and slow heating can be traced back into the Bronze Age. At Belverde, Tufariello and a number of similar sites stands dating to the Bronze Age of a type generally described as a 'milk boiler' have been discovered (fig. 31i). It is usually inferred that these were involved in some form of dairy production. The most important characteristic is an internal rim on which an inverted perforated funnel is placed. The late Bronze Age and Etruscan cooking stands do not have this specific use but simply stood between the cooking vessel and the fire. This technology made cooking much less restricted to one activity area. Generally hearths were sheltered in a hut between the twelfth and eighth centuries BC; then, as housing became more complex, the cooking area was shifted into a covered area outside the house itself, although food may have been brought in on braziers for eating. We should not, however, think of a kitchen as such until the Hellenistic/Roman period. A detailed and unique study has been made of the coarseware pottery from Murlo. Although Murlo may have been a high status site, it did contain a large quantity of seemingly lower-status, but nevertheless wheel-made, pottery. This has been divided into table ware and serving/kitchen ware (fig. 32). At table, bowls with either a flat base or some form of foot were in common use; for drinking there were many types of cup and chalice. Serving and kitchen ware took the form of jars. Finally, in addition to the small kitchen storage vessel, there are large storage vessels. Storage is of considerable importance for stabilized farming communities and reaches even greater importance as social and political complexity increases. The voluminous storage vessels *(pithoi)* most prominent in the seventh/sixth century tombs of Cerveteri are

part of a prestige technology showing the abundance of the reserves available to the élite. Storage is, however, also an insurance for continued eating and a political control on those who have lesser reserves. From the latest Bronze Age large storage vessels became an important part of ceramic technology. In the Archaic period specialist containers were developed, including amphorae and wooden barrels.

Domestic and industrial production

It is a modern conception to consider the house as a refuge from work. The Swedish excavations at Acquarossa have revealed how much the Etruscans worked at home, at least during the sixth century BC. We can even have a good idea of where in the household these domestic production activities took place. In the limited space inside the house, there was probably room and light enough only for sleeping, eating or feasting and shelter. Outside was the area where, apart from cooking, other chores and jobs took place. Prominent amongst these would have been the working of wool, in particular weaving. Other production activities were by this stage most probably more centralized. Between the twelfth and sixth centuries activities such as pottery and metal production and certain types of construction were increasingly controlled by a central authority and, where identified, can be seen to be located in particular zones of the settlement. We shall look at these three activities in detail.

Pottery

Pottery forms an important focus of much study of the period 1200–600 BC in the reconstruction of the chronology and trade patterns within central Italy, so it is odd that little work has been carried out on the basic technology of ceramics. There is clearly a transformation of production over the period concerned, but the precise steps in this transformation can only be outlined. The pottery of the latest Bronze Age includes both fine burnished wares, with more developed finish and decoration, and larger storage vessels, but the distinction is difficult to define, partly because the pottery was handmade

32 *The range of domestic pottery from Murlo.*
a–d *bowls;* **e–m** *drinking vessels;* **n–q** *cooking vessels (including storage) (after Bouloumié Marique 1978).*

and partly because standardization was not strongly developed.

Wheel-turned pottery appeared during the eighth century BC and, over time, a changed organization of production introduced clearer distinctions of pottery form. A considerable amount of the coarse ware known as *impasto* continued to be produced by hand modelling and slow turning on a wheel. Large quantities of temper were added to the clay to increase strength and to facilitate manufacture, and the vessels were fired in an open kiln with all the accompanying irregularities of shape and colour. This type of pottery was particularly suitable for domestic use, although it was sometimes upgraded by being painted or embellished with metal trappings. By the seventh century, the production of *impasto* in a centre such as that of Cerveteri was a specialist craft; here they made a high-quality product with a distinctive burnished sheen. One important change by the late sixth century was the transfer of the production of terracottas from the hands of the potter to those of a specialized artisan. The standardization of production was most prominent in the finer pottery such as *bucchero*, which was more centralized in its production and sought to imitate finer, more valuable, metallic products. These are all characteristics of a transfer from seasonal household to year-round workshop production and the beginnings of specialized industrial-type production with a large regional distribution.

Metal

Metal had a major impact on technology and production only in the latest Bronze Age. Initially, relatively few bronze forms were present and these are predominantly interpretable as prestige and decorative items. During the later part of the period (from the eleventh century), there was an increase simultaneously in the functional range and quantity of bronze objects: pins, fibulae, small metal tools (awls, etc.), knives, razors, more efficient axe forms (shaft hole and winged) and swords. An important trend is the increased quantity of specialized tools, such as small tools for woodworking, that are to be found towards the end of the latest Bronze Age. In spite of this increase in the importance of metals, flint still continued to play some role. Numerous arrowheads and some other simple flintwork items continued to be utilized, particularly in upland areas (fig. 33).

In spite of increased settlement excavation and many sporadic finds, hoards remain the most plentiful but ambiguous form of evidence for metalwork. The increase in the range of functions of metal artefacts over time can clearly be seen from such sequences. The hoards have also been interpreted in more socio-political terms. The general increase in hoards over the final Bronze Age may indicate a change in the organization of production. In the most prominent of these studies, the Ardea hoard of the eighth century BC has been considered an indication of a pre-monetary economy, where metal objects within the hoard had distinct values of weight. The earlier Contigliano (Piediluco) hoard has also been cited as evidence of some measure of wealth. In minimal terms, the hoards can be considered as the placing of an important, accumulated resource out of circulation.

The relationship of this increase in metalwork to the processes of extraction and production is difficult to establish. Modern geological studies have established where the copper and tin ores can be found, but no serious work has been carried out to identify precisely where extraction and production took place. Surface veins of copper near Pari (see fig. 6) could have been among the most easily detected sources, but it is not established even whether the one major tin source in central Italy at Campiglia Marittima was exploited during this period. It has always been assumed that the economic growth of the late Bronze Age was related to the accelerated exploitation of these deposits. Settlements located close to the modern copper sources of the Campiglia Marittima area do not, however, appear to be especially rich or socio-politically developed. The major density of late-Bronze-Age settlements was placed in areas such as the Val di Fiora and the Tolfa mountains, where it is possible that other copper-bearing deposits, which have a low commercial significance today, may have had a greater relevance to the late-Bronze-Age economy.

The processes involved in the first production and use of iron are even more difficult to tackle.

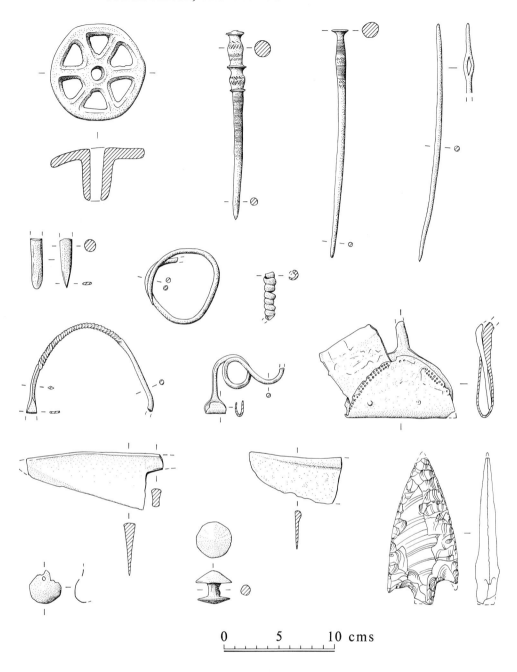

0   5   10 cms

33 *The range of metal and flint objects from the late Bronze Age site of Monte Ingino at Gubbio. Only the arrowhead in the bottom right hand corner is made of flint.*

There is the same lack of knowledge of sources and modes of production, compounded by the poor preservation of iron and the lack of settlement excavation. It is, however, clear that iron was at first a rare product. As in many parts of Europe, the definition of the beginning of the Iron Age is relatively arbitrary. Iron has been noted in the form of encrustations on bronze objects or as objects in contexts otherwise datable to the eleventh and tenth centuries. In the late tenth and early ninth centuries, iron was restricted to the manufacture of fibulae, iron rings and other decorative objects. Almost half of the objects are bimetallic (that is, made up of bronze and iron components). These objects are found frequently in graves of greater wealth. Some early iron objects also directly imitate the equivalent in bronze; this has been found most clearly in the case of fibulae and swords. Iron manufacture at this stage did not have a separate production identity but, in common with similar innovations in other parts of Europe, had a restricted functional role. From the late eighth century a wider range of objects was made from iron. The decorative and bimetallic components are reduced. Bronze, nevertheless, remains the dominant metal, particularly for functional and ritual items. With the development of social ranking in the eighth century (see Chapter VIII), iron became an important additional indicator of wealth. This innovation has its earliest recorded development in the southerly centres of Veii and Tarquinia; however, this must be interpreted cautiously even if it is paralleled by other changes in ritual, since it is for these two centres that the most refined cemetery sequences have been established. It is interesting to note that these centres are not directly associated with the important metal-ore areas of Tolfa and the Colline Metallifere.

There is no clear evidence of a developed mineral extraction and mining industry in Etruria before 550 BC; around this time slaves could have perhaps been brought in to intensify production and the manpower could have been collected to cut down the large amount of timber required for metalurgical work. The late date may be partly an artificial product of the few serious projects that have investigated the extraction and mining of metal in the Etruscan period, and also because modern extraction has been on a destructive scale. Severe doubt is now cast on whether one of these studies actually discovered a metallurgical extraction complex; the form of the kiln reported from Val Fucinaia is much more probably suitable for ceramic production and happened to be covered,

as much of surrounding area was, by slag from later metal smelting. Much more successful work has recently been undertaken at Populonia. Kilns suitable for the smelting of iron were found in the levels of the sixth and fifth centuries. Industrial activity of this type may not have been centralized in the primary centres; for example, recent finds at Scarlino suggest that metal smelting took place on this small hilltop site at a similar date. It is probable that earlier smelting took place closer to the source of the metal ores, such as the undated smelting deposits at Massa Marittima to the north of Vetulonia, and was only centralized with the extensive use of Elban ore towards the middle of the sixth century BC. Before the industrialization of smelting in the major centres, smelting may have involved few functional structures; open-air pile roasting may have been the major technique employed. This would explain the location of some sites, such as Massa Marittima and Scarlino, in windy, upland locations. Once intensive exploitation of iron was undertaken from the sixth century, iron must have been employed much more frequently for the manufacture of commonplace tools.

Construction

The Villanovan hut urn and Etruscan tomb with their architectural features were once the best evidence for constructional techniques in central Italy. The recent excavation of settlements has added to this limited source material and proved to be potentially complementary; such excavations are able to contribute detailed information on ground plans and cover a greater time span from the twelfth century BC, while the hut urns provide information on walls, doors and roofing. In the eleventh and tenth centuries in Etruria, wattle and daub was used predominantly to produce oval houses with footings or post-holes cut into the bedrock and covered by thatch. This use of wood was clearly quite sophisticated, as shown recently by the finds from the ninth-century lakeside site of Gran Carro. Where solid bedrock was not close to the surface dry stone footings were also employed. Two famous buildings from Luni sul Mignone and Monte Rovello are square and cut deeply into the bedrock. In the case of Luni sul Mignone the depth of the cutting (6 m or 6.5 yds) and stratigraphic problems have cast some doubt on the dating or nature of the structure. If securely Bronze Age, they provide the first signs of a trend towards rectangular constructions that increased in strength in the ninth and eighth centuries.

Larger buildings were approached through two solutions: either an oval or a rectangular form. The trend towards rectangular buildings and larger

34 *Two attempted reconstructions of late Bronze Age/Iron Age structures by Cozza and Davico.* **a** *no scale;* **b** *length of hut just under 6 m (6.6 yd) (after Battoloni et al. 1985).*

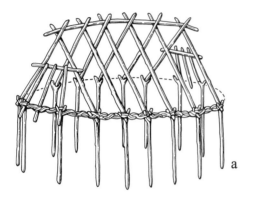

a

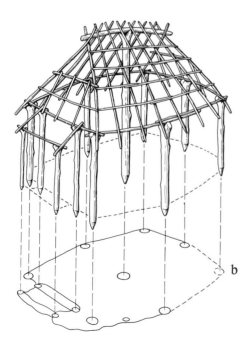

b

35 *Hut urn from Albano* (British Museum).

buildings appears to have been more powerful in Tarquinia and other central Etruscan centres. At first the oval form was employed here for the larger buildings and rectangular for the smaller. Circular ground plans appear to have been employed only in the southern part of Etruria at Veii and in Latium. The detailed reconstruction of the walls, openings and roofs has involved considerably more speculation depending on the amount of faith placed in funerary models and recent ethnographic accounts. Some reconstructions seem unnecessarily complicated, impractical and over-faithful to the hut urn (fig. 34a). It is highly probable that the hut-urn models showed a symbolic representation of the internal structure of the house outside its shell (fig. 35). Other reconstructions seem more practical (and stable) and better integrated with both settlement and funerary evidence (fig. 34b). The entrance to the hut was generally on the short side in rectangular houses and at the end of oval houses. Other openings are more difficult to define, but would include an aperture in the roof as a chimney.

The transition towards rectangular houses, which was clearly linked to the regular planning of settlements and certain social changes, was firmly

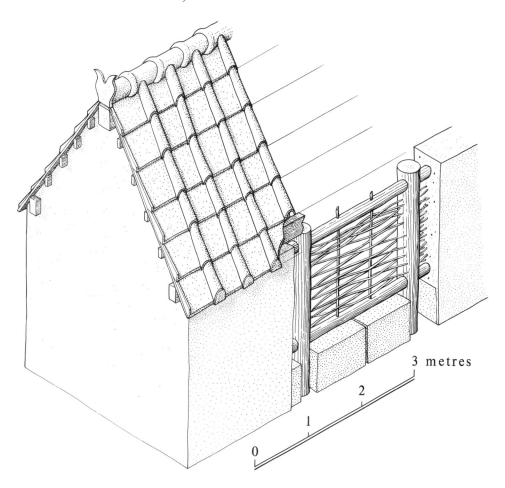

3 metres

2

1

0

36 *The reconstruction of an Etruscan House, based on information from Acquarossa. Cut-away to show wood and plaster construction on tufa foundations.*

completed in the late seventh century when rectangular structures became the rule and when tiles – often decorated – replaced straw as a roofing material. Two sites have contributed greatly to this knowledge of the building techniques of relatively humble Etruscan houses: S. Giovenale and Acquarossa. At S. Giovenale foundation trenches were cut into the tufa and blocks of the same local tufa, cut to a maximum width of 35 cm (14in.) placed inside. Little is known of the superstructure of these buildings, and what little is known has been gleaned from the architectonic forms of tombs. At

Acquarossa (fig. 36), there was a greater variety of construction methods. A foundation trench was usually dug, but then a pisé (rammed earth or clay), mud-brick or wattle-and-daub construction was built with or without stone footings. Wooden beams then suported tiles on the roof. There were probably some windows, but these were almost certainly restricted in size to increase insulation against cold, heat and damp. These simple construction techniques were used for the majority of Etruscan buildings: although there are good marble sources on the margins of Etruscan territory (especially at Carrara, which was later exploited by the Romans), the sort of heavy, monumental public building of which the Greeks were so fond was never developed in Etruria.

IV
TRADE AND EXCHANGE

A customary way of viewing Etruscan Italy is as a zone that received foreign manufactured products in exchange for raw materials. This standpoint reduces Etruscan Italy virtually to a colonial promontory and fails to investigate internally-derived trade. It also runs the danger of considering any social and political changes in Etruria as a response to outside interaction. The trade and exchange of Etruria must be seen in their own cultural context. A good illustration of this is the spread of literacy (see Chapter V). In the fields of literacy, myth and art, Etruria borrowed concepts but genuinely transformed them to fit a socio-political organization and a cultural milieu quite different from that of Greece or Phoenicia.

The first part of this chapter examines and rejects external influence as the underlying cause of the formative socio-political transformation of c. 1200–800 BC in central Italy, explored through changes in settlement organization in Chapter II. The evidence for the latest Bronze Age (1200–1000 BC) is rich but essentially repetitive; the finds from Gubbio are used to illustrate the general patterns. The evidence for the succeeding earliest Iron Age (1000–800 BC) is much less comprehensive, although when examined against the background of settlement change such evidence is some of the most crucial. The evidence for the Archaic period is very rich; the review has, therefore, necessarily been selective, taking those elements for which there is the best available spatial evidence.

The geographical position of Etruria in a maritime communication network between certain key resources (Chapter I) made it a natural focus of interaction. Etruria has, however, too frequently been relegated to the position of periphery in research on the ancient world. The final Bronze Age has even been seen in terms of 'invasion' because of similarities in styles of bronzework between different areas. The peripheral status of Etruscan Italy has an even longer history, if ancient commentators are to be believed: Dionysius of Halicarnassus apart, they like to indulge in speculation as to the Eastern origins of the Etruscans, and later we find writers like the fifteenth-century monk Annius of Viterbo concocting evidence that Egyptian gods (Osiris and his ilk) had brought civilization to the heart of Italy. The archaeological reality is not so exotic.

The latest Bronze age is noted for a similarity of metallurgical bronze forms over at least the peninsula of Italy. Typologists have attempted to carve a series of sub-assemblages out of this general uniformity by refining the criteria on which chronological and regional distinctions can be made. Many scholars have created their own individual frameworks into which new finds are placed. The work is very impressive until results are compared and it is found that similar premises have produced strikingly different chronologies and regional associations for the same artefacts. Furthermore, the distinction between regional and chronological variation is never fully established. No attempt will be made to enter these complex and unresolvable (without an independent chronology) debates at this point. Instead, some broad generalizations about the distribution of the better defined aspects of material culture will be presented.

The analysis of the material culture of most sites of the period 1200–900 BC from central Italy establishes two levels of interaction that grade into each other: strong intra-peninsular contact and the more

37 *Winged palstave at the moment of discovery in Gubbio.*

poorly defined locally-based identity. Over time, the local component became more important and was much more clearly visible. This network of interaction had as great an impact on sites in the upland mountain basins of the Apennines as on more coastally placed sites. Therefore, the finds (in course of study) from Gubbio can illustrate this phenomenon. Some of the domestic refuse from the midden of Monte Ingino and the settlement of Monte Ansciano suggests the presence of an exchange network with more distant regions of central Italy. One well-defined form, the winged palstave (fig. 37), has been found extensively over central Italy. Amber beads have an even more extensively distribution during the same period. The general characteristics of the pottery, although clearly locally made, are very similar to that found in the Val di Fiora, at Narce and other sites. Other items of material culture have a much more restricted distribution. Highly stylized bone combs have been found at Pianello and Gubbio. Distinctive pins of Casa Carletti type are restricted to the intermontane basins of eastern Tuscany and Umbria, including the site of Casa Carletti on Monte Cetona, the necropolis of Pianello and Gubbio. The glass beads seem to belong to a similar exchange network localized to inland central Italy, since their colour is distinct from a northern distribution centred on Frattesina in the Po valley. Certain decorative features of the locally produced pottery, such as the axe-shaped handles, are also found exclusively at Gubbio and mountain valleys to the east. It is difficult to distinguish the physical

exchange of objects from stylistic emulation, but it is clear that, whatever the mechanism, the whole peninsula forms a complex social network where peripheral zones are difficult to detect. In this respect, only north-west Etruria stands out as having a rather less well-defined pottery sequence and does not appear to be so clearly linked to the social network that covered the remainder of central Italy.

The economic and socio-political trends of the late Bronze Age extend well beyond the few areas where Mycenaean finds or finds of possibly Mycenaean/Cypriot influence have been made. One of the paradoxes for those appealing to external influence is that some of the areas with the highest density of material of Mycenaean origin in the central Mediterranean contain less marked evidence for later indigenous social evolution. In this respect, much future work needs to be carried out to establish the nature of Mycenaean contact with such areas as southern Italy (going as far north as Vivara near modern Naples) and eastern Sicily. By contrast, Luni Sul Mignone, Monte Rovello and S. Giovenale are renowned because they are the few north-central Italian sites that show the presence of Mycenaean material rather than for the quantity of material located (fig. 38). The intensity and duration of contact were not great; central Italy was at the end of a Mycenaean exchange network. Consequently any fluctuation in Mycenaean contact would not have had a significant effect on the development of central Italy, where an independently vibrant economy was already developing. The later existence of an extensive metallurgical *koine*, or network, suggests that the relationship with the rest of the Mediterranean was not one-sided. Common processes of metallurgical development were in progress.

The period 1050–850 BC was a fundamental phase of socio-political transformation, which can be measured in settlement change (Chapter II). This change is not, however, associated with a major period of trading contact with the remainder of the Mediterranean since the pre-existing networks collapsed. A few apparent exceptions can be readily explained. The possible Cypriot objects from the hoard of Piediluco-Contigliano appear to date to at least the early eleventh century, although the context in which they are found may be of the

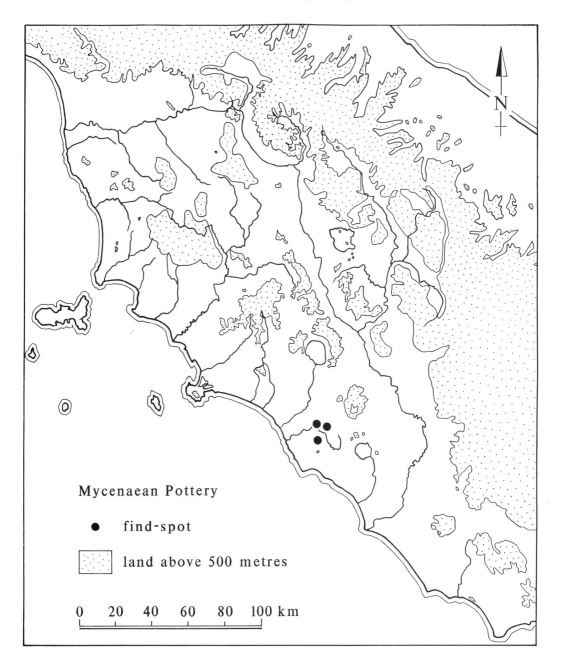

38 *The location of Mycenaean finds in Etruria.*

tenth or ninth century. Other objects in the same hoard show more localized interaction with Sardinia.

This phase appears to be associated rather with localized contact, in particular between the major Villanovan-period centres themselves and to a certain extent with the island of Sardinia. Items of material culture of various types have a wide distribution in this period. Ceramic styles, including hut urns, are very distinctive, but other items give more clear indications of exchange contact. In particular, pottery jug forms with metal attachments (*orcioli a lamelle metalliche*) have been found at Populonia, Vetulonia, Tarquinia, Cerveteri, Veii and possibly Bisenzio. The distribution of fibulae, stressed as important by some authors, seems somewhat less significant as an indication of contact and in fact seems to have had a much more diffuse and extensive distribution over northern Italy over a relatively long period (300 years).

Considerable attention has recently been directed towards the collection of data on the contact between the island of Sardinia and the Italian peninsula. Although the dating of material based on such contact is imprecise in traditional terms, the timing seems to fill a gap in the pattern of contact between peninsular Italy and the outside world. There is a wide range of objects involved that covers a considerable part of the metallurgical spectrum and is not restricted to a few ritual objects: not only small bronzes and askoid form jugs (*brocchette askoidi*), but also daggers, swords, axes, razors (*rasoi*), fibulae and an amber necklace. One set of ritual objects (*faretrine votive*) is restricted to northern Etruria.

The distribution of finds when viewed in the context of a socio-political relationship between exchange partners does not suggest the one-sided dominance of one group over another. It seems more probable that we are considering partners of equal power but set in different cultures with differing systems of value, a pattern that was to continue into later periods. At this particular period, a localized interaction sphere can be proposed that fills a vacuum following the 'collapse' of the Mycenaean exchange system.

The earliest evidence for renewed intensive contact in the form of imports from the eastern Mediterranean is only from the eighth century: the Cycladic cups of *c.* 800–760 BC or 780–730 BC or some time in between from Quattro Fontanili and Grotta Gramiccia at Veii; a Phoenician bronze vessel of the mid eighth century from Tomb VII of the Poggio della Guardia cemetery at Vetulonia; and other objects from Vulci, Tarquinia, Cerveteri and Praeneste. Furthermore, once contact was reestablished the Etruscan world did not adopt a passive role with respect to the Greeks and Phoenicians: evidence is accumulating for prestigious

objects of late Villanovan origin in Greek contexts, particularly sanctuaries: a horse bit at Olympia, helmet fragments at Olympia and Delphi, a belt from Euboea and fragments of bronze sheeting from shields from Dodona, Olympia and Samos. These are clear indications of exchange processes between societies of similar levels of socio-political development. Italian fibulae have been found also in the sanctuaries of Olympia, Perachora, Aegina (see fig. 13c), Rhodes and Samos.

The denial of external stimulus as the causation of evolution towards complexity in central Italy, however, appeals for a new cause of that change. The economic conditions for change can be fairly readily described (see Chapter III): an environment with a ready facility for intensification, previously underexploited in the Neolithic period. The causes of the important changes in settlement must be sought in the socio-economic momentum and interaction of the late Bronze Age, processes that can be studied in more detail by only settlement excavation. These changes may to some extent have been enabled by the vacuum created on the collapse of the Mycenaean system, even if Etruria was only very loosely connected with this system, but this in itself suggests an indigenous development. It is the localized interactions of the early ninth century that probably formed an important stimulus towards the new socio-political system, although caution is required before developing this into a more elaborate model.

In the second half of the eighth century there was an expansion of the early contacts mentioned above into an Orientalizing network, for instance in the case of the areas where goldwork has been found, stretching from Cumae in the south to Vetulonia in the north. This represented a common 'chiefly' ideology given material form through distinctive sumptuary items. Establishing the source and manufacturing centre of these sumptuary items is a separate if complementary problem that focuses on external relationships, using the methodology of art historical exegesis. It is clear that there was no administered trade at this stage: many small political units were competing on relatively equal terms in an exchange network. Access to this exchange network was restricted to a 'chiefly' élite but was not heavily centralized; the products exchanged, therefore, reached a relatively high proportion of central Italy, even if generally concentrated on the coast. That this interaction continued to be more intense on the coast is also illustrated by the distribution of the earliest onomastic inscriptions of the seventh century BC (see fig. 57, Chapter V).

39 *The distribution of decorated ostrich shell in Etruria (after Rathje 1979).*

The importance for the late eighth century is the common manipulation (if with different meaning) of motifs by both Eastern and early-Etruscan societies. The considerable controversy over the precise location of the production centre is an illustration of the nature of the process involved. In the art historical tradition, style and density of finds are the only clues. Unfortunately for this technique, the Orientalizing style was extensive and had a poor regional definition; the problems

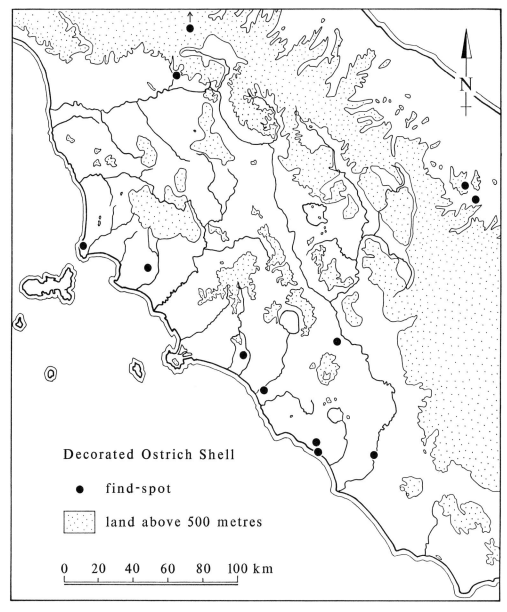

Decorated Ostrich Shell

● find-spot

land above 500 metres

0 20 40 60 80 100 km

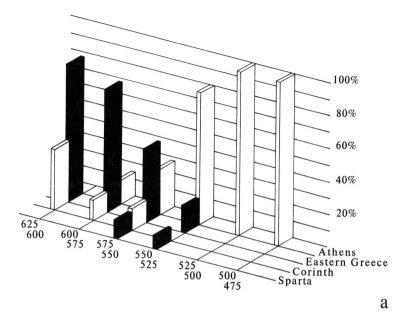

a

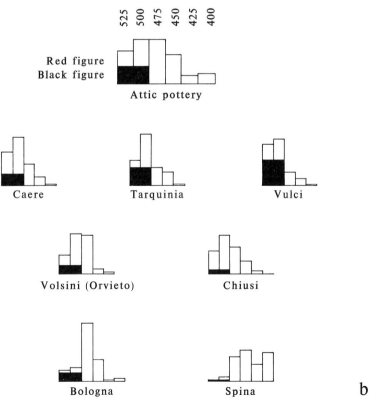

b

40 *Statistics for trade in fine Greek pottery during
the Archaic period according to source and destination
(after Martelli 1985).* **a** *sources for Etruria as a
whole (by 25-year period);* **b** *Black and Red figure
imports to major centres (by 25-year period).*

for the art historians arise out of the likelihood that there were many production centres. Decorated ostrich shell is one of the few products that escapes this problem; its source was certainly outside central Italy (fig. 39). We have a pattern of societies that shared some sumptuary elements of material culture, a situation that does not imply a peripheral status on the part of the Etruscans. The participant societies were of very comparable levels of social development, again pointing to the importance of the preceding and independent late-Bronze-Age and early-Iron-Age developments.

The good statistics that now exist for the distribution of later Greek luxury imports show clearly the succeeding cycles of contact with the different regions of the Greek world. The early contacts (625–550 BC) are with Eastern Greek and Corinthian centres. Two examples of products from this phase, *coppe ioniche* (ionic cups) and *balsamari plastici* (little unguent jars with relief decoration) are dealt with in more detail below. This is succeeded by the later domination of trade contact by the Athenians (550–475 BC). There is also a shorter, much less intense, period of contact with Sparta, *c.* 550–525 BC (fig. 40). In addition, Phoenician imports were important in the early sixth century at Gravisca. The distribution of these imports within the Etruscan centres conforms to a pattern that repeats itself for many imported items of material culture and locally produced ideological artefacts. A clear contrast is visible between the three principal coastal centres and the inland zones of central Italy. Attic pottery, one of the best calibrated imports, shows this most clearly. The peak for Cerveteri, Tarquinia and Vulci is between 525 and 500 BC, followed by a relatively sharp decline, with local production partly replacing the imported exotics. The peak of Attic pottery imports for the inland centres of Orvieto and Chiusi is at about the same time but was followed by a much more gradual decline in imports. The peak for Bologna and Spina is somewhat later (475–450 BC). Umbrian centres such as Gubbio were never in such close contact with the Greek world and instead received products of Etruscan origin, particularly from Volterra.

The distribution network of such imports is a fascinating problem that still requires much work,

particularly when interrelated to imitations of imports and products (such as *bucchero*) of clearly local production. Its future analysis should throw light on the organization of settlement discussed above (see Chapter II). As a working model, the major coastal polities seem to have administered luxury trade at first directly (in the late eighth and early seventh centuries BC) and then through the coastal emporia (from the late seventh century BC). Most of these luxury products were then used by the élite; we have the residue of these products in the cemeteries of the primate centres, and there is some indication that the exotic vessels may have contained equally exotic liquids. Under the same administrative control, some of these products passed to lesser settlements arranged spatially in a distant ring around the primate centres (figs. 41, 42) and, at least periodically, were under the political control of the primate centres. In North Etruria and Umbria, there appears to have been no such powerfully directed trade. For instance, Castelnuovo di Berardenga and Poggio Civitate received as many of these exotic products as the local primate centre of Chiusi.

A few of the more recently researched products illustrate these patterns. Unfortunately, this research extends to only a restricted set of imported products, distinctive coarse wares such as amphorae and rare detailed studies of local Etruscan artists such as the Micali painter. Inevitably, therefore, there are gaps in our treatment of the normal division of pottery into imports, imitations, *bucchero*, amphorae and coarseware. *Coppe ioniche*, an example of an eastern Greek import, made predominantly from between the late seventh and the middle of the sixth centuries, have been found in three areas: firstly the greatest numerical concentration is in the three coastal centres of Cerveteri, Tarquinia and Vulci and the entrepot of Gravisca; secondly, smaller numerical quantities are in centres most probably politically dependent on the three primate centres; and thirdly there is a dispersal of lower total quantities to centres such as North Etruria outside the political control of the coastal centres (fig. 41). A similar pattern can be seen for the distribution of the *balsamari plastici* of *c.* 625–550 BC (fig. 42), except that Populonia and Vetulonia are included more prominently in this

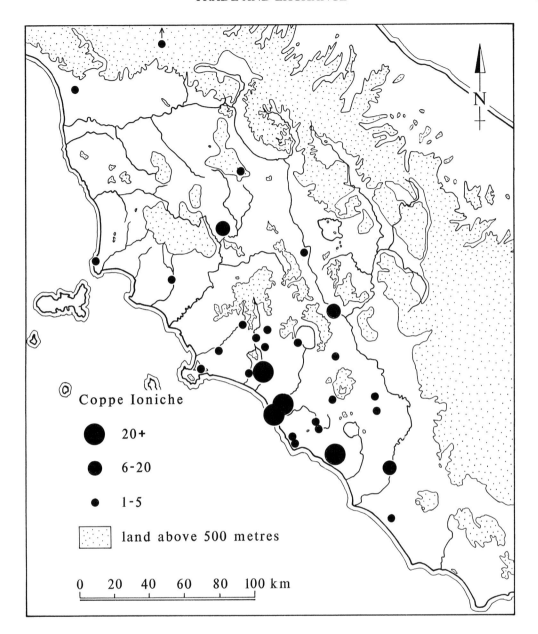

41 *The distribution of* Coppe Ioniche *in Etruria (data drawn from Martelli 1978).*

trade network. A less extensive network has recently been detected also for more bulky utilitarian products. Amphorae of Greek manufacture are found exclusively in the coastal centres (with a strange relative absence in Tarquinia) whereas amphorae of Etruscan manufacture are found in both the coastal and the inland centres. Over time, there is a decrease in the number of Greek amphorae in the coastal primate centres as the quantities in the coastal emporia increase, although the quantities of other, more exotic Greek imports continue to increase. The concentrations of Greek amphorae appear to indicate the locations from where the contents (possibly wine or oil) were distributed. On these grounds, early distribution can be

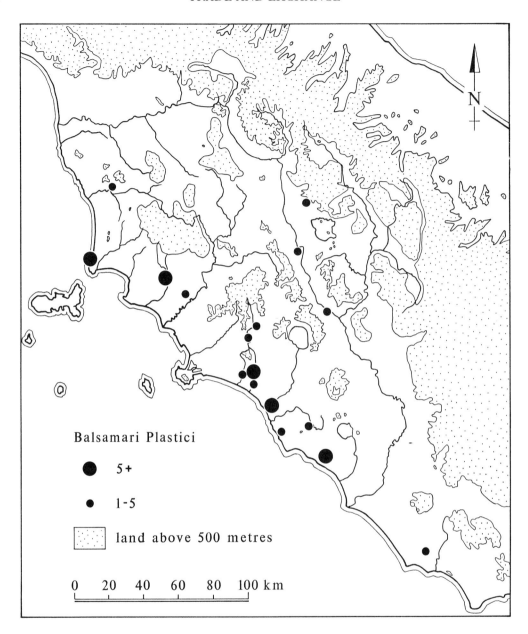

42 *The distribution of* balsamari *in Etruria*
(data drawn from Martelli 1978).

said to be from the primate centres themselves; later distribution, from the sixth century, with development of ports such as Pyrgi, was from the coastal emporia, and only the contents of the amphorae and other luxury products continued

their journey to the primate centres (fig. 43). Etruscan-made transport amphorae appear to originate from Vulci around 630 BC; since a number of these amphorae have yielded interior traces of tannin, it is supposed that the chief task of these vessels was to carry wine. If that is so, then it is plain that the Vulci vintage was widely esteemed, for it travelled not only to those minor centres under the political control of Vulci (Castro, Magliano, Pitigliano,

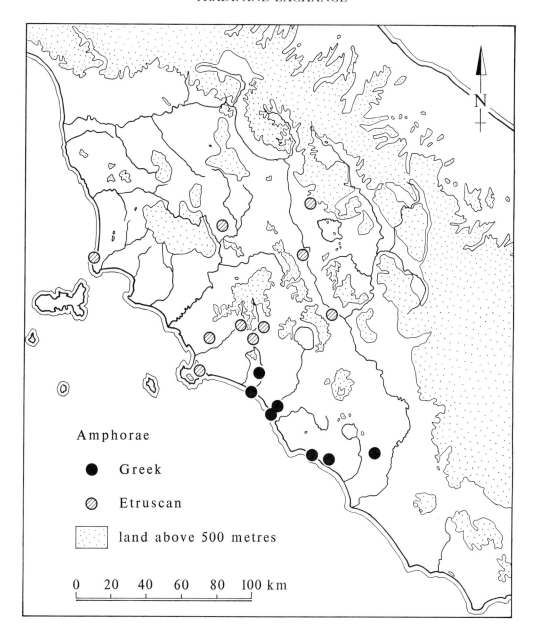

43 *The distribution of Greek and Etruscan amphorae in Etruria (after Atti 1985).*

Saturnia, Poggio Buco and Orbetello) but all along the Tyrrhenian coast and beyond: Sicily, Naxos, and Alicante are amongst the findspots of these amphorae. And the Etruscan wine merchants achieved what their Italian successors have failed to do: that is, to get the French to drink *vino italiano –*

sites in both Provence and the Languedoc have provided large amounts of sherds of Etruscan amphorae, substantiating the evidence of sixth-century BC wrecks off Cap d'Antibes and Bon Porte.

Bucchero started as a highly finished product designed in Cerveteri from *c.* 675 BC. From *c.* 650, the product becomes much more widespread in terms of both production centres and distri-

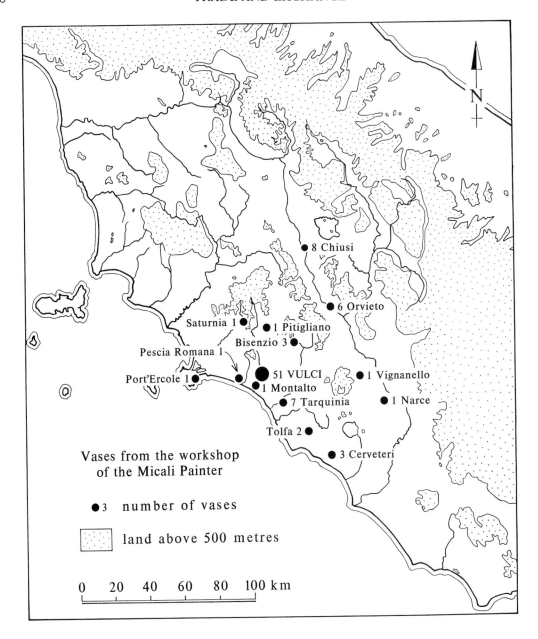

44 *The distribution of vases from the workshop of the Micali painter (after Spivey 1987).*

bution. This range of distribution reaches a peak *c.* 625–550 BC, entering North Etruria to an extent that the exotic imports described above never did. *Bucchero* has also been found at sites in the Aegean, on Corfu and within the Greek mainland (Athens, Sparta and Corinth); on the Iberian peninsula, and

in the South of France; and further east: Rumania (Istros), Syria (Ras-el-Bassit), Libya (Tocra), Egypt (Naukratis) and Cyprus (Kition) (fig. 13c). Some locally-produced prestige items, such as the vases of the Micali Painter, had a more localized distribution but with a greater penetration, particularly of certain areas of North Etruria, than the imported exotic products (fig. 44), even if probably produced and primarily present in a coastal centre such as Vulci. Other more generalized products such as the Etrusco-Corinthian *aryballoi* of the turn of the late seventh to early sixth centuries, although concentrated at Vulci and in the Val di Fiora, have a very wide distribution into northern Etruria (Populonia, Vetulonia and Poggio Civitate), inland southern Etruria (Orvieto and Castel d'Asso) and beyond.

Etruscologists have described the radiation of cultural attributes and the blending of art styles without proper explanation. This chapter has shown that there are underlying socio-political reasons for the spatial distribution of material culture.

There is clear evidence that independent types of evidence describe the same pattern of power relationships in the political landscape of Etruria and Umbria. Levels of economic development and political relationships, both internal and external, all play an important part in the acceptance of particular structures of artistic expression. This is not to reduce the study of art to a mere response to economic development: aesthetic studies are complementary. Furthermore, lines of communication, contact and distribution had an important effect on the spatial development of society itself, most readily visible here in the settlement system.

V

LANGUAGE, MYTH AND LITERACY: THE PROCESS OF CULTURAL CHANGE

Let any visitor to modern Italy enter a town or village in the hours of early evening and observe the young people as they conduct the traditional rite of the *passeggiata*. Witness how many of these young people sedulously adhere to the fashion of wearing jackets or sweat-shirts bearing some legend in English (or American), asserting them to be 'Best Company' or devotees of the 'Malibu Surfin' Fun Club'. The inquisitive visitor ought to stop some of these adolescents and ask them to read or explain the legends he or she is sporting. There is a fair chance that neither proper pronunciation nor correct meaning will be forthcoming. The garment has been acquired because it is deemed fashionable (a valid enough *raison d'etre*): but, like the arrival of fast-food in Rome's centre, and like the extreme quantities of Coca-Cola currently consumed by Italian youth, it is a token of something that runs deeper: the fact that learning to speak, read and write English has become an indispensable part of modern Italian education.

The consideration of this process of 'acculturation' (that is, adopting features of another culture) as it is happening in present-day Italy may be salutary prior to examining the analogous process as it occurred in Etruscan Italy. Modern Italians, without necessarily denying the value of their own culture, perceive the need to learn English for the purposes of commerce and all sorts of dealings with the wider world. This is especially true in cities, where the main transactions with foreigners take place. Some learn English well, others are more

shaky: as a general rule, the proficiency level rises more or less in accord with degrees of personal wealth and status. The poorly-educated and the provincial are not excluded: there is nothing to stop them from joining in with the fashion for shirts saying 'Best Company'. And when it comes to certain innovations, an Italian may find himself using English terms quite unwittingly: how else can he purchase the 'software' for his 'personal computer'?

The analogy could be further extended, but the point should already be clear. As Etruscan Italy opened to the increased volumes of Mediterranean trade, as colonists, refugees, artisans and merchants began to move more freely across the area from the coast of Asia Minor to the Iberian Peninsula, the catalysts of 'acculturation' caused a series of transformations on the face of Etruscan society, of which a phrase like 'Language, Myth and Literacy' gives only a partial idea. They are interrelated examples of the process of cultural change.

Contact zones and the spread of innovations

Cultural change is essentially bound up with the spread of innovations from one culture to another. These innovations may be classified in various ways: they range from what we would define as 'technological', such as engineering devices, weapons and agricultural tools, to what might be more generally considered as 'cultural', such as an alphabet.

Much of this book is concerned with cultural change in its broadest sense. The capacity of archaeology to chart such change is, on a superficial level, very strong. To talk of a 'culture' in traditional archaeological terms is to define a society by a series of specific artefacts or remains located at specific sites (hence 'Villanovan', for example); from that it is easy enough to note changes within a local pattern, although more difficult to recognize the changes as coming from without. Even if recognized, the question remains: Why do the people who form culture X take up features of culture Y?

If innovation is the basis of cultural change, then we need some reference to the theories of innovation adoption to assist our interpretation of the archaeological record. These theories were mostly drawn up for modern phenomena – the rate at which farmers in the American Mid-West took up certain innovations that enabled a more efficient grain harvest, for instance – but the terminology of modern cultural change will serve us for its ancient equivalent.

We need, first of all, the contact zones. These can be subdivided into primary and secondary, or direct and indirect, contact zones. The primary contact zones are the points of interaction between two cultures. They are areas where innovations may be displayed and considered. They are the fields of operation for the agents of change. We have already encountered these agents: in the Etruscan case, they are the traders and itinerant artisans, the colonists and the displaced persons. They came to Etruria for commercial gain or because the Persians had ruined their own homelands. To talk of a diaspora in the latter case is exaggerated, but there can be little doubt that the Persian sweep across east Greece at the end of the sixth century BC sent many eastern Greeks to seek new lives in the west, and amongst those who arrived in Etruria were some who left an enduring record of their talents for painting tombs and vases, for sculpture and for architecture. The primary contact zones will therefore tend to be ports of trade or, in Greek terms, *emporia*. Depending upon the attitudes of local 'opinion leaders', these zones will be the areas where innovations are adopted earliest.

The secondary or indirect contact zones will be the hinterlands or spheres of influence of these primary contact areas.

The determining factors of innovation adoption will be appreciated by those who think of modern examples. In particular, these include:

i) relative advantage: does the innovation offer perceptible improvements upon an existing pattern of things?
ii) compatibility: can the innovation co-exist with the established pattern of things?
iii) complexity: is the innovation readily understood?
iv) trialability or observability: can the innovation be tried out prior to proper adoption or observed in use elsewhere?

In general, there are certain socio-political factors that qualify the reception and adoption of an innovation. Talk of 'compatibility' and 'advantages' carries the implicit demands: compatible with whose system, advantageous to whom in a given society? The 'opinion leaders' are those who retain the power to screen innovations, to take them or refuse them depending upon how such innovations suit their own positions. Naturally there will be quick adopters and there will be laggards; there may also be refusal. The force of fashion is also a recurrent element: what we term an innovation could range from hairstyles to military formations.

What is important is that we take seriously such archaeological tokens as we possess of the innovation diffusion process, however trivial. So whilst we have no stadia or gymnasia yet excavated in Etruria, we should presume, when we come across a strigil – the hooked implement used by Greek athletes to scrape away dirt and oil and sweat after a wrestling bout or suchlike – amongst the contents of a fourth-century BC Etruscan tomb, that the object was used, and used more or less to the same purpose as it was in Greece.

This is often unpalatable to Greek-orientated archaeologists. The recovery of many artefacts of Greek origin or Greek type from Etruscan tombs is generally paid little heed by such scholars, who will portray the Etruscans as 'a rich but artistically immature and impoverished people', inhabiting a 'cultural vacuum' on the fringes of the Greek world. Greek traders, then, simply preyed on them: 'the Etruscans accepted all that they were offered, without discrimination ... and gave the Greeks the metal they wanted in return for what was often hardly more than the bright beads with which merchants are usually supposed to dazzle natives'. (John Boardman, *The Greeks Overseas*, London, 1980, p.200)

We shall attempt, in the course of this chapter, to demonstrate how an Etruscan cultural perspective can be put upon a Greek artefact found in Etruria. First of all, however, we need to establish the framework of contact between Greeks and Etruscans and the nature of cultural change and exchange that took place within that framework.

Pottery: a case study

Two sites on the coast of south Etruria may be characterized, after their excavation, as *emporia*: Pyrgi, the port-sanctuary of Cerveteri, and Gravisca, the port-sanctuary of Tarquinia. A third candidate, the site of Regisvilla, which would have served the city of Vulci, requires further exploration.

In the course of excavations at Gravisca, an anchor was found with an inscription. It appeared in a context of votive dedications at the site, whose donors include traders from Samos, Ephesus and Miletus. It was a dedication to the Apollo of Aegina and it was dedicated by one Sostratos. The find aroused much excitement, in so far as Sostratos is the name of a merchant known to the fifth-century BC historian Herodotus and winning mention in the *Histories* (Book IV, 152) on account of his prodigious amassal of wealth and his success in trading at Tartessos in southern Spain. By itself, the anchor dedication would mean little more than that this Sostratos of Aegina was one of the Greek merchants involved in traffic with Etruscan Italy in the last quarter of the sixth century BC, but our familiarity with this or some other Sostratos is increased thanks to some highly useful studies recently undertaken on the trademarks that are sometimes found on the bases of Greek vases. Amongst the repertoire of trademarks there are the letters SO (fig. 45), appearing on about 100 ex-

45 *Graffito on the base of a late-sixth-century BC Athenian krater, containing the SO mark of Sostratos.* (Cambridge, Museum of Classical Archaeology).

amples. These may be painted (*dipinti*) or scratched (*graffiti*); hence they are mostly either reserved for the particular trader before being fired in the potter's workshop or added subsequently. The SO examples occur on various types of Athenian-produced vases found in Etruria: most of the examples with a known provenance come from Vulci, but others come from Tarquinia and Cerveteri, and a few come from interior centres such as Bolsena and Orvieto. The script of the SO characters appears to be Aeginetan, and the vases mostly belong to the last quarter of the sixth century BC; so it is difficult to avoid the conclusion that these vases are amongst the cargo brought by Sostratos and signed by him with the abbreviation SO.

In the terminology we have espoused, we can see Sostratos as a prime example of an agent of change. What he took from the Etruscans is open to speculation, and the actual trading value of the vases is still a matter for debate. They were probably not his only commodity, but Sostratos does serve as the sort of middleman needed for cultural change and cultural exchange. The word 'exchange' is quite applicable here, for if it is evident that the Greeks (via characters like Sostratos) enriched and amplified the range of vessels used by the Etruscans, it is also becoming clear that some influence went the other way.

This is demonstrated by the changes in the morphology of Athenian vases resulting from Etruscan taste. Etruscan taste is measured by *bucchero* ware. It should be pointed out that there is a similar fabric, 'grey ware', produced earlier in parts of east Greece (Aeolis and Lesbos), and that Etruscan *bucchero* plagiarizes some of its shapes from various sources: native and foreign metalwork, Protocorin-

ETRUSCAN BUCCHERO ATTIC BLACK/RED-FIGURE

1
Carinated Kantharos
c.650/25 B.C. onwards

c.580 B.C. onwards

2
"Nikosthenic" Amphora
c.575 B.C. onwards

c.530-510 B.C.
(workshop of Nikosthenes)

3
Small Kyathos
c.650 B.C. onwards

c.530-480 B.C.

4
Tall Kyathos
or one-handled Kantharos
c.550 B.C. onwards

c.510-500 B.C.
(especially Perizoma Group)

46 *Shapes of* bucchero *ware in Athenian pottery.*

thian and Corinthian pottery, and east Greek pottery. Within the period of voluminous traffic in pottery between Athens and Etruria, certain shapes established in the *bucchero* tradition are copied by Athenian potters with a view to indulging Etruscan taste – perhaps as a result of market research carried out by the likes of Sostratos. Figure 46 shows how four shapes of *bucchero* were adopted by Attic potters.

The degree of particularity runs deeper than simply Etruscan taste, since it seems that the Attic versions of a certain *bucchero* shape were sent back to precisely that locality where the *bucchero* prototype was itself preferred. The distinctive amphora made by Athenean potter Nikosthenes copies a *bucchero* shape popular at Cerveteri, and the copies are found so far exclusively at Cerveteri; while the *kyathoi* (fig. 46,3–4), both small and high-footed, emerge from a *bucchero* tradition rooted at Vulci and tend to be sent to Vulci accordingly. The *kantharos* (fig. 46,1) presents a more complex case: it is not, as a basic shape, new to Athens (where versions go back to Protogeometric times) but it does acquire greater significance when it develops as the vessel-attribute of Dionysos. If Etruscan *bucchero* (which has been found at sites all over the Mediterranean) did not furnish the model for the carinated *kantharos* that became part of not only the Athenian but also the Boeotian and Laconian repertoire, then we might suspect that Etruscan metal prototypes did. One of the few records of the Etruscans in Greek literature is that their exported bronze vessels were ubiquitous in Greek households: such vessels rarely survive in the archaeological record, being too readily melted down, but they were (as some scholars have lately gone to great pains to point out) prized much more highly than terracotta equivalents.

Taste beyond types of shape is less easy to trace, but some Athenian painters probably turned out vases in a mannered or gaudy style to satisfy the Etruscan market, for there are some prolific workshops or particular painters (The Affecter, the Elbows-Out Painter, the Perizoma Group) whose vases are rarely found outside an Etruscan context.

Herodotus speaks of Sostratos, but he also relates some fairly eccentric trading practices in north Africa, notably a system of 'silent trade' –

whereby Phoenician ('Carchedonian') merchants used to unload their goods on a certain 'Libyan' shore, and retire to their boats, whence they put out a smoke signal: the local tribesmen came down and laid out a quantity of gold by the goods, and then retired themselves; the Phoenicians returned, and took the gold if it was sufficient for the value of the goods, or else retired again and returned when the amount had been topped up by the natives (*Histories* IV, 196). For Herodotus this is a curious example of trust without contact, but this cannot have been the case in Etruria. Not only do we have an archaeological record of contact: linguistically it is plain that the Greeks who operated in Etruria caused many changes.

The one piece of information which most people possess about Etruscan Italy is that the Etruscan language is an unresolved mystery. This makes most people badly-informed. Etruscan is an unusual language, in the same way that Basque is an unusual language, but it is generally comprehensible when inscribed (to say 'written' seems unfair, when no proper literature has survived). It can be read precisely because of Greek influence: the script is Greek. The Roman historian Tacitus thought that the Greek alphabet entered Etruria via the legendary Corinthian exile Demaratus, but the archaeological and epigraphical evidence points to the adoption of a localized script of Euboean type, rather than Corinthian: and the most likely transmitters of this alphabet would be the Euboean colonists at Cumae.

Greek contact may be measured also by the phenomenon of word-borrowing. A language is said to attest political and economic independence so long as it has a core vocabulary that is its own: that is, its own terminology of 'universally recognized everyday things and actions'. Sustained contact with users of an alien language, however, will lead to a certain amount of word-borrowing associated with specific areas of cultural influence.

We can test this within our discussion of pottery by examining the terminology of vases. The increasing corpus of inscriptions upon vases has made possible a provisional analysis of the Etruscan terminology of vases. It shows that there was a generic term in Etruscan for a drinking vessel, germane to the Etruscan language: *thafna*. This appears throughout all areas of Etruria, and Etrus-canized areas of Faleria (such as Narce), across a date range from the first half of the seventh century BC up to the third century BC, with some phonetic or graphic variations (*thahvna, tafina, thapna*). The shape to which it refers is like a cup or a chalice. This, then, belongs to the core vocabulary: if thirsty, ask for a *thafna* of wine or water. Greek traders were, however, assiduous in persuading Etruscans to use a wider range of vessels, especially when such vessels served as containers for goods being traded (wine, perfume, oils and various essences). Hence more specific terms had to be devised in Etruscan, and these turn out to be more or less transliterations of the Greek. The jug, or *oinochoe*, that the Greeks called *prochous* (or *chous*) becomes in Etruscan *pruchum*; the Greek *olpe* becomes the Etruscan *ulpaia*; the Greek *lekythos*, the Etruscan *lechtum* (or *lechtumuza* if small). The Greek *askos* simply means 'leather container', implying a further word to define the contents: hence in Etruscan we find *aska eleivana*, 'oil flask'. We find also an Etruscan vessel known as a *qutum*, which must be the drinking cup or flask known in Greek as a *kothon* and associated with soldiers and mariners. If it was part of a ship's service, we may readily envisage how the term gained parlance at a port where Greeks regularly did business with Etruscans.

A cultural package: the Aristonothos *krater*

The Aristonothos *krater*, a mixing bowl for wine and water (fig. 47), is celebrated as one of the earliest signed Greek vases; it is also celebrated as being one of the earliest representations of a recognizably Homeric story: the blinding of the one-eyed giant Polyphemus by Odysseus and his companions. The vase is usually dated to the middle of the seventh century BC; the script in which Aristonothos signs his work seems Euboean, and the Euboean colony at Cumae has been suggested as a possible source of the vase.

The Aristonothos krater was not found in Greece, however. Its provenance is Cerveteri, and this poses a number of questions from the Etruscan point of view. If it came from a tomb, one presumes its owner to have been Etruscan. So what did the krater mean to that Etruscan? Was it simply a splendid thing to possess and then deposit as a drinking vessel for the ideal afterlife? Was it acquired because it represented a familiar story, or did the story have to be explained by whoever was selling the vase? Were there Etruscan names for the protagonists, and did an Etruscan know what happened to Odysseus next? Reading the inscription, an Etruscan would have recognized the letters, but what was written was not the Etruscan language. Was it comprehensible as an artist's signature?

47 *The Aristonothos krater (detail).*

Objects such as the Aristonothos krater need to be viewed as objects in context. The context is Cerveteri in the mid seventh century BC. We must try to establish a meaning for the object in that context, irrespective of whatever merits the object might be claimed to have in the history of Greek art. The Aristonothos krater in fact vaunts two precise factors of prestige in seventh-century Cerveteri: the capacity to comprehend Greek myth, and the capacity to use Greek letters. It is of course impossible to say in this particular case whether the Etruscan owner of the vase gazed upon it with understanding or blank ignorance or something between the two. From the evidence available to us, we can establish a series of probabilities, based on the notion that the vase presents a package of cultural value.

Objects such as the Aristonothos krater stand at the beginning of an acculturative process that by the end of fifth century BC had the following singular result: a non-Greek society, rich and politically independent, but only partially literate, whose heroes, so far as we can tell, were almost exclusively drawn from Greek mythology.

Greek myth in Etruria

Classical archaeologists (including some Etruscan specialists) have tended to play down the Etruscan understanding of Greek myth. In the absence of a supporting literary corpus, they have characterized Etruscan figurative representations of Greek myth as blundering copies or banalizations of Greek models. This stems partly from the odd idea that Greek myth is some sort of codified, inviolable set of stories, a common heritage throughout the Greek world – which it is not – and partly from premature dismissal of such Etruscan images as we do not understand. Two examples of this failure or incapacity to understand may be cited with reference to the iconography of Etruscan painted vases:

(i) In the course of his pioneering work of attributing Etruscan vases to certain painters, J. D. Beazley came across a late-sixth-century BC representation of Kaineus – the hero who, in the battle between the Lapiths and the Centaurs, is ham-

mered into the ground by centaurs wielding boulders. This Etruscan Kaineus was depicted using two swords against his equine aggressors, and Beazley imputed the two swords to 'an excessive love of symmetry' on the part of his naïve Etruscan painter. Then the German excavators at Olympia came across a bronze relief dedicated there in the late seventh century BC and quite clearly showing Kaineus plunging two swords into the bellies of his assailants. Beazley reconsidered his vase. Kaineus, according to the myth, was granted invulnerability by Poseidon; therefore, logically, Kaineus does not need a shield; therefore Kaineus can double his offensive capacity and fight with two swords. Whether our Etruscan artist had thought this through for himself, or whether he was following a Greek image similar to that on the

48 *Late-sixth-century Etruscan vase:*
Troilos arrives at the fountain to water his horses.

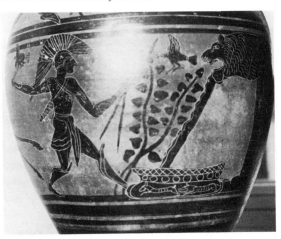

49 *(detail) Behind lurks Achilles, with bird.*

Olympia relief, is not the point here: the point is that we needed a Greek prototype before being, in Beazley's words, 'rather less ready to prattle about over-love of symmetry in the Etruscans'.

(ii) Another Etruscan vase, of the late sixth century BC shows the ambush of Troilos by Achilles (fig. 48a, b): where Achilles, lurking in wait behind the fountain to which Troilos is bringing his horses, appears to have a bird perched cheekily upon his raised fist. Well, we might think, birds are useful space-fillers: on numerous Etruscan vases, they seem to be flying about as such. There is, however, more to it than that: we know, from a note in Servius' commentary on Vergil's *Aeneid* that there was a tradition of the Troilos myth according to which Achilles not only sought to kill the Trojan prince (without his death the fall of Troy could not be achieved) but also had amorous designs upon him. Here the Etruscan painter shows Achilles holding a bird: this was a conventional token of courtship, especially homosexual

courtship – an older man inviting or luring a boy with the gift of a cockerel or a hare or suchlike. That the Etruscans knew this erotic nuance to the myth (which appears not to figure in the Greek tradition as we know it) is also indicated by the paintings in the Tomb of the Bulls at Tarquinia, with their emphasis upon the boyish nudity of Troilos and associated scenes of sodomy (figs. 49, 50).

Examples of the earliest Greek myths figured in Etruscan art are tabulated in figure 51. Without accompanying inscriptions, of course, some of these scenes are not definitively identifiable, but even if one removed the cases of doubt (indicated in the table by question-marks), we would still be left with a good range of figurative evidence at least for limited circulation of Greek myth in certain areas of Etruria. In terms of content, no one epic cycle

50 *Tomb of the Bulls at Tarquinia, main scene: ambush of Troilos by Achilles.*

seems to predominate: Herakles, the universal Mr Universe, is no surprise in the popularity stakes, but the provenance factor is worth noting. To claim Cerveteri as the epicentre for the diffusion of Greek myth in Etruria is fair enough. It is to be expected. Cerveteri was a primary contact zone. The only Etruscan city to be mentioned by Herodotus and the only Etruscan city to set up a treasury at Delphi, Cerveteri is imaginable as an area of early adoption. From the time that regular commercial contacts were established by the Greeks at the ports of Cerveteri, we may envisage a rapid, localized adoption of Greek myth; other Etruscan centres

with direct access to Greek coastal trading-posts, such as Tarquinia and Vulci, might also be expected to form an extension of this primary contact zone. Powerful cities inland, such as Chiusi, may also have commanded the efforts of traders. Thence occurs a secondary transmission: from the primary contact zones into their areas of hinterland.

The secondary transmission stage might well account for the errors and the *banalizzazioni* (banalizations) of Greek myths of which scholars complain. At Narce, for example, two early incised impasto fragments depicting a centaur fighting – perhaps the combat between Herakles and the centaur Nessos is intended (fig. 52) – have been described as 'misinterpretations' and 'mis-

51 *Earliest figurative representations of myth in Etruria* (c. 650–550 BC).

Myth	Medium	Provenance
Menalaus & Helen (?)	italo-geometric biconical krater	Cerveteri (Monte Abatone)
Odysseus & Polyphemus Odysseus & Scylla Geryon & herd	ivory pyxis	Chiusi (Tomba della Pania)
Odysseus & Polyphemus (?)	impasto amphora	Vulci
Medea & Dragon of Colchis	'Orientalizing' amphor	Cerveteri (?)
Birth of Athena Calydonian boar hunt	impasto krater	Cerveteri
Thesus & Ariadne (?)	incised impasto oinochoe	Tragliatella
Ilioupersis	Etrusco-Coninthian oinochoe (Bearded Sphinx Painter)	(?)
Oath of Seven Against Thebes	bronze relief	Castellina in Chianti
Theseus & Minotaur	i) impasto hydria ii) bronze relief iii) terracotta relief iv) nenfro relief	Vulci Chiusi Tarquinia Tarquinia
Thetis consigning arms of Achilles	bronze relief	Chiusi
Herakles & Hydra	Etrusco-Corinthian olpe	Tarquinia
Herakles & Alkyoneus Herakles & Cretan Bull	Etrusco-Corinthian krater (Rosoni Painter)	Cerveteri
Bellerophon & Chimera	incised impasto amphora	Narce
Herakles & Nessos (?)	incised impasto jug incised impasto sherd	Narce
Suicide of Ajax	2 nenfro reliefs	Tarquinia
Achilles & Troilos	Bucchero amphora	Cerveteri

52 *Incised impasto pieces from Narce (Faleria): centaurs fighting – with swords in hand (not to scale).*

understandings' of Greek myth because Greek centaurs are allowed to fight with boughs and boulders but never with swords. The local artist is supposed to have seen a centaur depicted on a Greek work and mistaken a branch for a sword. This is possible: but if our assessment of primary and secondary zones is right, it is more likely to have happened at Narce than at Cerveteri.

Our own knowledge of Greek myths comes primarily from books. There was once a thesis that the texts of Greek epics were in circulation in sixth-century BC Etruria, which was based upon some detailed epic references present in a series of vases (known misleadingly as 'Pontic') found exclusively in Etruria and probably painted there by immigrant Greek craftsmen. The reaction to this thesis was almost entirely negative, which is not surprising since it is unlikely that vase painters, be they Athenian or Etruscan, would have had a properly literate knowledge of Greek myth in the sixth century BC. The stories they heard whilst being dandled in their grandmother's lap are generally considered as their prime source, but a modified form of this thesis might have worked: that is, to present these 'Pontic' vase-painters acting in a sort of missionary capacity, settling at a certain Etruscan centre and acting as interpersonal communication channels for the oral (as well as for the figurative) diffusion of Greek myth. In the last

quarter of the sixth century BC there was an east-Greek pottery workshop at Cerveteri, producing the large colourful vases known as the 'Caeretan hydriae'. On these vases are depicted some fairly obscure episodes from Greek epics such as the *Iliad* and *Arimaspeia*. The author or authors of these vases did not work in hermetic isolation: he or they would have been to some extent Etruscanized through contact with Etruscan patrons and neighbours. Tales will have been told, and vases painted to illustrate them.

We know that the Romans Latinized Greek myth: in the third century BC, one Livius Andronicus translated Homer's *Odyssey*. The evidence for Etruscan verse is slight, though that does not entail that it never existed; but the iconography of the Tarquinian tomb paintings, and of a large series of funerary reliefs from Chiusi, suggests that musical recitation occupied a prominent position at Etruscan banquets or *symposia*, and in such a context poetic recitation or balladry may well have taken place. What we do know is that by the fifth century BC the nomenclature of Greek myth is fully assimilated in Etruria: that is to say, within Etruscan life and language. Hence *Truile* (Troilos), *Eivas* (Aias, or Ajax), *Tuntle* (Tyndareus) and *Ercle* (Herakles): genuine transliterations that do not necessarily imply some Etruscan Livius Andronicus turning Greek epics into the vernacular, but more probably a proper assimilation.

Greek myths, once introduced, would have been historicized on an Etruscan basis by subsequent retelling. By the fourth century BC it was possible for Etruscan cavaliers – real historical figures – to be assimilated in their deeds with the Greek heroes of the Trojan War, as evident from the paintings of the François Tomb at Vulci. Here the propaganda element is clear: as the Romans associated themselves with the Trojan heroes of Troy (Aeneas *par excellence*, of course), the Etruscans, as rivals to Rome, allied themselves mythically with Achilles, Patrokles and Ajax: 'chiefs, grac'd with scars, and prodigal of blood'.

The François Tomb (whose paintings are conserved at the Villa Albani in Rome) should be seen within a deeply-rooted process of adoption and manipulation of Greek myth. We may trace this at two levels: the personal and the public.

On the personal level there are the Etruscan carved gems. These scarabs and sealstones generously repay close examination, for they are very fine pieces of work. They too have their contexts outside of museum cabinets. They meant something to their owners. With regard to the images engraved on them – it is perhaps incidentally significant that so many myths can be recognized on objects where the field for specifying mythical detail was so minutely limited – we may note three important points:

i)   Whatever the consensus about the workmanship may be (the usual claim is for Greek craftsmen gradually giving rise to Etruscanized styles), it is clear that the myth-scenes were cut to Etruscan order. The Theban story of Capaneus – struck down by a thunderbolt for his pompous assertion that nothing could prevent him from scaling the walls of Thebes – may be depicted in what is a highly Greek manner, but it is inscribed with the Etruscan legend *Capne*. Achilles will appear as *Achele, Achale* or *Achile*, but never *Achilleus*. The lesson of this is that Greek myths, once adopted in Etruria, circulated in Etruscan.

ii) The mythical repertoire, from the end of the sixth century BC onwards, is not only extremely rich and varied, covering Herakles, Theseus and the Homeric and Theban cycles, but also refers to some sophisticated details – for example, the breaking-out of the Trojan Horse by the light of the moon (as it should be,

according to a fragment of the *Little Iliad*) – and some stories of which we do not have any Greek record, such as Herakles manning a raft of amphorae lashed together.

iii) As Richter observes: 'When a figure is represented engaged in a simple activity, such as an athlete practising, it is often transported into the realm of legend by having the name of a hero inscribed'. The process can happen vice-versa: an onomastic inscription may be placed next to a recognizable hero.

On the public level we should consider the nature of temple decoration in Etruria and the possibilities that it was 'programmatic' in its choice of myth: whether a particular myth was chosen for more than simply its decorative potential.

As with the gems, there are some unusual or unexpected examples of Greek myths in Etruscan temples. One is offered by Temple A at Pyrgi, datable to 490–480 BC, where the central pedimental focus is the cannibalistic attack of Tydeus upon Melanippus, an episode of the Theban saga that Euripides, when dramatizing it in his *Phoenissae* (410 BC), chose to eschew. What moral force the episode had for those who contemplated it at Pyrgi is open to speculation: but the local popularity of the episode may have something to do with the shadowy figure of Stesichoros, the 'chorus master' who may have been active in the sixth century BC in Magna Grecia, especially Sicily. Of his work we possess precious little: subsequent references to it by other writers, however, leave us in no doubt that Stesichoros worked up many episodes (such as the Tydeus-Melanippus tale) into full-blown and much-loved ballads. It may be that the sculptors hired to execute the Pyrgi pediment were Greeks, and we know that Greek traders frequented Pyrgi as both port and sanctuary, but the context is an Etruscan one, and we should assume that many Etruscans recognized the myth depicted on the pediment and were reminded of a poem (the necessary adjunct for pointing the moral: and we must bear in mind that temples are places of moral education).

Two Etruscan temples datable to the last quarter of the sixth century BC – the Portonaccio sanctuary of Minerva at Veii and the Sant'Omobono temple of Mater Matuta in the Forum Boarium at Rome –

feature terracotta pedimental or akroterial decoration (i.e. from *akroteria* or roof decorations of
houses or temples) that depicts the apotheosis of
Herakles: his admission to deified status on Olym-
pus, conducted by his divine protectress Athena
(or Minerva). Chronologically it is inviting to compare these with the limestone temple set up on the
Athenian Acropolis during the rule of Pisistratus,
where the pedimental decoration also shows the
apotheosis of Herakles. In the Athenian context, it
is suggested that Herakles is being proposed as a
mythical alter-ego of the tyrant Pisistratus: in the
apotheosis of Herakles we are to read the divine
protection and right to rule of Pisistratus. Later,
Alexander the Great and some of the Roman emperors were to adopt Herakles for this same propaganda purpose: for Herakles had a usefully
ambiguous status, being a mortal transformed into
a deity, and rulers might avoid charges of impiety
by choosing to model themselves on him rather
than one of the standard members of the pantheon.

So what is the meaning of the apotheosis at these
Etruscan temples? At Veii we cannot put names to
possible rulers (tyrannical or not), but at Rome the

date of the Sant'Omobono temple more or less fits
with the supposed period of rule of the Etruscan
king Tarquinius Superbus – 'Tarquin the Proud' –
whose name is enough to lend credence to the idea
that he, like his Athenian counterpart, saw in the
apotheosis of Herakles the chance to bolster his own
position by erecting a temple whose decoration
reminded onlookers that some men become gods.

Myth manipulation sounds insidious, but it is in
the nature of myth to offer the possibilities of adoption on a political, personal or localized basis. This
last factor may again explain what some scholars
see as 'mistakes' in Etruscan representations of
Greek myth. An early-fifth-century BC vase in the
Louvre (fig. 53) appears to depict Herakles (identifiable from his knotted lionskin and white-painted
club) taking on a half-man, half-bull figure: the
Minotaur, of course – but, we think, should it not
be the deed of Theseus? From our received knowledge of Greek myth, yes; but that does not mean
that the Etruscans need share such knowledge. In
the cultural ambience that produced this vase, it is
possible that Herakles as a hero counted for more
than Theseus (who by the early fifth century BC had
been claimed and manipulated by the Athenians
into being *their* special hero). This phenomenon of
subtracting exploits from one hero and giving them
to another (more popular, more acceptable or more
meaningful) would not be confined to Etruria. It
occurs in many marginal areas of the Greek world.
Interestingly, there happens to be a sealstone from
Cyprus (fig. 54) that depicts a Minotaur-like beast

*53 Etruscan black-figure vase: Herakles and the
Minotaur.*

*54 Cypriot gem, showing Herakles killing the
Minotaur (not to scale).*

being stabbed by a Herakles-like figure (the beard and the quiver slung over the shoulder are key Herakles attributes), and here the 'mistake' is simply explicable as owing to the superior popularity of Herakles over Theseus in east Greece.

It is clear that some myths enjoy a popularity in Etruria not matched in their country of origin. One of the early representations, the Suicide of Ajax, crops up subsequently on a whole series of vases, bronzes, gems and mirrors. Its details grow increasingly complex: there are references to Ajax's virtual invulnerability (having been once swaddled by Herakles), and so on one mirror (fig. 55) we see Athena considerately directing the hero to a point under his left armpit where he could still impale himself; references to the hyacinth that sprouted from the ground where his blood spilled; one bronze statuette looks to refer to an acrobatic routine, 'The Frenzy of Ajax' (known to later writers such as Lucian and Petronius), which was a banquet entertainment that involved a set of backward somersaults over vertical swords; and many gems feature the poignant single motif of Ajax doubled-up over his sword. We must wonder what it was about the myth that particularly appealed to the Etruscan consciousness. To speak of a 'heroic strain in the Etruscan character' to which such tragic figures made natural appeal is too vague. We

55 *Etruscan mirror with Athena and Ajax.*

might compare the eighteenth-century predilection for scenes of classical myth in oil painting, where such pictures offered 'a system of etiquette', 'examples of how the heightened moments of life – to be found in heroic action, the dignified exercise of power, passion, courageous death, the noble pursuit of pleasure – should be lived, or, at least, should be seen to be lived.' (John Berger, *Ways of Seeing*, London 1972, p. 101.) Greek myth may have been exemplary to certain Etruscans in this sense (though it is not necessary to suppose some inbuilt vacuity in such models, as might be claimed for the eighteenth century parallel): in the case of Ajax, a very specific code of conduct may be implied on the part of those who, for instance, used the motif of his suicide as their signet-seal. Like the Japanese Samurai, this could be a restricted and aristocratic code: but it is important to relate some meaning of the tragedy for those who adopted the myth-symbol. The possibility of the drama being played out on stage is not remote: one Etruscan red-figure vase (fig. 56) shows Ajax striking a very theatrical pose, addressing Athena (who stands with one foot on one of the sheep that Ajax has slaughtered in mistake for his fellow Greek commanders), and with his sword ready to take his act

of suicide, and a very Etruscan-looking demon ready to usher him off the worldly stage.

Myths should be taken to work in a paradigmatic manner as much in their Etruscan as in their Greek context. The message of the Suicide of Ajax is, 'Ajax brought shame upon himself and killed himself: in such circumstances, I would do the same.' Less stringent paradigms may be sought in some of the myths apparently favoured by the Etruscan purchasers of Greek vases. Herakles returns on a large number of these vases, and one Athenian painter (after Beazley, the 'Priam Painter') seems to specialize in scenes of the apotheosis of Herakles by chariot. The context of these vases is not the context of temple decoration, however: it is the context of tombs, death and burial. We know from a variety of sources (amongst them the numerous alabaster sarcophagi produced at Volterra) that the Etruscans conceived of death as a journey and often represented it as a chariot-ride (reflecting, perhaps, the actual funeral cortege that took the deceased out of the precincts of the society of the living and off to the necropolis, the community of the dead), so is it possible that those who owned these vases saw in the apotheosis of Herakles a paradigm of their personal immortality, achieved at the moment of death? If Athenian pottery workshops were shrewd enough to produce special shapes for

56 *Etruscan red figure vase with Ajax.*

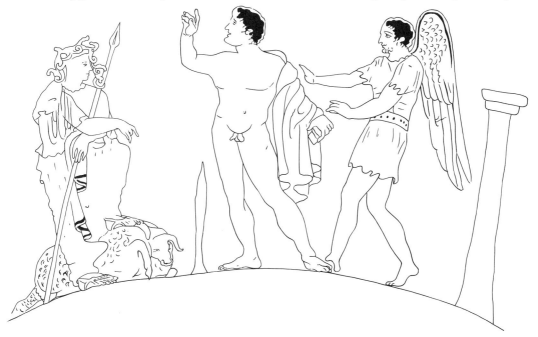

the Etruscan market, they could also produce specially-favoured subjects: if the Etruscans were sensitive to the morphology of their imported vases, they were sensitive also to the iconography.

The prestige and uses of literacy

The transmission of myth forms part of a package in which, as we have said, literacy and language are inevitably bound up. If we do not realize this, we shall find ourselves locked into some of the ludicrous hypotheses launched by respectable Greek-oriented archaeologists. Witness a specialist in Greek iconography trying to explain why so many images of Herakles prevail in Etruria: 'The "cyclic" narrative of the deeds of Herakles was probably matched by a work in which the story was told in simple pictorial form especially for the barbarians who did not know Greek. We must assume the existence of such "picture-books" in order to understand the familiarity of the Etruscans with the Greek legend.' (Karl Schefold, *Myth and Legend in Early Greek Art*, London 1966, p. 74.)

Without pushing the idea that Greek myths were circulated as texts in Etruria, we can still reject this absurd comic-strip theory, although the degree to which oral knowledge was matched by literal knowledge is a question worth exploring. Many of the Greek vases that were purchased by the Etruscans not only told myth-stories but also had inscribed or painted names for the protagonists of those stories. Were the Etruscans baffled by those names?

The answer is that it must have depended on which Etruscans, which part of Etruria, and which period. Literacy in the Greek alphabet is an innovation, the rate of adoption of which in the Etruscan sphere depends upon not only the activity of the agents of change (who may, if the notion of craft-literacy is accepted, have been openly didactic: the *grammatistai* – teachers of writing – of the Greek world who went out like commercial missionaires to the illiterate), but also the perceived advantage of letters in an oral situation. Archaeology can do little to illuminate literacy if literacy is understood in the 'lettered' or 'literary' sense – that is, we cannot say how many young Etruscans were

schooled to read Homer – but it can throw light upon 'pragmatic' literacy, the literacy bound up in political, religious, commercial and family affairs.

There are two schools of thought here. One ascribes the development of literacy, in particular onomastic literacy – the ability to read and write the names of people – to the growth of urban society and the need to define increasingly complex social and familial structures within the Etruscan *polis* (city-state). The other sees the onomastic system as pre-dating the introduction of the alphabet, serving as an oral protocol of patronymics reserved for an élite, who recognized the hereditary transmission of a family name as a social privilege and sought to accentuate the prestige by adopting, as an élite, the extra power of literacy.

This notion that literacy is a source of almost magical power – that it was, in Etruria as in parts of the ancient near East, the prerogative of a priestly ruling class – is a tempting way of explaining the fact that the alphabet entered Etruria at roughly the same time that it entered most of Greece, i.e. the mid-seventh century BC, but in Etruria spread more thinly within society. So while in Greece by the fifth century BC a good number of relatively humble craftsmen (pot painters being amongst their number) are well-versed in writing skills, literacy in Etruria still seems restricted from that class. There are, it is true, some physical indications to the contrary – odd letters on objects distinctly removed from an élite context, such as letters scratched on loom-weights and spindle-whorls, which also raise questions about female literacy – but more obvious qualifications are to do with chronology and locality. Chronologically, we may see literacy in the seventh century BC as being a 'chiefly' acquisition. The contexts of the early abecedaria (the Marsiliana ivory tablet, a practice slate of Greek letters, which is in fact the earliest of its kind to be found anywhere in the Greek world; the *bucchero* flask from the Regolini-Galassi tomb), being rich and unusual tombs, would confirm this. In the sixth century, as the city takes shape, the ceremonial functions of literacy may be seen as giving way to business and bureaucratic needs. This pragmatic change may be symbolized by the manner in which the *economia del dono* – the system of gift-exchange, strongly tied up with ritualized

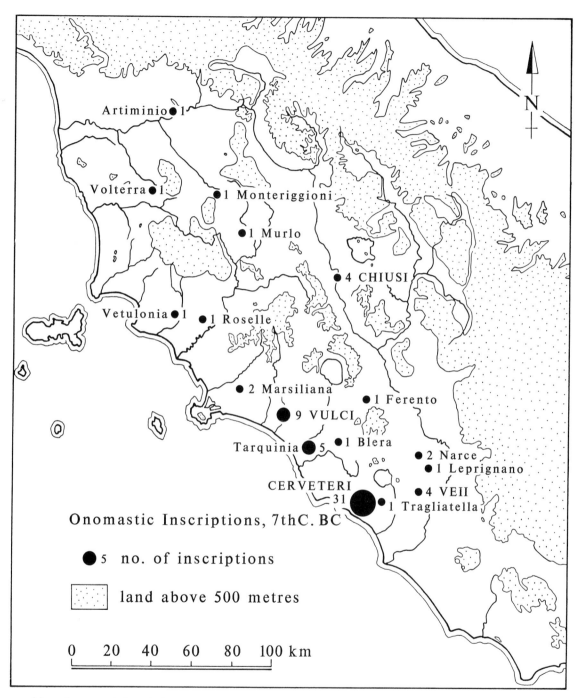

57 *Map of onomastic inscriptions.*

friendship between kinship groups and peer groups and characterized in many inscriptions by the *mi mulu*, 'I was given', formula on *bucchero* drinking vessels and the like – yields to the more abrupt graffiti used by traders like Sostratos.

The Etruscan scripts that have survived all relate to 'pragmatic' literacy, referring to religious functions, litigation between families, the marking of territory and so on. We have only indirect testimony of what must have been a substantial body of literature, the family histories: thanks to the *elogia* that the Romanised Etruscans of Tarquinia set up to commemorate their ancestors. To go back as far as the fifth century BC (as in the case of the *elogium* for Velthur Spurinna), these nostalgic Etruscans were not inventing false respectability but probably translating into Latin documents of family history that already existed in Etruscan. As a practice this should be compared to the *ricordanze* set down by the patrician families (and sometimes aped by the bourgeois) of Renaissance Florence: 'memoranda', events and accomplishments and deeds pertaining to a particular family.

There is also a spatial qualification to the spread and use of literacy in Etruria. As we have seen with regard to the transmission of myth, the primary contact zone is by definition more cosmopolitan and the reasons for wanting or needing to read and write are more varied and more pressing, with characters like Sostratos regularly calling. And if we make a simple mapping of the onomastic inscriptions so far found that belong to the seventh century BC (fig. 57), it is clear where this contact zone lies. If Cerveteri is deemed the epicentre for the spread of Greek myth in Etruria, it may also be seen as the pioneer zone of literacy in Etruria, the first Etruscan centre where a need to legitimize possession was met by the adoption of writing skills. It follows, therefore, that some of the abecedaria found in the hinterland are roughly done, being at a phase of secondary transmission: hence

58 *Leprignano inscription.*

our queer centaurs from Narce are matched by a very straggly set of letters from Leprignano in the Agro Capenate (fig. 58), judged to be 'the work of a barely literate writer'.

The death of the Etruscan language

A postscript on this process of cultural change should be given, though it goes beyond the chronological scope of this book. What was left of the Etruscan language by 90 BC, the date at which Roman citizen-rights were extended to the Etruscan cities? It has been described as 'on the one hand a learned tongue, and on the other a peasant patois'. Philologists sometimes claim that the phonetics and phonology of Etruscan account for the so-called *gorgia toscana*, 'the Tuscan burr', that even if Etruscan itself is not a substratum of Tuscan Italian, the natural tendency of Etruscan speakers to aspirate certain consonants was carried over into their localized pronunciation of Latin.

This seems unlikely, although the motto, 'Everything is older than we think', may apply as reasonably in linguistics as in any other historical field. The archaeological picture of the process of cultural change as it occurs with the Roman conquest of Etruria does, however, reveal the prominence of primary contact zones again (if it is fair to characterize conquest as contact!): the first city to demonstrate a general adoption of Latin, as far as we can tell from inscriptions, is Cerveteri. Cerveteri was the first Etruscan city to become a Roman *municipium* and appears to have adopted Latin in pragmatically literate terms by the end of the second century BC. The change of language anticipates many other aspects of cultural change (as has been pointed out: 'We know in almost all cities of Latin inscriptions written on Etruscan monuments; but nowhere Etruscan texts inscribed on Roman monuments'). And it probably occurred as a pragmatic choice: like the citizens of Cumae, who in 180 BC petitioned the Roman senate to make Latin the *lingua franca* of their town, the inhabitants of Cerveteri will have perceived advantages in using Latin.

The elements of space and time are again important to note. Cerveteri goes Latin by the end of the second century BC; at centres like Chiusi the process is delayed by a further half century or so. Perugia has yielded some valuable tomb-evidence for this period: in the nineteenth century, the Rufia family tomb, which contains 39 inscriptions of which one is bilingual and five are Latin, the change taking place about the mid first century BC; and more recently, the Cutu family tomb, which contains the burial urns of a family through the third to the first centuries BC, shows the Etruscan family name *Cutu* becoming the Latin family name *Cutius*. And then there are the hinterland areas, where the use of Etruscan persisted longest: hence the Hepni family tomb at Asciano, in the Clusine hinterland, where Roman coins of 15 BC were found in conjunction with some burial urns inscribed in Etruscan: at the end of the first century BC, therefore, a century's lag behind Cerveteri.

VI
RITUAL

It is probably the profane tenor of twentieth-century existence that induces us to imagine that the material remains of an ancient society will tell us whatever we want to know about that society. Only a very foolish archaeologist would claim, however, that a structure of beliefs can be dug up from the ground. Archaeology can encourage a certain at-homeness with the material expressions of belief, both minor and monumental, but beyond the basic establishment of sanctuary sites, and beyond the typologies of votive gifts and dedications made at such sites, we rarely achieve more than inklings as to the ideas and intentions underlying ancient ritual.

This admitted, we have a choice of approaches. We can take a consistently flippant or rational line: whenever we come across some image or building that perplexes us we can assume that if it is meaningless to us then it was originally meaningless. This approach is generally allied with an aloof, no-nonsense attitude towards metaphysics of any kind; it is the kind of approach exemplified by the young German archaeologist encountered at Tarquinia by D. H. Lawrence:

'He is a modern, and the obvious alone has true existence for him. A lion with a goat's head as well as its own head is unthinkable. That which is unthinkable is non-existent, is nothing. So, all the Etruscan symbols are to him non-existent and mere crude incapacity to think. He wastes not a thought on them: they are spawn of mental impotence, hence negligible.' (*Etruscan Places*, Penguin ed. 1950, p. 103.)

We do not know what progress this German scholar later made – he may have abandoned ar-chaeology in favour of Logical Positivism – but his attitude is still shared by plenty of classical archaeologists. A related approach to this dismissal of meaning is more cynical: it involves consigning whatever excavated material that we do not understand to the sphere of ritual simply on the grounds that it is a mystery to us. Once consigned, there's an end on it: it is the hocus-pocus we have transcended, or else it is the exploitation of simple people by a cunning priesthood. A Marxist-inclined analysis of this type is attractive to those of a lazy intellectual disposition, and again plenty of present-day advocates might be cited.

Refusing to take these options – which are grossly dissatisfying whenever one meets them in action, or rather in inaction – requires us to shake off some of our twentieth-century enlightenment and make proper efforts of imagination. Limits upon what we can know should not impose limits upon our curiosity. In themselves, the archaeological remains of Etruscan ritual say little. We look upon the Gorgon's face (fig. 59) not as an image of the Gorgon but as an artefact: without imagination, we shall examine its moulding and colouring, the manner in which the ears and nostrils have been rendered; we shall compare it with other terracotta masks or antefixes of the region, or even of the Mediterranean world; we shall classify it, date it, exhibit it. We may name the workshop that produced it; we may even go on to identify the social factors involved in its production. But it would probably take a child to ask what is really the most important question: What does it mean?

The hurried adult reply is: 'It's *apotropaic*' – an image put up to ward off evil – but this is an incomplete answer. Is this the mask of the Gorgon, or a

59 *Temple (?) antefix of Gorgon's face, late sixth century* BC.

gorgon? Is it Medusa, freshly decapitated by Perseus? Why does an exposed tongue ward off evil? And if the image is frightening, why should one be frightened when approaching the place where it was mounted?

Finding answers to these and like enquiries is not simple, and the answers are not likely to be definitive. We are talking about things that we cannot touch, clean or classify. In the passage cited from Lawrence, what defies comprehension is literally the chimerical. If archaeology provides a sense of at-homeness with the past, it seems pernicious to insist upon the *otherness* of that same past by imaginatively exploring the rites of its religion, but this is precisely what we must do: admit the otherness, and seek to understand it as best we can.

The cities

The archaeologist is bound to take the scope of ritual in terms of its dictionary definition: 'of, with, consisting in, involving, religious rites': no more and no less than what is implied there. It seems right to begin with the establishment of cities. When Romulus ploughed out the extent of his new city on the Palatine, he was believed to have been following the ritual practices of the Etruscans: certain procedures laid out in the *disciplina Etrusca* (the Etruscan religious system) which determined and sanctified a city foundation. This is not easily accommodated by the usual historical-geographical theories of the morphogenesis of cities, so what can archaeology do to substantiate Roman tradition?

We can glean some evidence from the 'iconography of power'; when political institutions are indentified with religion, they carry the icons of religious authority. It needs only superficial study of Etruscan art to see how certain 'symbol systems' worked. The augurs, for example, carried long crook-staffs (fig. 60), so even when they are not depicted gesturing up at the flight of birds in their ritual stance, the presence of the staff is enough to invest them with a particular political-religious status. And it is these augurs who would have been responsible for the city foundation rituals. The nature of such rituals is possibly suggested by an extraordinary series of bronze tablets found at Gubbio in the fifteenth century and preserved there as 'The Iguvine Tables'. They are inscribed partially in Latin but mostly in a local Umbrian script akin to Etruscan: their date seems to be around the second century BC, but of course they may derive from much older documents.

Reading the Iguvine Tables is a grand game for philologists and fraught with uncertainties. It

appears, however, that one section of the Tables does refer to the ritual protocol involved in consecrating a city. This has been read as follows: A fixed point of reference is made by the natural eminence, the *arx* (or, in Umbrian, *okri*) of the city. It is here that the augural stones or platforms (*sellae augurales*, or *vapersos avieklos*) are located, as well as the principal altar (*ara divorum*). These in turn furnish fixed points for the taking of an upper angle (*angulus summus*) and a lower angle (*angulus imus*). Hence the practice of augury: for the angles will be drawn according to the flightpaths of specific birds; the point where lower angles intersect with upper angles should then determine the sacred limits of the city. The city walls as such may matter less than the *pomerium*, the area immediately behind and beyond the walls (*post moerium*) in which no building was done and which in Latin terms marked the formal delimitation of magisterial powers. Figure 61 gives some idea of how this procedure looks in diagram form. The reader will appreciate how ab-

60 *Augur (detail of the Tomb of the Augurs, Tarquinia, c. 510 BC).*

61 *Reconstruction of ritual on Iguvine tables.*

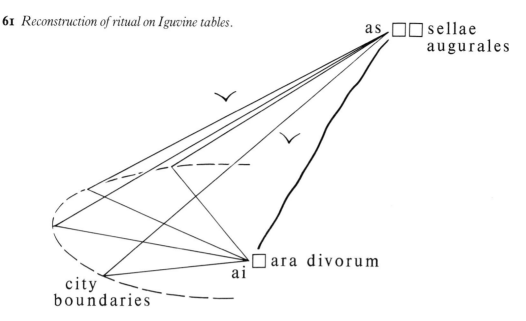

as   sellae
      augurales

ara divorum
ai

city
boundaries

as   angulus summus

ai   angulus imus

∨   bird flight

stract this seems and will perhaps feel incredulous that a city's boundaries can be determined by a combination of pure geometry and bird-spotting. Two things should be borne in mind: first, that the maintenance of an ideal in city-building is perfectly congruent with a general failure to meet that ideal – true as much in Etruscan Italy as it was later in Renaissance Italy; and second, that the Iguvine Tables are retrospective documents. However they are interpreted, they still look like religious formalizations of a political *status quo* established in early-Roman Gubbio: in a sense they are themselves icons, probably made public or invoked only on special occasions.

The notion that ritual procedure can work in a retrospective way is important to our understanding of Etruscan cities within a landscape. It is quite clear that the foundations of most Etruscan cities lie not in the rites prescribed by the *disciplina Etrusca* but in the synoecism, or coming-together, of divers settlements on a single plateau. This is plainly the

case at Tarquinia, and is becoming clearer at Cerveteri: beneath the large buildings currently being explored there are the circular remains of Villanovan period hut-houses. It is during the sixth and fifth centuries BC that an axial arrangement is imposed, a process mirrored in the principal necropolis of Cerveteri, the Banditaccia, where the large circular tombs of the seventh and early sixth centuries BC give way to regular 'streets' of tombs. It remains to be seen whether at Cerveteri the orientation of temples determines the orientation of streets; certainly it looks as if the large edifice currently being explored – probably a temple with three cellas, erected in an area of formerly domestic habitation – was deliberately set in alignment with the late-sixth-century BC 'Sanctuary of Hera', a good stone's throw to the north. The building is dated to *c.* 500 BC: is it the result of some ritual codification of the city of Cerveteri at that period?

Our best example of an 'ideal' city in Etruscan Italy, a city laid out from its inception according to ritual conventions, is Marzabotto. Etruscan colonists from Chiusi or some other part of Central Etruria arrived at this small site on the River Reno, not far from Bologna (Felsina), towards the end of the sixth century BC. They built Marzabotto as a 'New Town' (see Chapter II), and the result, a neatly orthogonal layout, has been well-known ever since its excavation in the last century. Marzabotto is not unique: it is simply a very good example of the same 'ideal' planning that the Etruscans brought to Campania when they occupied Capua during the late sixth century BC. A miniature version of this orthogonal procedure is evident at the colonial foundation of Bagnolo S. Vito, near Mantua, as well as at the later city of Musarna in South Etruria, which is currently being excavated by French archaeologists. Interesting for our present purposes, however, is that at Marzabotto the points of alignment for the whole city (see Chapter II, fig. 25) are provided by the altars and temples on the *arx*, or acropolis, of the site. These cast the north-south orientation of the settlement and hence determine the pattern of roads and houses. Furthermore, excavators in 1856 are known to have found an isolated platform (now destroyed and cryptically referred to as Y), which stood on the highest point of the acropolis: this would be a good candidate for the *auguraculum*, the vantage-point from which the augurs took their signs.

Few Etruscan cities are known archaeologically, and indeed few are knowable, so we shall be excused if we cite, as further evidence for the ritual procedure of city foundation, the case of Cosa. Cosa is not an Etruscan town, nor even an Etruscan colony: it was built *ex novo* by Roman pioneers in 273 BC on a promontory south of the Etruscan port settlements of Talamone and Orbetello, and it is fair to assume that Etruscan city-founding ritual influenced its building. We find, amongst the very few buildings that can be identified as belonging to the first phase of the colony, a square precinct, cut into the highest point of the colony site, and an adjacent pit or crevasse. This platform, chosen for the panorama it affords, eventually becomes the foundation of the *arx* of Cosa, and the pit, which evidently served as a receptacle for sacrifices, determines the central point of the subsequent

capitolium or temple, as its excavator notes, 'forcing upon its designers both adaptation to a steep and unbalanced site and a series of unusual adjustments of its approaches' (fig. 62). This would fit with what we have inferred at Marzabotto: that the establishment of the *auguraculum* is the ritualistic conception of the city, even when it causes difficulties for later development.

Within the city walls, sites of cult are not necessarily confined to a separate eminence that we might term as an acropolis, but temple buildings have been found to occupy the high points as a rule. This is the case at Veii (Piazza d'Armi) and Tarquinia (Ara della Regina). At Orvieto, no less than eight temples are attested inside the city boundaries, distributed more or less along the spine of the plateau and culminating with the Belvedere sanctuary, which – as its name suggests – commands impressive views from the north-east edge of the city.

The cemeteries

The nature of such views leads us to an important consideration of the topography of Etruscan ritual. Those who go to the sites of Etruscan cities will realize that a certain pattern is operating. If one stands anywhere within the precinct of ancient Cerveteri – precincts now mostly occupied by the parochial vineyards – the view in every direction includes, quite conspicuously, the tombs of former inhabitants. Here Etruria strikes us as a landscape of commemoration. The effect is typically registered by George Dennis; this passage, taken almost at random, describes a visit to the site of Norchia:

> 'At length we turned a corner in the glen, and lo! a grand range of monuments burst upon us. There they were – a line of sepulchres, high in the face of the cliff which forms the right-hand barrier of the glen, some two hundred feet above the stream – an amphitheatre of tombs!' (*Cities and Cemeteries of Etruria*, London 1883, I, p. 196.)

This is still how Norchia strikes one, and of course the effect is heightened when nothing or little is left of the city and only the cemetery remains (fig. 63). The question that emerges is, was

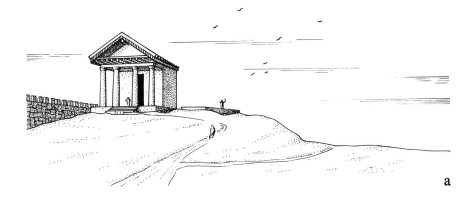

a

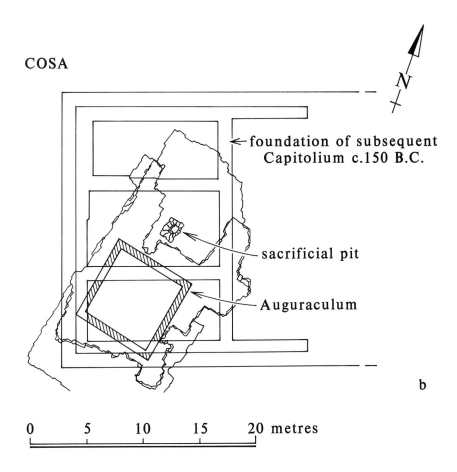

COSA

foundation of subsequent
Capitolium c.150 B.C.

sacrificial pit

Auguraculum

b

0   5   10   15   20 metres

62 *Arx at Cosa.* **a** *reconstruction;* **b** *plan (after Brown 1980).*

63 *The West cemetery, Blera.*

it the intended effect? Were the cemeteries intended to dwarf the cities, either physically or sym-
bolically? Does the concept of *necropolis* bulk larger
in the ideology of the Etruscan landscape than the
concept of *polis*?

We can accept that the tombs outside Etruscan
cities represent, in various ways, considerable
investments of labour and other resources, but
having accepted that a choice of interpretation
faces us. In the case of the cliff-cut façades of sites
like Norchia and Castel d'Asso, profane enlightenment sees nothing more than the expression of conspicuous urban consumption, families amongst an
urbanized élite, competing with each other to produce the most impressive façade. It is not easy to
see how this interpretation would work when
applied to cemeteries such as those at Tarquinia or
Vulci, where the investment in painted walls or
Greek vases and other luxury items remains closed
from general view. The stranger to Etruscan religion naturally cannot understand the sheer effort

of these cemeteries, nor, probably, could the
Romans. Pliny was outraged by the labyrinthine
tomb set up by the legendary Lars Porsenna of Chiusi: it is all so much *vanitas*, or even lunacy (*vesana
dementia*: see Pliny's *Natural History* Vol. XXXVI,
19, 91–3).

If we approach matters of ritual sympathetically,
however, an alternative interpretation opens to us.
Suppose these cemeteries to embody a genuine
faith. Suppose the dead and buried to have their
own dominion in Etruscan ideology, a dominion
that can be physically located. Suppose the physical relationship between city and cemetery to be
underwritten by a metaphysical structure: the relationship between *polis* and *necropolis*, between the
society of the living and the community of the
dead. At the risk of literally idealizing the past by
appropriating or approximating the Etruscans to
our own systems of metaphysics, this is what we
shall here attempt.

In recent years there has emerged a self-styled
'archaeology of death', but its exponents have
mostly shied clear of tackling mortuary rituals in
Greece, Etruria and the Roman world. Moreover,
it has rarely probed beyond death as a 'social
event': so whilst analysing the ceremonial or formal
behaviour of a given community, and interpreting
the appurtenances of this formality or ceremony, it
has failed to tell us much about actual eschatology –
what really motivated those who behaved in this
way, and what they conceived of the afterlife.

Recourse to anthropological theories proves
more fruitful. This too has some bearing on social
organization, given the implications of ancestral-
ism – and remembering G. K. Chesterton's definition of tradition as 'the democracy of the dead'.
For a proper understanding of ritual behaviour, an
essential anthropological concept is that of *liminality*: literally, a being-on-the-threshold, a being-
neither-in-nor-out. The importance of this concept, expounded and popularized by Sir Edmund
Leach, has already been grasped by classical archaeologists, and its relevance to the study of cults
of the dead will readily become apparent. For
death is a rite of passage; or rather, it brings about a
rite of passage. The act of funeral and burial is a
ritual intended to assist the passage from one status
to another: from the status of living person to the

64 *Etruscan black-figure vase, c. 510 BC, depicting a* prothesis. *The deceased is laid out on a couch: on a stool underneath are left the deceased's summer sandals and winter boots.*

status of deceased ancestor, from the society of the living to the community of the dead. The passage implies a period of liminality, of being neither one status nor yet the other. The Greeks, when they laid out a deceased person on a couch for a period of mourning prior to interring or incinerating the body, termed this rite the *prothesis*: it is their stage of liminality. There is evidence, both archaeological and iconographical, that the Etruscans organized something like the Greek *prothesis* (fig. 64). In certain cases (depending on social status) this period will have been accompanied by special and unusual events: *ploratores* (professional mourners) will have been called in (figs. 65, 66), and games and feasts laid on. Much of Etruscan art has been

preserved in the context of tomb-decoration, and it is to be expected that the meaning of such art ultimately lies with Etruscan funerary rites.

Reading Etruscan funerary art is not always straightforward, however. The interpretation of the banqueting scenes frequently encountered in painted tombs at Tarquinia (and less frequently at Orvieto and Chiusi) is tricky because the meaning of the banquet changes over the three centuries during which it is depicted. In the fifth-century BC versions, it is clear that an outdoor and temporary setting to the banquet is intended, with many festooned drapes and garlands and patterned backgrounds indicating the texture and structure of a tent or catafalque. We, the onlookers, are meant to see the banquet held in honour of the deceased, celebrating the rite of passage, of which the painting offers itself as a permanent record. By the fourth century BC, however, these scenes of banqueting are taking on more symbolic meaning, as

65 *Grieving figure, from the Tomba del Pulcinella, Tarquinia (c. 510 BC).*

66 *Professional mourner, from the Tomb of the Augurs, Tarquinia. The inscription beside him reads* tanasar: *later we find the same word corresponding to the Latin* histrio, *'actor'.*

they include tokens of the underworld in anticipation of the arrival of the deceased there. In the Tomb of Orcus at Tarquinia, for example, the banquet is laid out under a pergola, but demons are in attendance; and as one passes into the ensuing rooms of the tomb-complex, it is like being in the Underworld. There is Cerberus the three-headed dog, there Sisyphus endlessly pushing his boulder, there Hades and Persephone; and beyond them, the Elysian Fields, the fine side of it: the pleasure of meeting with Theseus, Ajax, Agamemnon and Tiresias.

The differences in effect between the later and the earlier tombs have caused scholars to postulate changes in Etruscan eschatology over the period, but it is likely that beliefs regarding the afterlife changed less than the modes of painting. The most recently discovered painted tomb at Tarquinia has been christened the 'Tomb of the Blue Demons', and it indicates that the entry of demons took place

before the end of the fifth century BC. And that should not come as a surprise, when we remember that the Greek painter Polygnotus, who in the early fifth century BC decorated the walls of the Lesche at Delphi with scenes of the trip made to the underworld by Odysseus, included in his depiction not only Charon the Ferryman but also a demon whose appearance corresponds closely to the Tarquinian sprites. As Pausanias describes it: 'His colour is between blue and black, like that of the flies that settle on meat.'

Tombs such as the Tomb of the Blue Demons and the Tomb of Orcus indicate the extent to which Greek imagery and terminology permeated the Etruscan cult of the dead. Those buried in the Tomb of Orcus – which was the family tomb of the Spurinna clan – believed, as Socrates is reported to have believed shortly before his end, that death

67 *(above) Multi-teated lioness/leopardess, from the Tomba delle Leonesse, Tarquinia (c. 520 BC).*

68 *(below) Multi-teated feline on an Etruscan black-figure vase, c. 520 BC.*

69 *Winged genitalia: from the Tomba del Topolino,
Tarquinia (c. 500 BC).*

beginning of another, reaches its logical symbolic
expression with the depiction of the phallus, often
in stone at the entrance to a tomb or else painted
inside (fig. 69). Death hereby becomes the beginning of a new cycle: copulation, conception and nutrition. What emerges is both an old and a new
figure: the deceased takes on new status as an
ancestor, heroized and then worshipped for the
new heroized status.

Some Etruscan vases depict this epiphany. It
appears like the Greek 'entry' (*anodos*) of the god
Dionysos, like a head breaking up through the
earth (figs. 70, 71). The Etruscan cult of the dead

70 *Etruscan black-figure* oinochoe: *note vertical row
of teats along border, emphasizing the 'rebirth' of the
venerated ancestor (whose head is rising from the
ground).*

brought the chance to join the eternal community
of past souls. The achieved status is by implication
a heroized status. The characterization of heroized
status may be done either with references to Greek
epic (though names, of course, are transliterated
into Etruscan) or by combining Greek mythical
figures with celebrated men of Etruscan history (as
evident in the paintings from the François Tomb at
Vulci). The funerary process establishes the
deceased as a figure of cult worship. It is a new status. And if many of the objects deposited in the
tombs seem to us quaintly domestic – wine strain-
ers, cups, plates – it is because such objects were
installed in the tombs to mark not the finality of
death but the beginning of a new type of life. Even
heroes need to strain their wine.

The decoration of the Archaic tombs contains
this message as much as the more sophisticated imagery of the later period. The symbols may be less
direct but they are there. Take, for example, the
depiction of multi-teated animals on a tomb-wall
(fig. 67) and on a vase deposited in a tomb (fig. 68).
These are not painted for caprice: they have
obvious connotations of fertility. More specifically,
they allude to the condition of infant growth and
nutrition: the raising of new life. The alignment of
death with fertility, the end of one life with the

71 *Etruscan black figure* oinochoe, *early fifth century* BC: *the* anodos *of Dionysos? Note figure with vine or ivy strands acclaiming the rebirth.*

is a cult that transforms the dead into objects of veneration: the ritual creates from the dead a transcendent force that is both above society and at its very foundation.

The sanctuaries

If cemeteries are the locations for the cult of the dead (about which more will be said in Chapter VIII), then sanctuaries are the places where the living pay attention to their own earthly well-being.

This should very often be taken literally. The reasons for frequenting a sanctuary will include wanting a child, wanting a successful pregnancy, wanting to erase the pain of an arthritic limb, wanting a trouble-free voyage to Spain, and wanting to win a battle against another person, city or people. The invocation naturally involved some personal or collective cost.

It is a regrettable truism that the practical workings of even a well-excavated ancient sanctuary, such as Delphi, remain obscure to us. This is as true for Etruria as it is for Greece. We know that healing cults were practised at many sites; we know about the spread of the specific cult of Asclepius, especially in transapennine Etruria; we may even know which particular maladies were catered for at certain sites, thanks to patterns of votive material. What we do not know is just how much practical business was conducted at one of these sanctuaries: that is, whether it was residential, whether specialized physicians were available for consultation, and so on.

The range of sanctuary sites may be outlined according to a classification that seems to be becoming standard. This supposes three categories of sites: urban, extra-urban and rural. 'Extra-urban' is used to denote such sites of ritual activity as are located in the immediate environs of a city: Veii and Civita Castellana provide some good examples of this. Within this triple categorization (which is not terribly useful in itself) there are further variant factors. Along the coast there are cult sites associated with ports of trade, whilst inland the sanctuaries can be mapped according to road networks, water-sources and mountain tops. What constitutes a rural sanctuary is arguable: some of these 'rural sanctuaries', such as Monte Falterona and Brolio (both in Tuscany), are designated by virtue of deposits of bronze statuettes; others have altars or minor structures associated with them, such as Pieve Socana, to the north of Arezzo, and Grotta Porcina, near Blera; and others, such as Montetosto, a large and as yet poorly-explored plateau site between Cerveteri and Pyrgi, rank as monumental. There is also the *fanum Voltumnae*, traditionally cited as the chief pan-Etruscan sanctuary and confederate forum-place: it is supposed to be situated near to Orvieto or Bolsena, but so far no decent archaeological evidence supports this location.

The most ubiquitous cult of the living in the ancient Mediterranean world generally is the cult of birth. In Etruscan Italy this conflates, as we have seen, with the cult of death, in so far as death may be seen as a form of rebirth; to some extent a similar conflation takes place in modern Italy. The image of *Madonna con bambino* (mother with child) carries much more symbolic value than the *Madonna del parto* (mother of the pregnancy), who is specifically invoked by expectant mothers. So it is difficult to place a number of artefacts: when we come across an urn from Chiusi that is surmounted by the figure of a woman cradling a child – a cinerary urn, used to contain the ashes of a deceased person – we must wonder whether this be the urn of a prematurely-deceased child or a more symbolic reference to new birth in the afterlife.

The Etruscan equivalent to the Madonna is Hera. As in the Greek world, Hera is much more than the wife of Zeus. She is often seen on Etruscan mirrors, suckling Herakles at her breast. Sometimes she seems to be labelled as Hera, as at her supposed temple in the city of Cerveteri; or else she appears in her proper Etruscan guise as Uni, as at Gravisca, where she is the recipient of many votive terracotta swaddled infant-effigies. These are also numerous at Capua and Cerveteri.

If not Hera, then it is the mother-goddess figure who receives the cult. Mater Matuta (as she is known at the sanctuary of the Latin settlement at Satricum and at other central Italian sites) often figures as a child-carrying image (*kourotrophos*): at Satricum the range of votives dedicated to her includes not only models of swaddled babies but also reproductions of cockerels, doves and pomegranates. Real gifts are recorded in the Greek equivalent to this cult: worshippers of the mother-goddess took to the cult site special cakes, pomegranates, birds and snakes.

The ambiguity of the votives should be noted. It

72 *Votive terracotta: couple with child.*

is not always clear whether the votive is intended as an image of the goddess or as an image of the human supplicant to the goddess. Some votives from Etruscan sites show a couple with a child between them (fig. 72): is this a couple with one child hoping for another or a couple projecting a desired state? Or indeed is it the image of a divine couple with their divine offspring? Other votives present few problems by getting down to the basics of midwifery: hence the simple models of the uterus (fig. 73). Some sanctuaries, however, do appear to relate more to death than to life: there are, for instance, a number of swaddled-baby figurines from the Castelsecco site near Arezzo and the extra-

73 *Votive terracotta: model of uterus.*

explored. The site is coastal and is now half-swallowed by the Tyrrhenian Sea. Although some distance from Cerveteri, Pyrgi was linked to that city by a direct road and probably served as the principal port or *emporium* for Cerveteri and the Caeretan hinterland.

Pyrgi's importance lies not so much in its Etruscan character as in the fact that it was a cosmopolitan site. The key discovery came in 1964, when a triptych of gold laminate plaques bearing bilingual inscriptions was revealed. The two languages were not, as one might have expected, Etruscan and Greek but Etruscan and Phoenician: they attest the dedication of the Archaic temple (in fig. 74, Temple B) by Thefarie Velianas, ruler of Cerveteri, to Astarte (the Phoenician mother-goddess) and Uni (the Etruscan Hera). The dedication follows close on the first signs of monumental building at the site, in the second half of the sixth century BC: it is reasonable to suppose that the initiative for the building came from Cerveteri. The possible motives are varied: there may have been political motivation (sealing an alliance with the Phoenicians); commercial motivation (if Phoenicians traded on a regular basis at the port, they will have wanted a familiar place of cult); or it may have been bound up in some expiatory foundation (we are told by Herodotus, for example, that the Delphic oracle commanded the citizens of Cerveteri – Greek Agylla – to expiate for the crime of stoning to death on the shore a batch of Phocaean prisoners, prisoners taken, we may note, by a combined Etrusco-Phoenician force).

It is not unusual for a sanctuary to host more than one deity: hence it is not unusual for a sanctuary to perform a variety of cult functions. Pyrgi's history or prehistory as a cult site prior to the erection of Temple B is not clear, but its development between the early fifth and the late fourth centuries BC (it was annexed, along with the rest of the Caeretan coastline, by Rome in 273 BC) is providing much ground for discussion. The terracotta decorations to Temples A and B are arguably 'programmatic' in relation to cult practices. Amongst the votive material there are anatomical terracottas from the area of Temple A, suggestive of a healing function, and from the small area C (marked on fig. 74) there came numerous lanterns, which indicate

mural 'Oriental' sanctuary at Latin Lavinium that have mature adult faces and which must pertain to a chthonic cult. They were presented in the hope of securing rebirth for a deceased person. If Hera suckling the fully-grown Herakles is a model, then the hope is for immortality by divine adoption; this divine adoption leading to rebirth and immortality is a key theme of the cult of Dionysos, which has been traced as gaining credence in Etruria from the late sixth century BC onwards.

The sanctuary at Pyrgi

The best-known of Etruscan sanctuaries is Pyrgi. It has been under excavation for many years and is still producing surprises, even though the area adjacent to the sanctuary has yet to be properly

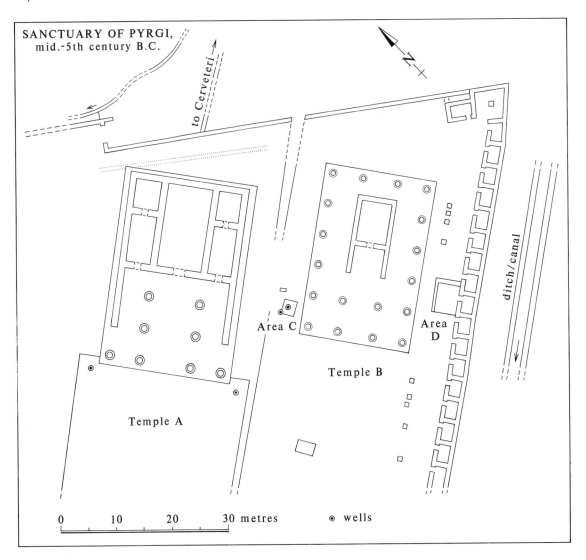

SANCTUARY OF PYRGI,
mid.-5th century B.C.

to Cerveteri

N

ditch/canal

Area C

Area D

Temple B

Temple A

0   10   20   30 metres   ⊙ wells

74 *Plan of temples at Pyrgi.*

some ritual conducted nocturnally. Throughout the sanctuary there have been plentiful finds of pottery cups and bowls, that is, small vessels for the pouring of libations.

While it is normal to think of a temple as the home of a particular deity, the fact that Pyrgi is a coastal and therefore cosmopolitan site should lead us to expect a considerable diversity of dedications. Ancient sources tell us that Pyrgi was variously the sanctuary of Leucothea, Eilithyia and Lucina. Dedications recovered from the sanctuary mention not only Astarte and Uni but also Thesan (the

Etruscan Aurora), Tinia (the Etruscan Zeus) and Suri (presumably related to the Faliscan *pater Soranus*, father Soranus, the Apollo-god worshipped on Mount Soracte). If the ambiguities and connections between these deities seem complicated, it is only a reflection of the flexibility of the sanctuary: it was built to serve an international community.

The cult associated with Astarte should be understood in this light. Astarte shares sites with Aphrodite at Eryx (Erice) on the west coast of Sicily and at Kition on the southern coast of Cyprus. Aphrodite is a favourite cult goddess for major port sites around the Mediterranean: she was wor-

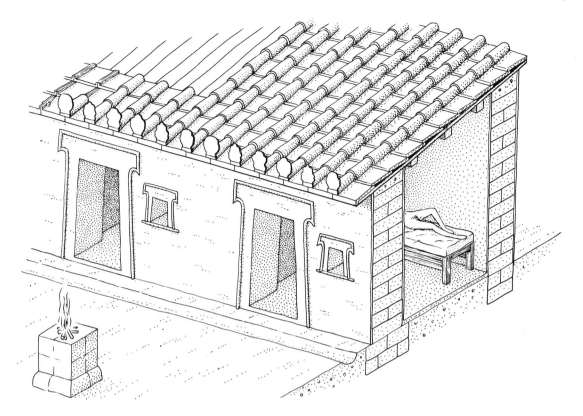

75 *Brothels at Pyrgi.*

shipped at Troezen, Piraeus (the port of Athens) and Naukratis, amongst other places. Most notoriously, she was worshipped at Corinth, and it now seems that what shocked St Paul at Corinth was also being practised at Pyrgi. As figure 74 shows, alongside Temple B (the temple dedicated to Astarte) there is a structure divided into multiple small cells. A charitable interpretation of these would be that they are shops, or perhaps hostel accommodation for those seeking a medical cure; but ports are never very salubrious places, and given that there is a Roman reference to the *scorta Pyrgensia* ('the Pyrgi harlots'), and given the presence of the Astarte-Aphrodite cult, it seems likely that the structure was a brothel of some official nature within the scope of the sanctuary. Figure 75 gives the excavator's idea of how these little love-nests may have looked.

The practice of a sacred prostitution, of course, is only one facet of the cult. A mariner may have

gratified his lust after a long journey but we would also have paid thanks to Astarte with certain sacrifices. We cannot say precisely what these were at Pyrgi, but no doubt they were not unlike those at Kition, where an inscribed bowl records that the devotee to Astarte had his head shaved for her and sacrificed a sheep and a lamb in her honour.

Tarquinia: the sacred area of Pian di Civita

Once upon a time, in the district of Tarquinia, a field was being ploughed; and when the ploughshare at a certain point sunk deeper into the ground than usual, a figure sprang up from the earth and immediately began to speak to the farmer. This figure was Tages, who according to Etruscan tradition had the appearance of a boy but the wisdom of an aged seer. The peasant, unnerved by the sight, raised a crowd of witnesses, and soon virtually the whole of Etruria was gathered at the spot. They formed an eager audience for Tages, who addressed them on the art of soothsaying and haruspicy: and his exposition formed the basis of the written *disciplina* of the Etruscans, later added to and expanded by further experiences.

Thus wrote Cicero in his treatise on divination (*De Divinatione II, 23*) and in scornful tones, for this seems to him all so much bunkum (*refellenda*) – what holy being could appear in this bizarre way, and what man would lie under the clods waiting to be discovered? Quite: and what man could be killed on a cross and return to life? Cicero's pompous rationality is almost as foolish as the attitude of some archaeologists in searching for the site of Tages' appearance at Tarquinia ('the quest for the historical Tages'), but indeed the myth – which seems entirely aetiological, since the peasant at the plough is given the name Tarchon, and hence the role of founder of Tarquinia – has been invoked by those excavating the Pian di Civita area of Tarquinia city. This area, some 700 m (750 yd) downhill from what later figures as the acropolis of Tarquinia (the Ara della Regina temple, whose fourth-century BC foundations are still imposingly visible) was certainly given over to some ritual activity and in its ninth-century BC phase does feature a natural cavity, which it might be tempting to view as the site of the appearance of Tages. One might as well search for the rag with which Athena wiped her thigh clear of the semen of Hephaistos, and threw to the ground – producing Erichthonius, one of the cult figures of Athens: these myths were not meant for archaeological investigation, and in the case of the Pian di Civita we do not know what was the scope of the ritual practised there. We can, however, trace the essentials of what took place there. To the end of the ninth century belongs a sacrificial deposit within the afore-mentioned cavity. This included a quantity of sawn-off animal horns, and the skeleton of a child, probably about eight years old, probably a boy and probably suffering from epilepsy. The first buildings in stone are erected at the site at the beginning of the seventh century, including a rectangular enclosure about the cavity. The finds from this period are made up of numerous libation bowls, traces of further infant burials and some important bronze votive objects, including a trumpet and a 'killed' shield, that is, a shield deliberately crumpled up and rendered useless. At the begining of the sixth century, the buildings are extended to include a large altar and the hollowing out of another pit, 2 m (2.2 yd) in diameter. The cult continues with further traces of cut-off horn pieces and more infant burials.

The suggested cult figure here is Uni, whom we know to have been worshipped at the Tarquinian port of Gravisca. Only small scraps of epigraphical evidence support her nomination, but it is plausible enough: Uni as goddess of shepherds is an appropriate recipient of goat and ram horns; Uni as mother goddess will accept the 'exemplary corpse' of the diseased child or still-born infant. More interesting than the melodramatic discovery of 'human sacrifice', however, is the significance of the three bronzes: the axe, the trumpet (*tromba*) and the shield. These are precisely the 'icons of power' of which we spoke with regard to city-founding ritual. The axe is the symbol of the chief magistrate (which puts the *fascis* into Fascism); the embossed shield symbolizes the chief warrior; and the trumpet has a part-civic, part-military and part-religious function – an emblem of the power to call meetings, start battle or initiate rituals, like Piggy's conch-shell in *Lord of the Flies*. These are not from a tomb, 'killed' when their owner died: they must have dedications to an apposite divinity by some Tarquinian leader by way of thanks-offering, consecrations or placed there to bring good luck.

VII
WARFARE

Military historians are generally unskilled in archaeology, and archaeologists are astoundingly slow to grasp the essentials of military history. This mutual incompetence has left us confused about Etruscan warfare. One strand of Roman tradition holds that the Etruscans were the first in Italy who 'fought with round shields of bronze and in phalanx formation', and although this claim is by no means held as a substantial consensus amongst Roman historians it has encouraged archaeologists to hunt for the types of weapons and armour that might furnish proof of it. The context of the tradition is in fact one of the standard tenets of Roman history: that the Romans were 'pupils who always outstripped their masters' (*fas est ab hoste doceri*) – a satisfying thought for Roman readers, but its rhetorical nature should make us immediately suspicious. The tenet could be as readily applied to the Samnites as to the Etruscans: the literary tradition varies.

Three types of evidence may be invoked for the reconstruction of Etruscan warfare: literary, iconographical and archaeological. The literary evidence is untrustworthy, and the iconographical evidence is to be treated with caution. Constructing Etruscan realities from depictions of warriors on either imported Greek and near-eastern artefacts or Etruscan imitations of such artefacts (fig. 76) is dangerous. The approach taken here will eschew as far as possible the iconography of warfare, whether Etruscan or otherwise, save where a ritual or mythical function can be ascribed to the images.

The archaeology of warfare deals principally with two sorts of remains: i) the deposition of arms and armour in graves; and ii) the fortifications put up around settlement areas. Before addressing the problems posed by the archaeological evidence, it is, however, worth spelling out just what is implied by claiming that the Etruscans brought the phalanx to Italy. The phalanx was a deployment of foot soldiers or, to use the original Greek terminology, hoplites. A hoplite was armed in such a way as to make it impractical and dangerous for him to fight outside the phalanx unit. He would have been heavily encumbered with bronze body armour (including greaves to protect the legs); he wore a helmet designed to cover as much of his face as possible (sacrificing sideways vision for added protection); and he carried a large round shield, which would have overlapped with those of the hoplites either side of him in the formation, and, as his main offensive weapon, a long spear. The phalanx moved forward as a unit, jabbing with the spears. It was logistically simple and easily raised from a state whose citizens were supplied with the requisite armour and trained together. Battles were often settled by the first clash. If the political and topographical terrain were suitable, hoplite warfare was an effective means of settling disputes between city-states.

The socio-political implications of the phalanx are as important as its implications for military strategy. Bronze armour is expensive. For the phalanx to be effective, large numbers of men must possess it, and the status of those men must be at least above the servile. This is why the Roman adoption of hoplite strategy is usually linked to the social legislation of Servius Tullius sometime around the sixth century BC, a programme of reforms that was said to include the issue of citizen armour. The first known Latin reference to the *palangis* is Republican and is a direct transliteration

76 *Detail of Greco-Etruscan amphora, c. 530 BC, in Basle Antikenmuseum. A file of hoplites advancing.*

of the Greek. There is no solid evidence to show that the Etruscans introduced the phalanx to Rome, and there is no real reason why the Romans should not have adopted it directly from the Greeks.

Studies in the typology and diffusion of armour have produced some highly inconsistent results.

The appearance of elements of hoplite armour in Etruria is taken to include 'revolutionary effects', while the appearance of such armour in neighbouring areas of central Italy, for example Picenum, and the area north of the Po means simply that 'Greco-Etruscan weapons were integrated into the existing warrior-equipment as rank- and status-symbols for the chieftains'. This is a sloppy analysis, and we need to examine the context of our evidence more carefully.

Assessing the evidence from graves

One basis for supposing that hoplite tactics were brought to Italy by the Etruscans is archaeological: the first hoplite panoplies known in Italy come from Etruscan graves.

With a few exceptions, these panoplies are poorly documented, but what precisely do they demonstrate? Deposits of arms and armour in graves are well-attested in the eighth and seventh centuries BC and provide important tokens of rank: amongst the more spectacular burials are the Tomba del Guerriero (Tarquinia: *c.* 680 BC), the Tomba del Duce (Vetulonia: *c.* 700 BC), the Regolini-Galassi tomb (Cerveteri: *c.* 675 BC), Tomb 43 from Narce (*c.* 680–650 BC), Tomb 94 from the Esquiline Cemetery, Rome, and Tomb 871 from the Grotta Gramiccia necropolis, Veii (both *c.* 700 BC). An eye-witness account of the discovery of the Avvolta tomb at Tarquinia (fig. 77) in the nineteenth century poignantly records how its excavator momentarily gazed upon the flesh of the interred warrior before it dissolved. The draughtsman's impression of this find gives us a full set of body armour (helmet, corselet, greaves), two circular bronze shields embossed with multiple concentric friezes, eight javelins, a double-edged sword and, inside a bronze-lidded vase, the remains of a 'killed' chariot. On a stone table adjacent to the deceased was laid a bronze diadem, overlaid with gold.

The body armour from this discovery has not survived, but the chances are that it resembled that preserved from Tomb 43, Narce (fig. 78). This is a rare survival of helmet and corselet together. The helmet, as we shall see, is of a recognizably 'Villanovan' type. The corselet is hammered out of a single sheet of bronze, riveted and reinforced: it probably follows a prototype in hide. But it is ornamental sheet bronze: as protection, it is undoubtedly less useful than thick leather. It is not functional and it is expensive. It is conspicuous display, not advanced military technology. Like the French general who witnessed the Charge of the Light Brigade, we are tempted to say, *'C'est magnifique mais ce n'est pas la guerre'*.

If we look at the 'Villanovan' helmet from Tomb 871, Veii (fig. 79), what should impress us most of

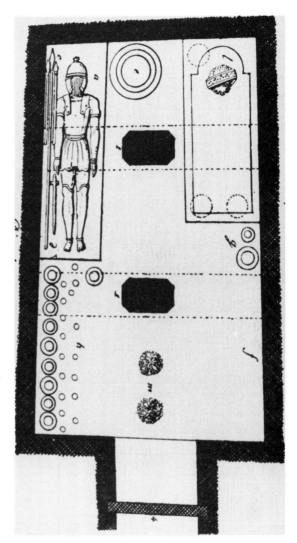

77 *The Avvolta tomb, Tarquinia. During its discovery in 1823, a thunderstorm broke out and while the excavators sheltered, the tomb was plundered and its contents dispersed.*

all is the fact that the height from base to top of crest is 64 cm (25 in.). Such a helmet would have been simply impossible to wear in a combat situation. Its context is not with actual warfare but with ritual. This is something that archaeologists have been slow to appreciate: that arms and armour as grave goods serve as enhancements of burial, as indicators of rank; amongst the deposits of domestic

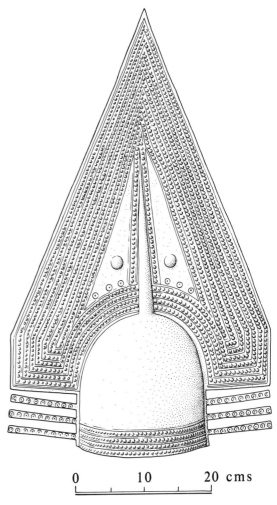

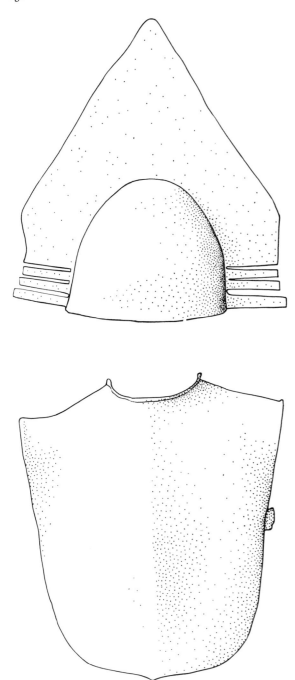

78 *From Tomb 43, Narce.*

79 *Villanovan helmet from tomb 871, Veii.*

0   10   20 cms

effects, the arms and armour are objects inspiring pride and reverence, objects that the Greeks would have termed as *agalmata*. Hence we find in the Villanovan period cemeteries of Tarquinia and elsewhere helmets actually used as covers for cinerary urns or, if the deposit of a metal helmet is too much, its imitation in clay.

Viewed in this light, the evidence from graves is likely to be misleading when it comes to claiming that the Etruscans fought with hoplite phalanxes. The burial of arms and armour in itself is a form of ritual, but the nature of the armour buried suggests that in the world of the living it was primarily an appurtenance of ritual; some of the weapons should perhaps be similarly classified. We can now recognize that the palstaves recovered from a grave such as the Tomba del Guerriero at Tarquinia belong to a sequence of Villanovan period weapon-types, but the nineteenth-century excavator of the tomb may not have been far wrong in identifying them as the blades of an early *fascis*, that is, as tokens of social rank and government. The palstave has no evident place within hoplite warfare but it

80 *Stele of Aule Feluske, from a tomba a circolo at Vetulonia, now in the Museo Archeologico, Florence.*

survives, in the form of the double axe, throughout the various changes to Etruscan equipment (fig. 80).

Figure 81 charts the development of weapons and armour in Etruria as revealed by actual archaeological finds. It shows that types of hoplite panoplies are owned by some Etruscan warriors by the end of the seventh century BC, but this does not demonstrate that Etruscan warfare was hoplite warfare. There is no perceptible increase in the deposition of armour in graves, although this may be a fact of little importance: it is one thing to be able to afford hoplite armour for military service, another thing to be able to afford to bury it. As it stands, the archaeological evidence cannot sustain the theory that there was in the sixth century a considerable body of 'middle-class farmers' who could afford to equip themselves in the 'newer fashion'. Panoplies such as that from the Osteria necropolis at Vulci (fig. 82), datable to 630–620 BC, should be understood as luxury acquisitions either from the Greek world or produced under Greek influence for the same ritual purposes as the extravagant 'Orientalizing' panoplies.

If we isolate one particular element of armour, the helmet (fig. 85), the superficial nature of the Etruscan 'adoption' of the hoplite panoply becomes clear. Some exquisite examples of the Corinthian-style helmet, with its built-in protection for neck, cheeks and nose, are known from Etruscan contexts: these are examples of the bronzesmith's craft, but as a type the Corinthian helmet did not make redundant the helmets that had developed from the bell-shaped Villanovan types. In fact these are the sorts that are commonly found (fig. 83): high, ovoid, with inset brim and with or without separately-attached cheek-guards. Another shape that stays with the Etruscans despite Greek influence is the so-called 'shrapnel' helmet: one of the early examples of this comes from the seventh-century BC Tomba del Duce at Vetulonia, and with minor variations it survives well into the fifth century BC – one such variant was taken from an Etruscan casualty at the battle of Cumae (c. 474 BC) by the Greek tyrant Hieron of Syracuse and dedicated by him to Zeus at Olympia (fig. 84).

The tactical implications here are clear. A soldier

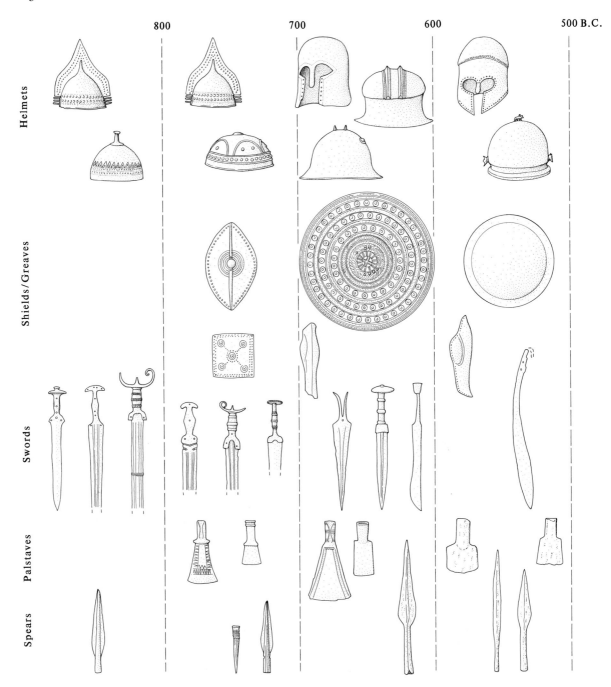

81 *Chart showing development of Etruscan military equipment (after Stary, 1979).*

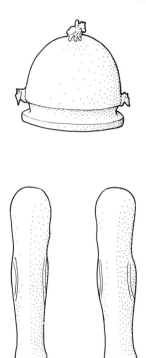

82 *Panoply from Osteria necropolis at Vulci.*

83 *Fifth-century BC Etruscan helmet* (The Vatican).

84 *Etruscan helmet dedicated at Olympia by Hieron of Syracuse. 'Hieron, son of Deinomenes/and the Syracusans/to Zeus, for victory over the Tyrrhenians.'* (British Museum).

Helmet-Types in Central Italy

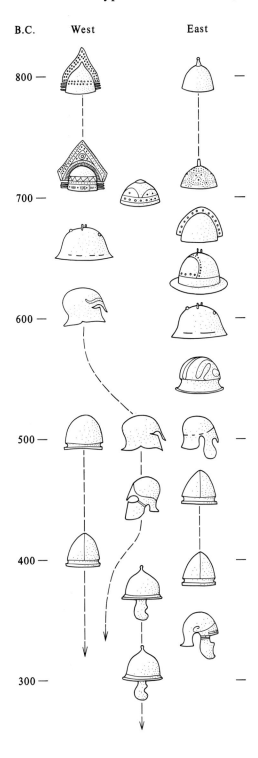

B.C.   West   East

800 —

700 —

600 —

500 —

400 —

300 —

85 *Etruscan helmets (after Stary, 1979).*

moving forward as part of a human tank, that is, in a phalanx, would be better served by the Corinthian helmet. A warrior engaged in a more fluid and open combat would find that the restrictions on his vision and hearing imposed by the Corinthian helmet made it more of a liability than a safeguard. The Etruscans ultimately preferred their own less restrictive design.

Finally, it is worth adding the following caveat: tanned or boiled leather hide makes for lighter and more effective protection than bronze armour. It was probably the best battlegear, but we shall never know how many men possessed it because it does not survive in the archaeological record.

The clan factor

The practice of warfare 'may favour both intensification and the emergence of hierarchial institutions.' (Renfrew, *Peer Polity Interaction and Socio-Political Change* Cambridge, Cambridge University Press, p. 8.) Like other areas of early-Iron-Age Europe, the identification of a warrior-based aristocracy from tomb deposits seems justified for Etruria in the eighth century BC, although it is less easy to imagine how battles were accordingly conducted. If, as we have suggested, the model of Greek hoplite strategy is unsuitable in the Etruscan context, what options remain open to us?

The clan factor is invoked here as an alternative terminology to the Latin *gens*. What precisely a *gens* constitutes in either Etruscan or Roman society is still imperfectly understood, but it is customary to consider the warrior aristocracy of the eighth century BC crystallizing, during the seventh and sixth centuries, into a gentilician structure, that is, a system of extended families effectively retaining aristocratic control of political and religious functions. We can see this crystallization in other areas, such as literacy, and in archaeological terms it is evident that the possession of bronze arms and armour was, like literacy, controlled by clan membership. An important extension of this is of course the culture of horses: in pre-colonial Africa, 'horses were the possessions of a politically dominant élite that was usually of immigrant origin and had established its domination over a land of peasant farmers.' (Goody *Technology, tradition and the state in Africa*, Cambridge, Cambridge University Press, pp. 48–9.) Tokens of aristocratic horse-culture in eight-century BC graves are the bronze bits of bridle and harness and, in exceptional cases, the two-wheeled chariot. Aristotle saw it as a political truth that aristocratic governments had a power base in the military culture of the horse, and there is, naturally, the same problem of defining the relics of horse ownership as there is for arms and armour. How much pertains to ritual and how much to the actual practice of war? How, for example, is a chariot deployed? Does an interred chariot signify the exceptional warrior status of the deceased when part of the society of the living, or is its presence in the tomb primarily to facilitate the passage from life to death – and hence simply imply exceptional wealth accrued by the deceased in the society of the living?

We have seen that the success of the phalanx system depends upon the arming of a body of middle-class citizens and that in Etruria there is no archaeological evidence for such an egalitarian move. If the possession of weapons, armour and horses were confined to aristocratic clan units, then the strategies of warfare in Etruria must be defined more by the models of medieval Italy than by those of Classical Greece. Some historians have already anticipated this by referring to certain semi-historical Etruscan characters, such as the Vibenna brothers from Vulci, as *condottieri* (cavaliers with private armies for rent). The military implications of this must be envisaged along the following lines: that in the event of a dispute between two competing Etruscan centres the ruling families of the respective centres mobilized their own members as the principal protagonists of the battle, backed up by ranks of lightly-armed and probably lightly-protected retainers and slaves. The warriors would have fought chiefly on horseback, with various types of body armour (including parts of the panoply described in Greek terms as 'hoplite'), and the contest would have been settled by their personal defeats or victories.

For an oligarchic society developed out of a warrior aristocracy, this is the most reasonable model of warfare. It should be pointed out here that by the fifth century BC the clan size could be considerable,

86 *Part of the Etruscan walls of Cerveteri.*

87 *Walls at S. Giovenale, during excavation (British School at Rome).*

and that the confinement of military equipment and training to the aristocratic sections of each Etruscan centre does not preclude their coming together in the face of an enemy without. Whilst such warfare may have proved a workable 'channel of communication' between the Etruscan centres, and a basis for raiding parties and amphibious expeditions, it was ultimately a top-heavy structure and unsuited to meeting the challenge of Rome, whose capacity to arm and mobilize properly a greater proportion of her citizenship was probably the most decisive factor in her conquest of Etruria.

The fortification of cities

Plato did not like the concept of cities being walled, but Aristotle, writing in the mid fourth century BC, puts his finger on an archaeological problem when he chides Plato for not seeing that walls are essential for both the 'embellishment of the city' and the city's 'military needs'. He is thus delineating the ideological and functional nature of city walls – and giving preference to neither.

Influenced by near-Eastern practice, the Greeks began to put up walls around their cities as early as the ninth century BC. Those at Old Smyrna are datable to c. 850 BC, and provided a prototype for the first Etruscan walls. Those at Roselle, built c. 600 BC, consisted of large mud bricks mounted upon a stone plinth, following the pattern of Old Smyrna; later a more substantial structure of tufa blocks was put up at Roselle and this was in keeping with such stretches of walls as survive at Veii (late fifth century), Cerveteri (fifth to fourth centuries, fig. 86), Tarquinia (sixth century), Vulci (fifth to fourth centuries) and San Giovenale (fifth century, fig. 87). Walls very rarely extend right around the plateaux of a given city: the plateaux themselves furnish excellent defences where they drop as sheer precipices (as at Cerveteri), and artificial defence-works – not only walls but also ditches and terraces – need be erected simply to fill in vulnerable areas. The effectiveness of the part-natural, part-artificial walls will be readily appreciable to those who visit the sites, especially the more compact settlements (Luni sul Mignone is a good example).

The antiquity of the practice of wall-building in Etruria is probably underestimated. Recent excavations at Cerveteri suggest that the first system of enclosing walls was laid out as early as c. 700 BC. These are massive affairs of tufa blocks and would be coeval with the first signs of synoecism on the plateau of Etruscan Cerveteri. Synoecism (from the Greek synoikismos, 'dwelling together') implies that the walls enclose a community or, more realistically, provide a point of refuge for a certain territory. In the event of raids or aggression, those within the territorial bounds would come together behind the walls.

The military implications of these early walls are less easy to visualize. The walls provide shelter well enough, but it is no comfort to those behind them to know that, while they are sheltering, their farms

88 *Armed dancers; Etruscan black-figure* oinochoe, c. *500 BC.* (Louvre).

and houses in the territory – and their sources of food and livelihood – are being wrecked by an enemy. For this reason, no doubt, Homer's Trojans did not sit out the Greek siege of their city but rather emerged to confront the enemy outside the city walls.

The pitching of strategy upon walled cities occurs later. Historians attribute the refinement of siegecraft to Dionysius of Syracuse, who in the early fourth century BC hired engineers to construct the landing-bridges with which he conquered the island stronghold of Motya. The development of catapults and mobile towers seems to belong to this period, and it is certainly the period in which Etruscan cities consolidated their fortifications, although there is nothing in Etruria comparable to the great Euryalus fortress constructed by Dionysius at Syracuse. At Veii, prior to the decisive Roman attack of 396 BC, the laying down of a block-built substructure below the ground level of the city settlement (that is, down to the bedrock) must have made possible much higher walls than previously established. Further evidence of consolidation in this period comes from Populonia and Tarquinia. And yet, as field survey shows, city walls such as those at Veii can only ever have provided temporary relief for the belts of countryside around the city contained numerous small settlements, and when they went a genuine lifeline was severed.

Walls were as much symbolic as they were useful. More practical were towers. The very name of the port-sanctuary of Pyrgi (*pyrgoi*, 'the towers')

89 *Tragliatella* oinochoe.

90 *Etruscan black-figure amphora*, c. *500 BC* (Karlsruhe).

indicates that it served as a garrison with surveillance of the sea, and it is likely that inland cities too had watch-towers incorporated into their fortification systems.

What archaeology cannot really substantiate is the political option of defence, the federation between city states. The effect of federation upon the conduct of warfare is something that must remain subject to historical speculation.

War and ritual: the armed dance

For a single small artefact, the Tragliatella *oinochoe* (fig. 89) has provoked a tiresome amount of scholarly activity. Some would like to see the band of warriors with spears and shields as a prototypical phalanx: the fact that each shield bears the motif of

a boar is said to reflect the devices of Greek hoplite shields. It is also claimed to indicate connections with Tarquinia (of which the boar would be a symbol), despite the fact that Tragliatella is a site that lies in the hinterland of Cerveteri, not Tarquinia. But if the overall interpretation of the scenes on the oinochoe remains difficult, it is at least clear that the warriors with shields and spears are executing some sort of dance. The homogeneity of their shield devices may well signify that they all belong to the same clan, but the representation is of ritual rather than war.

The impracticality of the high-crested helmets such as that from Tomb 871 at Grotta Gramiccia has been noted, but in fact much of the armour that has survived from Etruria is thin-walled bronze, ornamentally-embossed and decorated. Its quality appears more ceremonial than useful. In the late sixth century, we find a fashion recorded on Etrus-can vases that seems quite unique: the attachment of crests to shields as well as to helmets (fig. 88). These belong to the world of spectacle and display, like the great plumed helmets, or *pinnirapi*, of Roman gladiators, and should remind us once more of the ritual background to Etruscan warfare. If the analogy of the Middle Ages were pursued, then these dances and ritual combats should be seen as the jousting tournaments of Etruscan Italy. They include not only elements of athletic contests and tests of nerve, such as chariot racing, but also functions of aristocratic breeding (fig. 90). George Orwell's definition of sport as 'war minus the shooting' finds ample illustration on Etruscan tomb- and vase-paintings.

The occasions for armed dancing are manifold: as part of funerary celebrations; to mark the turning-points of the seasons; to propitiate the gods of war before or after a campaign; or to initiate new

91 *'The Tuscan mariners transform'd'. Detail of Etruscan black-figure vase* (Toledo, Ohio).

members to the status of warriorhood. The Latins had a priesthood, the *Salii*, the members of which performed rites in honour of Mars whilst wearing conical helmets and carrying archaic-shaped shields; this may reflect Etruscan practice. It is a short step from such an armed dance to the mock combat or 'sham-fight', and thence to gladiatorial spectacles. The Romans thought these derived from Etruscan funerary customs, and this is plausible, so long as we remember that the origins, whether they be bound up with local cults, funeral games or agrarian purification, are essentially rites of passage, not mass entertainment.

War at sea

Archaeological substantiation of the Etruscan *thalassocracy*, or military domination of the Tyrrhenian seaboard, is difficult to muster, although archaeology has revealed the volume of trade between Etruria and the eastern Mediterranean and has furthermore revealed the ports where it was conducted. The reputation that the Etruscans have amongst Greek writers for piracy looks like romance. In the cases where these histories are Sicilian-based, one must acknowledge that they are also Sicilian-biased; otherwise, the Greeks were simply irked to discover a barbarian people as adept at seafaring as themselves. The conflict of commercial interests between Etruria and the Greek colonists of southern Italy naturally involved the Etruscans in naval combat. The attempt to take Lipari in the early fifth century BC is recorded by two dedications made by the Cnidian colonists at Delphi, thanking Apollo for their victory over the *Tyrsanoi*, the Etruscans. The Etruscan side of the story is only indirectly reported in the Latin inscription (from late-sixth-century BC Etruscan sources) eulogizing a member of one of the great Tarquinian clans:

> *V[elth]ur Spurinna [L]artis filius pr[aetor]*
> *[(bis);in] magistratu Ale[riae] exerc[i]tum habuit,*
> *alte[rum in] Siciliam duxit; primus o[mnium]*
> *Etruscorum mare c[um legione] traie[cit]* etc.

(Velthur Spurinna, son of Larth, twice magistrate of the city, conducted Etruscan expeditions to Aleria (Corsica) and Sicily: he was the first of the Etruscans to 'take troops on the sea'.) There is an Etruscan presence attested archaeologically at Aleria around the end of the sixth century BC, and, as we have seen, Spurinna's expedition to Sicily/Lipari was repulsed in the early fifth century.

Piecing together these splinters of epigraphical testimony gives a rather unsatisfactory picture of the Etruscan *thalassocracy*, if such a thing ever existed. The patterns of trade, discussed elsewhere in this book, are sufficient to offset the picture given by Thucydides and others of a people rooted in 'piratical habits'. The Etruscans went to sea to protect their interests and, probably, in search of slaves. And they seem to have known the moralizing Seventh Homeric Hymn, which illustrates the perils of piracy: a party of *Tyrsenoi* that attacks the god Dionysos at sea meets the singular fate of being metamorphosed into dolphins. It is a late-sixth-century BC Etruscan vase-painter who has left us with the most explicit depiction of this story we know (fig. 91).

SOCIAL ORGANIZATION

Etruscan society is often described in terms of either the coeval Greek society or the Roman society that overlaid it by conquest: hence one comes across references to the Etruscan *polis*, the Etruscan *gens*, the Etruscan *nobiles*: 'city', 'clan', 'nobles' respectively, terms which have meaning in Greek and Latin and English – and which we more or less understand. Speak of a *zilath*, however, and you might as well speak of the Akond of Swat or the jabberwock. Who, why or what is a *zilath*? An Etruscological definition will come up with something like an annually-appointed magistrate, but such a definition gives little idea of the socio-religious nature of the office of *zilath*, glimpsed through formulaic inscriptions but frustratingly difficult to relate to, say, the *archons* of Athens or any ancient or modern institutional structure. And yet there is no reason to suppose either that the Etruscans modelled themselves on the Greeks in their social organization (as suggested in the previous chapter, the Greek military technique of fighting with a phalanx was unacceptable in Etruria for largely social reasons) or that Roman society contains more than trace elements of Etruscan institutions (despite Latin traditions that many of the symbols of power, such as the *fascis*, were inherited from the Etruscans).

We have no fresh epigraphical interpretations to bring to bear here in the assistance of a better definition of Etruscan oligarchic society. From what has already been touched upon in the spheres of settlement, ritual and warfare it should already be clear that the key to Etruscan society is kinship: if an Etruscan were stopped at the border and questioned on his identity, he would probably not lay claims to hailing from Rasenna (the supposed Etruscan name for what we call Etruria) nor even declare himself a man of Tarquinia. The chances are that he would state a family or clan name, such as Spurinna. This taxes our imagination – but is it any less peculiar than the mechanism by which Englishmen may advance in business and politics according to the name of the school that they attended in youth?

Archaeology may illuminate social structures in various ways, of which we shall present two examples: i) differentiation in burial, and ii) the iconology of power. A standing caveat is that general statements about Etruscan society must be tempered by regional and chronological factors. To describe it as 'oligarchic' seems broad enough to allow for local interpretations; beyond that, we shall leave the readers to their own preferred approximations.

Burial evidence

Burial evidence is at one level an aspect of ritual, the rite of passage from life to death (see Chapter VI). At another level the organization of burial, provided it is not considered in isolation, also affords valuable evidence of the nature of social organization. A glance at our own society signals the caution that must be employed in using this burial evidence out of context. The ideology employed in contemporary rituals of death can mask and transform many differences in life. Christian practice and the sanitized approaches to death by other modern ideologies have created many complexities in the way in which burial occurs. It is, therefore, crucial that the whole pattern of death ritual must be viewed against the wider patterns of society (in particular settlement and territory) that have already been described in this book. With these reservations, social organization can be assessed not only from the range of the wealth of graves but also in terms of the degree of access by age, sex and status accorded to formal bounded burial.

The final Bronze Age

During the final Bronze Age, formal cemeteries appeared for the first time since the Chalcolithic. These communities cremated their dead, placed the ashes in simple decorated pottery urns with a few offerings of personal ornament and set the urns in small, although probably demarcated, cemeteries of less than 50 graves. There was clearly a sense of community to create this common identity, but it is impossible to assess the social links that linked the buried populations. It is, though, clear that the sense of community was neither sufficiently great nor sufficiently long lived to produce substantial cemeteries, with the major exception of Pianello di Genga to the east of Etruria where over 500 cremations have been found (fig. 92).

A study of the other evidence of society (see Chapters II, III and IV), suggests that there was probably an increasingly competitive social atmosphere, but there is little evidence that this

92 *Late-Bronze-Age cemetery of Pianello di Genga (after Peroni 1963).*

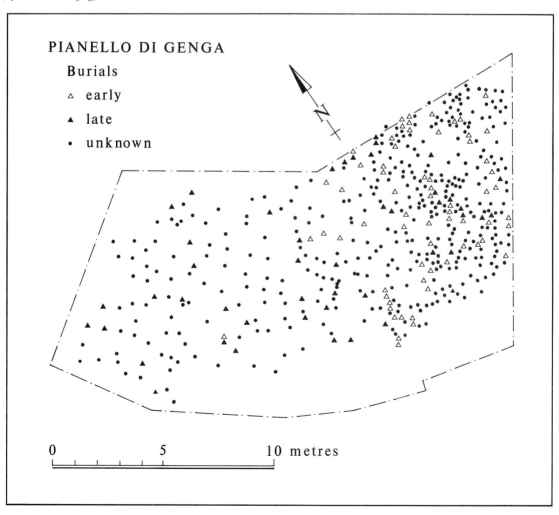

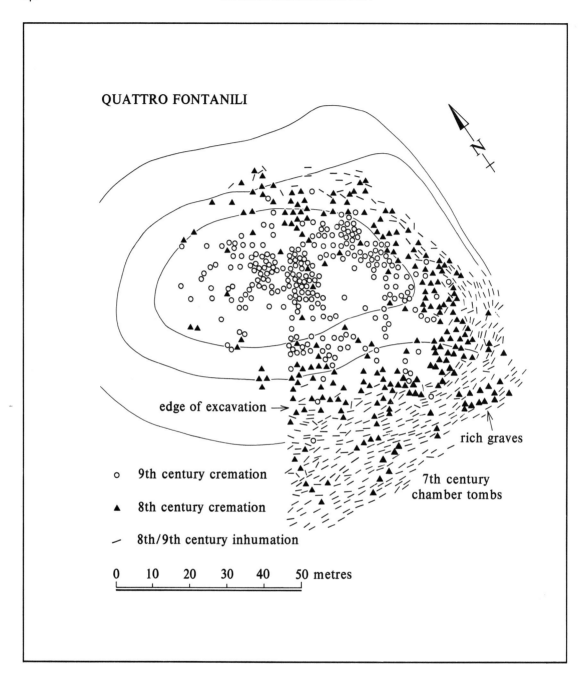

93 *The Villanovan cemetery of Quattro fontanili*
(after Potter 1979). This does not take into account
the revisions recently made by Toms (1982).

expressed itself in material culture or, more particularly, in a display of wealth in tombs. Some slight tendency towards differences in grave goods and prominent tumulus graves does appear towards the end of the period. Nevertheless, the more prominent disposal of surplus wealth appears to have been in the metal hoards of the same period and thus not so overtly associated with individuals in society. This image of an 'egalitarian' society is in agreement with the relatively small villages of the period and their apparent lack of internal differentiation. In a few cases, the association of a cemetery with a settlement can be inferred, suggesting a strong association of the area with both the local living community and their ancestors. There is, furthermore, some evidence that a few late-Bronze-Age burials formed the earliest depositions in the major cemeteries that expanded to form the foundations of recognizable Etruscan society.

The Villanovan period

The formality and size of the cemeteries greatly increased at the same time as the major changes of settlement organization of the beginning of the ninth century BC. For the first time in the development of central Italian society, large groups of people saw sufficient common identity to bury themselves close to one another over many generations (fig. 93) (in the case of Quattro Fontanili, over 650 individuals in one place). From this moment we have the first of many cycles of highly-recognizable large (more than 100 cremations) cemeteries that are clearly associated with settlements of similarly large dimensions. Much has been made of the fact that characteristically there was more than one of these cemeteries associated with each major settlement. Each has been claimed to represent a distinctive group that retained a separate identity within the greatly enlarged community.

This phenomenon is distinctive for most of the later major Etruscan centres as widely separated as Cerveteri and Perugia. In social terms this can be interpreted as the formation of new corporate groups bound together by a common social structure, probably on lines of kinship, expressing in-

itially no visible differences in wealth. The most prevalent rite of cremation may have masked some of the differences of status that must have been incipient in the stresses of these newly-formed communities.

In the eighth century BC, differences began to be expressed in the material culture of the cemeteries. Early exotic imports were placed in some of the cremation graves, rich metalwork of local manufacture was placed in others. The best studied case of this phenomenon is the cemetery of Quattro Fontanili at the Etruscan city of Veii (fig. 94). It appears that once exotic valuables became available (see Chapter IV) certain members of the indigenous society reserved access to these valuables and that some were 'killed' or placed out of circulation on death.

Etruscan society

In the seventh century, in a process that is also evident in the early use of writing, there was a phase of large prominent chamber tombs that were clearly restricted to élite families. These generally appear earlier in the major coastal cities (such as the Regolini Galassi tomb at Cerveteri, fig. 95a, and the Tomba del Duce at Vetulonia). Valuable commodities (which can often be identified by short naming inscriptions) were placed exclusively in these tombs. Visible burial appears to have been restricted to a small selected group within society.

From this moment Etruscan society cannot be seen as uniform: great differences developed both between individual cities and more broadly over regions. For instance, the pattern of restricted burial that was already present in Cerveteri at the beginning of the seventh century BC appears to have taken place later in the same century and at the beginning of the sixth century on the fringes of the Etruscan world. By this time in Cerveteri access to the burial rite has been extended to a greater range of family groups. A strongly regionalized pattern of social organization developed that is indicated by on the one hand the long-standing extensive cemeteries of Cerveteri funded by many rich families and on the other the single prominent chamber tombs at Comeana, Quinto Fiorentino

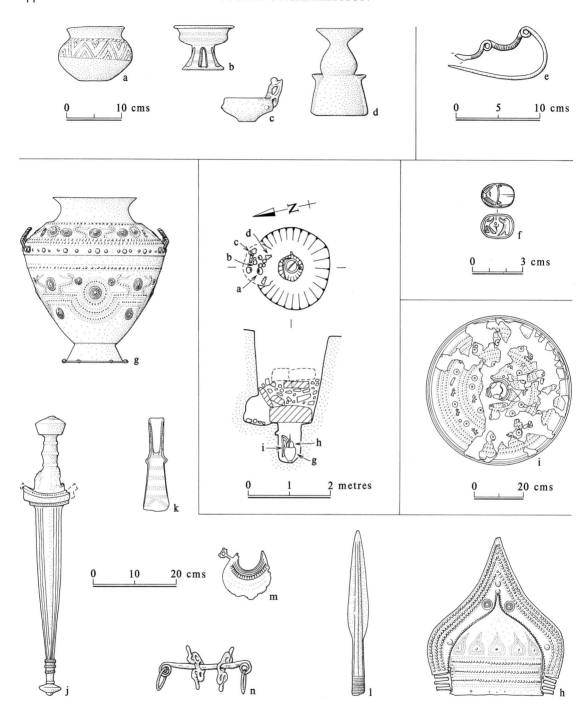

94 *The contents of a wealthy tomb from Quattro Fontanili (Tomb AA 1).* **a–d** *pottery;* **e** *fibula brooch;* **f** *scarab;* **g** *bronze vessel;* **h** *helmet;* **i** *shield;* **j** *sword;* **k** *axe;* **l** *spearhead;* **m** *razor;* **n** *horse bit (after Notizie degli Scavi 1970).*

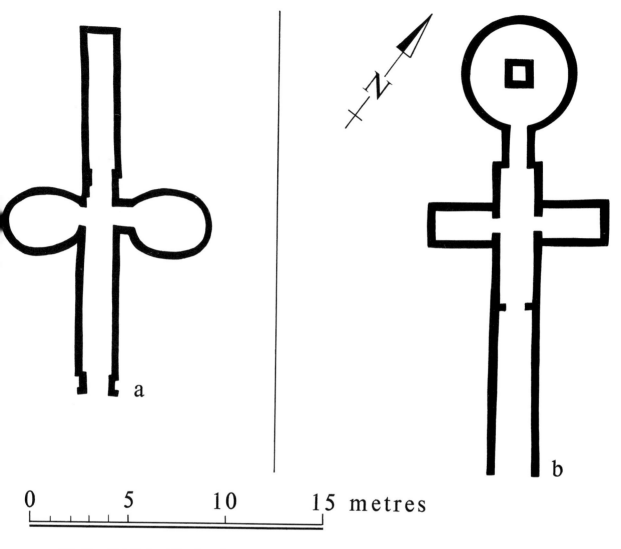

0   5   10   15 metres

95 a *The Regolini-Galassi Tomb at Cerveteri.*
No orientation in the original publications;
b *The Montagnola tomb at Quinto Fiorentino*
(after Prayon 1975).

(fig. 95b), Casal Marittimo, Volterra, Populonia, Castellina and Cortona funded by a much more restricted élite in northern Etruria.

The differences between individual cities further demonstrate the lack of unity of social organization between the different Etruscan centres. The extension of cemeteries has normally been seen as a measure of the prosperity of individual cities. The range of cemeteries is also a measure of the degree of access to formal burial that was permitted within the context of the local society. At Cerveteri this privilege was accorded early; at Arezzo and Perugia it was accorded very late and not on a wide scale until Hellenistic times.

Cerveteri

The first evidence of burial at Cerveteri dates from the final Bronze Age. It was only with the Villanovan period that substantial numbers of burials have been found in the cemeteries surrounding the settlement area (especially the Sorbo and Pozzolana necropoleis). The burials are mixed: in the Sorbo cemetery, some 230 incinerations may be

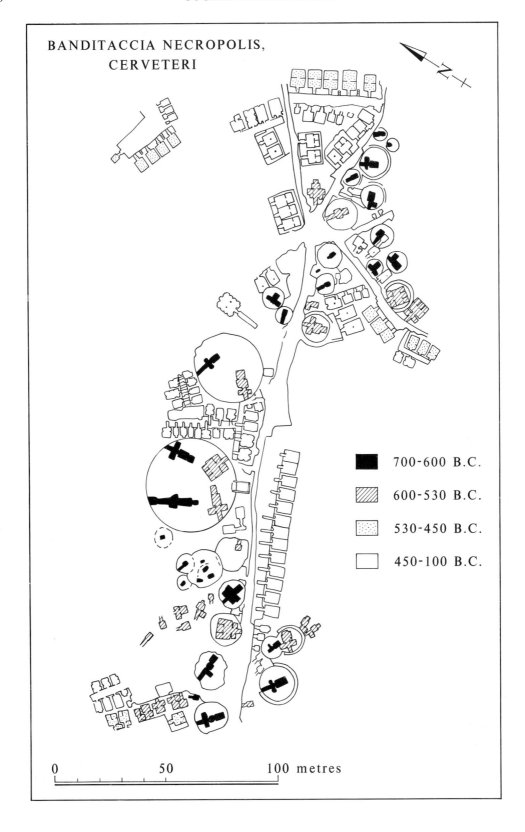

BANDITACCIA NECROPOLIS,
CERVETERI

700-600 B.C.

600-530 B.C.

530-450 B.C.

450-100 B.C.

0   50   100 metres

96 *The chronological distribution of graves at the Banditaccia cemetery (after Prayon, 1975).*

compared with some 200 inhumations. The form of burial is simple enough: a circular or rectangular hole was sunk into tufa bedrock, and the body or urn containing ashes was then inserted, and the grave sealed up, often with clay. It was worth noting the comparative poverty of these burials; though numerous, they do not show the wealth of grave goods that were present in other centres of South Etruria. It was only from *c.* 700 BC that new riches began to be present in the cemeteries of Cerveteri (fig. 96). This is the period of the first appearance of the monumental tumuli that contained the rich architectonic funerary displays of the restricted élite. Burial was arranged so as to maximize the visibility of élite authority. Towards the end of the sixth century BC the privilege of formal interment in the major Banditaccia cemetery was dramatically extended if only in more modest architectural surroundings. Rows of similar tombs were erected in alignment, allowing the incorporation of more associated members of the

élite social group. These new funerary arrangements were more in the form of a planned city of the dead, which more effectively paralleled the city of the living. It entailed in certain ways a greater representation of the living community, in as much as there are not only more members of more families buried but also probably some of their retainers. The niches and simple little tombs cut into the rock around the main family burial-places may well be the graves of nannies, cooks and grooms. The complex is extended towards the city by the Via degli Inferi; those wishing to appear more conspicuous had to go elsewhere, as recently revealed by the evidence of cliff-cut tombs in the Greppe S. Angelo area close to the modern town, done in the manner of the great façades at Norchia and Castel d'Asso and datable to the second half of the fourth century BC.

Cerveteri affords the best example of structural change within a necropolis, but perhaps the best example in isolation is the Crocifisso del Tufo cemetery at Orvieto, with its onomastic lintels (fig. 97).

97 *Crocifisso del Tufo Cemetry.*

Chiusi

The inland city of Chiusi had a different development of access to formal burial. The first burials date from the Villanovan period (ninth century BC) since the local Bronze Age populations were established to the south on the upland area of Monte Cetona. In common with the coastal cities the Villanovan period cemeteries of Chiusi were placed in several locations around the city, although far fewer individuals were buried here. The smaller buried population does not seem to be purely a result of the smaller size of this inland centre. The low level of access to burial continued through into the sixth century, incorporating changes in burial rite (simple cremation urns to elaborate anthropomorphic urns to chambered tombs), and from the seventh century BC the few individuals with access to formal burial show an increasing access to prestige items, but these gradual changes appear to have affected the whole Chiusi area: similar changes were taking place at Chianciano and other local sites. A more marked social change took place in the fifth century when the access to formal burial increased dramatically. The number of chambered tombs rose from 29 in the sixth century to 475 over the rest of the Etruscan period. The aristocratic control over formal burial had been relaxed.

Populonia

The burial evidence at Populonia shows a third distinctive pattern that could be repeated severalfold by taking examples from the remaining Etruscan cities. The access to formal burial has familiarly modest beginnings in the late Bronze Age, restricted to a few cremations in one small cemetery. This access to formal burial increased between 900 and 750 BC (including the Villanovan period) when four to five slightly larger cemeteries were founded, but the total number of individuals so far recovered does not exceed 150. Within this restricted group with access to formal burial a few individuals began to be treated preferentially. Monumental chamber tombs replaced individual graves. Some of the monumental chamber tombs became the depositories of rich grave goods (including gold) suggesting the beginnings of social differentiation. This pattern was accentuated in the seventh century with the introduction of circular

drum tumulus tombs that emphasized the status of the most privileged access to formal burial. A number of tombs founded in this phase continued to be employed in the sixth century BC, intimating the genealogical continuity of certain social groups. The relaxation of access to formal burial only took place in the fourth century when burial became a much more common procedure along with a greater range of wealth employed in tomb construction.

Elite images and the symbols of power

A major symbol of power was the use of literacy (see Chapter V). It is therefore not surprising to find that Etruscan inscriptions contain clues about the development of kinship relationships. One important change took place in South Etruria in the second half of the seventh century BC, when it became customary to employ both first and second names. Whereas in the first part of the century inscriptions (in common with burials) were a means of communication amongst a small élite, in the second half of the century social access was broadened, necessitating the adoption of a second name to allow greater accuracy in personal identification. A further change took place towards the end of the sixth century BC when the range of first names was reduced by 40 per cent as the importance of second family names assumed the pre-eminent importance in the identification of members of society. In this type of society, it is not surprising to find the web of inscriptions that can be reconstructed as family genealogies in such tombs as those of Asciano and Perugia.

The iconology of Etruscan art can also point towards some notions of Etruscan social organization. Art requires patrons. Assyrian and Hittite kings commissioned great friezes to record their deeds; Roman emperors ordered not only private friezes but also friezes on arch-ways and columns, reminding citizens throughout the Empire who Caesar was and what ought to be rendered in his direction. There is every reason to believe that Etruscan art, particularly in its monumental manifestations, expresses through a basis of symbolism some socio-political hierarchy.

The fact that only 2 per cent of the known tombs

at Tarquinia are painted says something in itself about élitism. The paintings are bound to hold up a mirror to an élite life-style, and there are some facets of élite lifestyle that will be readily understandable to the modern 'reader' of these tomb-paintings. Hunting, for example – whether the deceased bagged wild boar by the dozen or whether he was an appalling shot, his tomb will state an accepted idea of bliss, with depictions of the hunt in full cry, the prey or simply the game hung up for prospective consumption. The participation in hunting implies possession of horses and horse-riding skills, weapons, and no doubt beaters, batmen and all that goes with flushing out and recovering the prey. Hunting is both an alternative to and a sublimation of war: if the practice of war was effectively confined to an élite, as we have suggested, then it is not surprising that the hunt appealed to the élite as indicated by the paintings on the walls of

their tombs or the Greek vases what they took to the tombs with them.

Banqueting has a ritual significance in the iconography of tombs and vases, but it is also bound up with the symbolism of status, with claims to luxury and affluence. The aristocrats of the Tarquinian tombs were setting themselves up as part of an *internationale* of the Mediterranean élite: for banqueting figures prominently not only on Greek vases of the period but also on such tombs elsewhere whose paintings have survived, such as in Lycia. The extent to which this affectation went may be illustrated by the depiction, in Tarquinian tombs, of the game of *kottabos*. This game, beloved of rich young Athenian louts, and presumably played in the posteriors of a symposium evening, involved twirling a wine cup in one's index finger and aiming to shoot the contents into a receptacle balanced in another part of the room. It was the epitome of wastefulness, a status to which the person commissioning the image aspired. The images of banqueting tell us about Etruscan aristocrats apeing their Greek counterparts but they also

98 *Scene of courtship on a late-sixth-century* BC *Etruscan vase: boy offers a hind; girl is carrying* lagobolon, *a hare, in exchange* (Deutsches Archäologisches Institut).

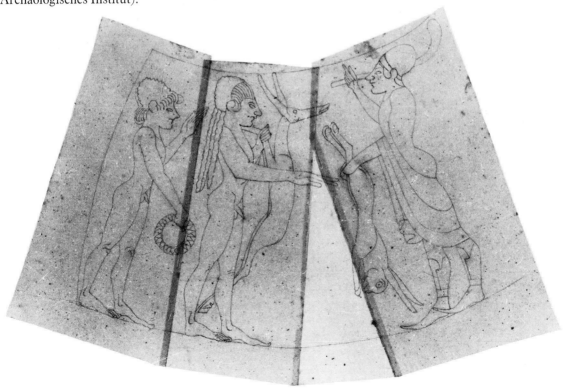

reveal an important difference between Greek and Etruscan society. At Etruscan banquets, the women who participate are the wives (as inscriptions reveal): they are not the *heterai* or 'professional ladies' featured in Greek banquets (so far as women feature at all). The images support the shocked Greek opinions recorded in literary tradition. Women as equals of men! The very thought appalled the Greeks. We know that the legal status of women in Etruria was stronger than it was in Greece (in the event of no male succession, the family *heredium* passed to the female line), and the social position of women in Etruria may also explain the noticeable relative absence of homoerotic images in Etruscan art. Plenty of images of courtship exist (fig. 98), but images of pederastic courtship, ubiquitous on Greek vases, are extremely rare. The Etruscan aristocratic affectation of 'the higher love' or 'Athenian vice' was curtailed by social factors, therefore.

Certain social indicators are easily spotted in the tomb-paintings; slaves are lower down the social scale and when depicted they are done to smaller graphic scale. But the recognition of symbols of power as such is more complex. Take the file of dignitaries – or so they seem, to judge by their garb and general air of *gravitas* – in the Tomba Bruschi

99 *Detail of the Tomba Bruschi, Tarquinia (late third to early second century BC).*

(fig. 99), for example: that they are togate figures says something about them; that some carry trumpets, and others hooked staves, says something more specific: appurtenances of status are there, but to be precise about their socio-religious role within civic life is not easy. In diverse media of Etruscan art, hats are sported that are evidently invested with status: the Hermes-style *petasos*, the apparently priestly headpiece or *apex*. And as we have already seen, crooks are carried. These may look like the long staves used by Greek trainers to referee wrestling matches; they may look like shepherds' crooks, when carried by augurs (see fig. 60); in more truncated form, they appear like the Greek *lagobolon* as a general attribute of aristoc-

100 *Etruscan black-figure amphora, late sixth century BC.*

racy. And yet when we come across an image featuring a youth with lagobolon in hand standing amongst livestock (fig. 100), how should we read it? A boy minding cattle, whose switching stick happens to look like the swagger stick of the élite? An aristocrat whose wealth is based in stock? A mythical figure, engaged in a rustling expedition of some sort?

The difficulties of interpreting possible 'symbols of power' are compounded in the case of the architectural terracottas figuring processions, which have been found at many Etruscan and central Italian sites: Pitigliano, Cerveteri, Veii, Tuscania, Tarquinia, Murlo, Acquarossa, Satricum, Rome (Sant'Omobono, in the *Forum Boarium*), Palestrina (*Praeneste*), Velletri and Cisterna. These plaques are stylized but are not meaningless on that account: their imagery includes banquets, assemblies, horse-racing and departures in chariots (whose drivers may command both normal and winged horses). Obviously there is a measure here of the fantasy involved in the commemoration of rites of passage: but what sort of rite is actually being represented? One attractive suggestion is that these plaques feature an Etruscan prototype of the Roman triumphal procession: the reception of the *trionfator* (triumpher) by city officials and by city deities too, which may very well be conflated with the reception of the heroized dead and the apotheosis of Herakles. In any case, a form of divine affiliation is being claimed by those in the ruling class. Whatever the precise connotations of their symbols of power, they thought themselves gods – or gods as near as damn it.

A TRAVELLER'S GAZETTEER

For those now tempted to visit Etruria, the following gazetteer serves as a guide to the sites and museums that are at the time of printing most worthy of a visit. The visitor is advised to take a portable guide such as M. Torelli's into the field and consult the other volumes in the general section of the bibliography. *Etruscan Cities* by F. Boitani, M. Cataldi and M. Pasquinucci (London, Cassell) is an older volume (1975) and perhaps too bulky for the tourist, but nevertheless still useful. Care has been taken to give mention of most Etruscan sites discussed in the text (if only to remark on the beauty of the landscape!) together with some of the principal museum collections.

The sites (fig. 2).

Acquarossa. (fig. 26) A major Etruscan centre of the second rank, located in a central position within inland South Etruria. The subject of important excavations by the Swedes, parts of the excavated city are now preserved *in situ*, although a visit needs to be accompanied by some of the original field reports for a proper understanding.

Adria. The museum houses many finds from the cemeteries of this extensive Etruscan trading post at the head of the Adriatic.

Arezzo. A beautiful medieval and Renaissance town that should be visited by those in search of the artist Piero della Francesca and his Story of the True Cross. Etruscan remains are difficult to find, but the museum is worth a visit mainly for its collection of Etruscan bronze figurines, Roman Aretine pottery and its view over the Roman amphitheatre.

Asciano. An interesting site for its late Etruscan tombs, but not worth a visit unless the museum is open.

Bisenzio. The area is worth a visit for those with an eye for the volcanic landscape of Lake Bolsena, but little is archaeologically visible.

Blera. (fig. 63) A small centre in inland Etruria which is a good location to visit Archaic and Hellenistic rock-cut tombs. The wooded terrain and tufa outcrops are very attractive.

Bolsena. The surviving remains are principally Roman in date, but the location above Lake Bolsena provides excellent views of the volcanic caldera.

Brolio. A wet, waterlogged location where an important deposit of votive figurines was found, although there is nothing to see on the ground today.

Casentino. The basin of the upper Arno where the Florentines escape the summer heat. The Etruscans left little trace (except Pieve Socana – see below), but this is an area of great beauty occupied by monastic orders such the Franciscans.

Castel d'Asso. A small, mainly Hellenistic centre of inland South Etruria, remarkable for the quantity of its rock-cut tombs. A beautiful location in the wooded dissected tufa topography.

Castellina in Chianti. The location of a major seventh century BC burial tumulus which may be entered.

Castelnuovo di Berardenga. An important site

similar in character to Murlo but only suitable for the visitor armed with the original site report. More remarkable for the beauty of the Chianti region than for visible archaeological remains.

Castro. A small centre in the Fiora valley but known only from its tombs.

Cerveteri. (figs. 95–6) One of the important South Etruscan cities. The layout of the city is relatively unknown, although this is likely to be changed by the new excavations. A visit to the famous Banditaccia cemetery is particularly worthwhile. The museum illustrates the development of the city.

Chianciano. A small museum provides an impression of the tombs of a small centre near Chiusi. The famous local spa water provides refreshment.

Chiusi. One of the most important Etruscan cities of North Etruria. The museum has a good range of the distinctive grave goods of the important Etruscan town, and a guide is usually available to take you to some of the tombs.

Comeana. Together with the neighbouring centre of Artimino, this was an important early nucleation in North Etruria. Impressive burial tumuli can be seen from outside and some of the recent finds from the area, seen within a splendid Medici palazzo on the summit of the hill.

Cortona. A medieval town well worth visiting with the added attraction of the museum of the Accademia Etrusca (including the famous bronze lamp) and several local tombs. The town has a fine position overlooking the Val di Chiana and is a good place to stay.

Cosa. (figs. 5, 62) A good example of a Roman colonial town in this boundary area between major Etruscan cities.

Doganella. (fig. 23) An important site, but ploughed fields (hence the recent successful field survey) await the enthusiast!

Elba. A modern holiday island that was an important source of Etruscan iron ore. Little to see of Etruscan date, even for the determined.

Faliscan territory. A picturesque area to the north-east of Veii containing many small centres contemporary with the Etruscans: Capena, Civita Castellana, Nepi and Sutri. Many of the finds are in the Villa Giulia museum in Rome, but the sites themselves are generally fine medieval towns set in beautiful wooded volcanic terrain. A further site, Narce, was recently excavated by the British School at Rome but is best visited only with a guide.

Felsina (the Etruscan name for Bologna). The museum is one of the richest for the Etruscans north of the Apennines. The modern food is some of the most prized in Italy.

Fiesole. This town has long proved attractive to British visitors to Florence escaping the summer heat of the Arno Valley. Relatively few, perhaps, realise the ancient Etruscan origins of the town which are best understood by a visit to the museum. Some tombs are visible as well as the monumental quarter of the town that received a strongly Roman imprint.

Florence. There is no space to speak of the Renaissance and later town. Its importance for following the Etruscans is principally through the Archaeological Museum, although the Prehistory Museum is also worth a visit.

Gran Carro. (fig. 19) An interesting, although submerged, Villanovan settlement on the ancient edge of Lake Bolsena.

Gravisca. The emporium that served the city of Tarquinia which is remarkable for its Greek sanctuary.

Grosseto. Not an Etruscan town, but contains one of the best topographical museums on the Etruscans. The visitor gets a good impression of the different characteristics and layout of centres, large and small, in the Maremma area.

Gubbio. Not strictly in Etruria, but one of the most beautiful Umbrian towns of central Italy. Famous for a ritualized race every 15 May which, some say (not the authors), continues the traditions described on the ancient bronze tablets housed in the Palazzo dei Consoli. These same tablets are the indirect source of some interpretations of Etruscan religion described in Chapter VI.

Luni sul Mignone. (fig. 15b) A naturally delimited location occupied both in the Late Bronze Age and in the Archaic period. The subject of important Swedish excavations.

Magliano. A small Etruscan centre in the Albegna valley, best known from its tombs.

Manciano. The location of an important new museum that offers an excellent chance to understand the prehistory of the Fiora valley.

Marsiliana d'Albegna. A famous early Etruscan centre in the Albegna valley known for its fine grave goods of the eight and seventh centuries BC, including an early writing tablet. The finds are in Florence.

Marzabotto. An important site to visit north of the Apennines, both for its museum, and for the layout of the city.

Massarosa. An interesting waterlogged Archaic Etruscan site in North Etruria, but no longer visible.

Monte Falterona. An upland Etruscan sanctuary in the Casentino (see above) that has produced many bronze figurines. The finds have been dispersed around the museums of the world (including the British Museum in London).

Monte Rovello. An important Late Bronze Age site in South Etruria, but not worth visiting without a guide.

Montepulciano. A beautiful Tuscan town, but the visible traces of the Etruscans are limited to some cinerary urns preserved in the walls of later buildings.

Montetosto. A large seventh-century burial tumulus, 4 kilometres (2½ miles) from Cerveteri.

Murlo (Poggio Civitate). A site of great importance for its seventh/sixth century palace-like structures (fig. 22a), but only worth a visit for the enthusiast with a good map. The site is heavily wooded, but traces of the occupation area and

recent excavations can be made out.

Musarna. An interesting planned Hellenistic town, but, on the ground, only some tombs and recently excavated areas can be distinguished.

Narce (see Faliscan territory).

Norchia. Another typical small centre of inland Etruria that flourished in the Hellenistic period. The rock-cut tombs make a visit worthwhile.

Orvieto. The approach to this important Etruscan city (located on an ancient volcanic plug) from Lake Bolsena is particularly impressive. Little remains of the Etruscan city, dominated by the medieval town and the cathedral that contains famous paintings by Signorelli. The Crocefisso del Tufo cemetery (fig. 97), the Belvedere temple and the local Museums, however, give a good impression of the ancient city.

Perugia. An Umbrian town with impressive Etruscan gates that houses the University for Foreigners where courses can be taken on the Etruscans. The museum is remarkable for an impressive collection of Bronze and Iron Age material, giving a full coverage of Etruscan origins.

Pienza. The birthplace of Pope Pius II who transformed the town into a Renaissance masterpiece. Little remains of the Etruscan period.

Pieve Socana. The site of a small sanctuary at the entrance to the Casentino. The surviving altar next to the Romanesque church has great charm.

Pitigliano. A beautiful medieval town of Etruscan origin with some rock-cut tombs.

Podere Tartucchino. A sixth-century farm with evidence of wine production. This is the neglected part of Etruscan studies, where much research can be expected in the future. Nothing is visible on the ground, even if you have the guide to locate it.

Poggio Buco. A small Etruscan centre in the Fiora valley, mainly known from its cemeteries.

Poggio Civitate (see Murlo).

Populonia. An important coastal Etruscan city in

North Etruria, whose acropolis is placed in a spectacular position above the sea. The cemeteries were covered by the waste products of iron production and have been well preserved. Access is now possible to some of the tombs.

Pyrgi. (fig. 74) A second important coastal emporium similar to Gravisca, but connected to Cerveteri and the Phoenician world. The foundations of an impressive sanctuary have been discovered.

Quattro Fontanili (see Veii).

Quinto Fiorentino. The location of several impressive seventh century burial tumuli in the Arno valley which can be visited. Nothing is known of the settlement.

Regisvilla. The probable emporium of Vulci, but little is yet known of this centre.

Rome. Two museums are of crucial importance, both housed in fine Renaissance and later settings. The Vatican contains, amongst many other treasures, important Etruscan collections. The Villa Giulia, the fine sixteenth century AD villa of Vignola, houses extensive collections from Etruria and Umbria. Rome is also the co-ordinating centre of many important Etruscan projects undertaken by the Italians, French, Swedes, British (especially the British School at Rome) and many other nations.

Roselle. One of the most important centres of North Etruria that gradually took over from neighbouring Vetulonia. The early development of the city has been investigated and some details are visible to the visitor.

S. Giovenale. A naturally defended position not far from Luni sul Mignone and also occupied in the Bronze Age and Archaic periods. The subject of important Swedish excavations.

S. Giuliano. Another significant, although small centre investigated by the Swedes in inland South Etruria. Remarkable for fine rock-cut tombs.

Sarteano. A small Etruscan centre in the Chiusi area whose visible remains are mainly medieval.

The site is located on the flanks of Monte Cetona, an important occupation area in the Bronze Age whose artefacts can be seen in Perugia museum.

Saturnia. A small Etruscan centre in Albegna valley, mainly visible today in the form of its cemeteries.

Scarlino. A small site in the territory of Vetulonia with fine views over the Gulf of Follonica. The castle has recently been excavated with the unexpected discovery of Etruscan and Bronze Age remains.

Siena. The famous city of art is also the university centre of major fieldwork into the development of the human landscape in Tuscany. Little is known of the Etruscan centre in Siena, but the small national museum houses local material and the palazzo comunale houses material from Murlo (see above).

Sorgenti della Nova. (fig. 16b) A interesting Late Bronze Age and medieval naturally defended settlement excavated recently by the University of Milan. The general visitor is advised to visit the museum at Manciano.

Sovana. Another small Etruscan centre in the Fiora valley largely known from its necropolis.

Spina. A major emporium in the Po valley. Wooden piles can still be seen occasionally in the sides of canals, but the most rewarding visit is to Ferrara museum, to see the rich products of the cemeteries and Etruscan trade down the Adriatic.

Talamone. The site of a small Etruscan centre on the coast to the north of the Albegna valley. Most of the finds are in Florence museum.

Tarquinia. (fig. 21 etc.) One of the principal Etruscan cities of South Etruria, famous for its painted tombs. The area of the ancient city is also worth visiting with recently uncovered monumental remains including walls, temple area and, on a less monumental scale, the domestic quarters of the city. A fine museum in the modern town contains many of the finds.

Todi. A beautiful medieval and Renaissance town

on the boundary of Etruria and Umbria which had Etruscan and Umbrian origins. The museum is usually closed, so visitors may have to be content with the attractions of the town itself.

Torrionaccio. (figs. 15a, 16a) The site of an important Bronze Age excavation, but not worth visiting, without a good guide, and then only to see the location.

Tragliatella. A small Etruscan centre of significance in South Etruria, but little researched.

Tuscania. The site of a medieval city known for its Romanesque churches, but also important for its Etruscan origins. Some tombs can be seen close to the town, but the city is more significant as the focal point of recent field survey work by the British School at Rome.

Veii. The closest major Etruscan city to Rome and a major rival to ancient Rome. Field survey has been carried out in the local area by Italian and British (British School at Rome) groups. Some significant excavations such as that of the Villanovan cemetery of Quattro Fontanili are now invisible, but interesting hydraulic engineering

works and the temple of the Portonaccio can be seen.

Verucchio. An outpost of the Villanovan 'culture' in the north-eastern Apennines where a small museum of local finds has recently been opened.

Vetulonia. An important and distinctive centre on the southern boundary of North Etruria. The most prominent remains to be visited are the monumental tombs and the local museum.

Volterra. A large Etruscan centre in North Etruria of increased importance in the late Etruscan period. The local museum has an overpowering quantity of mass-produced alabaster urns, but gives a good coverage of the development of the city. The acropolis area, the walls and gates are also worth attention.

Vulci. A major Etruscan centre of northern South Etruria, whose finds are now dispersed around the museums of the world. The site has produced more fine Greek pottery than many parts of Greece. Many of the visible remains are post-Etruscan in date and the museum is not always open.

GLOSSARY

alluvial deposits   sediments deposited by the action of rivers

Archaic period   defined here as lasting from *c.* 580–400 BC

Bronze Age   the period when bronze was used without iron (2000–900 BC). A less precise term than it first seems since bronze was only used in large quantities from *c.* 1300 BC. Divided into the 'early' (2000–1500 BC), 'middle' (1500–1300 BC) and 'late' (1300–900 BC) Bronze Age. The late Bronze Age is further subdivided into the Recent (1300–1200 BC) and 'final' or 'latest' (1200–900 BC) Bronze Age

bucchero   a finely burnished, distinctively Etruscan, black (including the internal fabric) pottery probably made in imitation of metal

carinated   a description of pottery vessel with a sharp or acute outwardly turned angle in its body

Chalcolithic   the period when copper was used without the addition of other metals such as tin or lead (3000–2000 BC)

chiefly   a term used to describe differences in wealth before the establishment of the city state

colluvial deposits   sediments deposited by water not concentrated in a stream bed, generally on slopes

Diorites   coarse grained igneous (volcanic) rocks employed in antiquity for making polished stone axes

einkorn   a single grained wheat used in early agriculture

electrical resistivity   a technique for locating subsurface remains, based on the electrical resistance of subsurface deposits

emmer   a two grained wheat used in early agriculture

interfluves   the higher ground between one river and the next in the same drainage system

lacustrine (deposits)   lake (deposits)

marl   a sedimentary rock largely composed of clay

Mesolithic   the period at the end of the Palaeolithic accompanied by a warming climate and changed hunting and gathering practices before the onset of Neolilthic farming (*c.* 10,000–6000 BC)

Neolithic   technically the period when polished stone tools were introduced, but also associated with onset of farming practices (*c.* 6000–3000 BC), before the use of metals

Orientalizing period   defined here as lasting from *c.* 750–580 BC

orthogonal   on grid plan

Palaeolithic   the longest period of human development, based on a hunting and gathering economy and stone tools (750,000–10,000 BC in Italy)

pie chart   a circular diagram divided into segments that represent the percentage present of each constituent of the whole

Pleistocene   an epoch of geological time extending from *c.* 10,000 years ago

Pliocene   an epoch of geological time extending from *c.* 1.8 million years ago to *c.* 10,000 years ago

Plio-Pleistocene   the Pliocene and Pleistocene combined

pollen diagrams   charts that show the changing percentages of pollen present through time

resistivity   a surveying technique based on electrical resitivity that can be used to detect subsurface remains

Rinaldone   a cultural group within the Chalcolithic

Schists   a coarse grained metamorphic (changed under pressure) rock with many mica minerals

tectonic valleys   deep valleys formed by faulting in the earth's crust

Tertiary   a geological period from 65 to 1.8 million years ago containing the Pliocene epoch

Thiessen polygons   a technique used to estimate the territory of settlements by bisecting a line between the each pair of settlements

travertines   deposits of calcium carbonate formed by precipitation from hot springs

tuffs   consolidated ash from volcanic action

Villanovan   the early Iron Age phase in central Italy, roughly 900–750 BC

BIBLIOGRAPHY

Introduction

The literature on the history of Rome in so far as it touches Etruscan Italy is large: distrust of Livy and his sources is best expressed in A. Alföldi, *Early Rome and the Latins* (Ann Arbor 1963), but for a more defensive view, see T. J. Cornell, 'The formation of the historical tradition of early Rome', in *Past Perspectives* (eds. Moxon, Smart, Woodman: Cambridge 1986). M. I. Finley, *Ancient History: Evidence and Models* (London 1985), especially pp. 7–26, gives probably the most balanced opinion. For the variations within Greek historical traditions, see H. H. Scullard, 'Two Halicarnassians and a Lydian', in E. Badian (ed.), *Ancient Society and Institutions* (Oxford 1966), pp. 225–31. On 'the Great Divide': S. Dyson, 'A Classical archaeologist's response to the "New Archaeology" ', in *Bulletin of the American School of Oriental Research* 242 (1981), pp. 7–13; A. M. Snodgrass, 'The new archaeology and the Classical Archaeologist', in *American Journal of Archaeology* 89 (1985), pp. 31–7; P. Cartledge, 'A new classical archaeology?' in *TLS* 12 Sept 1986, pp. 1011–12. Some discussion of the problem in Etruscan terms will be found in the *Journal of Roman Studies* 76 (1986), pp. 281–6. The most accessible and concise account of Etruscan history in English is David Ridgway's contribution to the *Cambridge Ancient History*, Revised Edition, Vol. IV (1988). The classic account remains Massimo Pallottino's *The Etruscans* London 1975).

Chapter I

A good essay on the physiography of southern Etruria is by Carl Fries, to be found in A. Boethius (ed.), *Etruscan Culture, Land and People* (New York/Malmo 1962); see also T. Potter, *The Changing Landscape of South Etruria* (London 1979), pp. 19–51. For a military eye cast over the landscape, K. Mason (ed.), *Italy: Geographical Handbook Series B.R. 517*, Vols. 1–4 (Oxford, Naval Intelligence Division/OUP 1944–5); and an eye both military and scholarly is cast by J. B. Ward-Perkins in 'Landscape and History in Central Italy' (Myres Memorial Lecutre, Oxford 1964). The best regional synthesis of the economy of central Italy up to the Middle Bronze Age is G. Barker, *Landscape and Society: Prehistoric Central Italy* (London 1981). A related approach by Italian authors is Cazzella, A., Moscoloni, M., Cassano, S. and Manfredini, A. *Paletnologia* (Rome 1986).

Chapter II

For South Etruria, the best account remains T. W. Potter, *The Changing Landscape of South Etruria* (London 1979). The fieldwork of the British School at Rome is not finished, however: see G. Barker and T. Rasmussen, 'The archaeology of an Etruscan *polis*', in *Papers of the British School at Rome* 56 (1988), pp. 25–42; also G. Barker, 'Archaeology and the Etruscan countryside', in *Antiquity* 62 (1988), pp. 772–85. For recent work on the settlement of the Villanovan period at Veii, see M. Guaitoli in *Quaderni dell'Istituto di topografia antica dell'Universita di Roma* 9 (1982), pp. 79–87. For the huts behind the hut-urns, see G. Bartoloni *et al.*, 'Huts in the central Tyrrhenian area of Italy during the protohistoric age', in C. Malone and S. Stoddart (eds.), *Papers in Italian Archaeology* IV (B.A.R. International Series 245, 1985), pp. 175–202. In the same volume, see also A. Guidi, 'An application of the rank size rule to protohistoric settlements in the middle Tyrrhenian area', pp. 217–42; and *Dialoghi di archeologia* 2 (1986), pp. 193–200. Forthcoming is S. K. F. Stoddart, *Power and Place in Etruria* (Cambridge University Press). On the Albegna valley settlement of Doganella, see L. Walker, 'Survey of a settlement: a strategy for the Etruscan site at Doganella in the Albegna valley', in Haselgrove *et al.* (eds.), *Archaeology from the Ploughsoil* (Sheffield 1986), pp. 87–94. The most recent accounts of development north of the Po are to be found in an important set of exhibition catalogues centred on individual modern cities such as

Bologna, Mantova (Mantua) and Modena: R. De Marinis, *Gli Etruschi a Nord del Po* (Mantova 1987), A. Cardarelli *et al.*, *Modena dalle origini all'anno mille* (Modena 1988), G. Montanari *La formazione della città in Emilia Romagna* (Bologna 1987).

Chapter III

The only account of Etruscan eating is the catalogue edited by C. Cerchiai, *L'alimentazione nel mondo antico: gli Etruschi* (Rome 1987), which gives a useful summary of archaeological, iconographical and literary evidence. The basics of cooking are discussed in C. Scheffer's study of the Acquarossa material: *Cooking and Cooking Stands in Italy, 1400–400 BC* (Swedish Institute at Rome 1981); further by B. Bouloumié in his publication of the Murlo material in the *Melanges de l'Ecole Française de Rome*, Vol. 84 (1972), pp. 61ff., and Vol. 90 (1978), pp. 113ff. For an honest assessment of the state of our knowledge of Etruscan metal-working, see P. G. Warden's contribution to T. Hackens, N. D. and R. R. Holloway (eds.), *Crossroads of the Mediterranean* (Providence 1984) pp. 349–64. The achievements of Etruscan engineering are well-known: the most useful essay remains that of J. B. Ward Perkins in *Hommages à Albert Grenier*, Collection Latomus 58, III (1962), pp. 1636–43. For the drainage systems around Veii and elsewhere, see the *Paper of the British School at Rome* 31 (1963) pp. 74–99. A reliable account of Etruscan building generally is given by A. Boethius, *Etruscan and Early Roman Architecture* (Harmondsworth 1978); for house construction in particular, the exhibition catalogue *Architettura etrusca nel Viterbese* (Rome 1986) publishes the results of the Swedish excavations at San Giovenale and Acquarossa. The exhibition catalogue *Case e Palazzi* (Milano 1985) covers similar ground since most house excavations have been carried out by the Swedes. For more detailed site reports: for late Bronze Age Torrionaccio, *Notizie degli scavi 32* (1978), pp. 1–382; for Narce, T. W. Potter *et al.*, *A Faliscan Town in South Etruria*, (British School at Rome 1976); for late Bronze Age Luni, *Acta Instituti Romani Regni Sueciae* (1969).

Chapter IV

Mycenaean contact is most comprehensively covered in A. M. Bietti Sestieri, 'The Mycenaean connection and its impact on Central Mediterranean societies', in *Dialoghi di archeologia* 6 (1988), pp. 23–51. For the Orientalizing period, see A. Rathje, 'Oriental Imports in Etruria', in F. and D. Ridgway (eds.), *Italy Before the Romans* (London 1979), pp. 145–83. Archaic trade is amply discussed

in M. Cristofani (ed.), *Il commercio etrusco arcaico* (Rome 1985); see also A. Johnston, *Trademarks on Greek Vases* (Warminster 1979), and J. Boardman, *The Greeks Overseas* (2nd ed., London 1980). Still worth consulting is a pioneering essay by A. Blakeway, 'Demaratus', in *Journal of Roman Studies* 25 (1935), pp. 129–49.

Chapter V

The outlines of the innovation theory adopted in this chapter are to be found in E. M. Rogers and F. F. Shoemaker, *Communication of Innovations* (New York 1971). For the context of Greek colonization, see J. Boardman, *The Greek Overseas*, (2nd ed., London 1980), esp. pp. 161–224. A succinct report on Gravisca is given by M. Torelli in *Parola del Passato* 26 (1971), pp. 44–67; and for Sostratos and others, see A. Johnston, *Trademarks on Greek Vases* (Warminster 1979). The influence of *bucchero* on Attic potters is discussed by T. Rasmussen, 'Etruscan Shapes in Attic Pottery', *Antike Kunst* 28 (1985), pp. 33–9. For Greek myth in Etruria, the *banalizzazioni* theory (chiefly espoused by G. Camporeale) was last stated in *Studi Etruschi* 43 (1975), pp. 357–65: previous bibliography will be found there. Against the theory: J. D. Beazley, 'Two Swords: Two Shields' *BABesch 14*, 1 (1939), pp. 7–8; I. Krauskopf, *Der thebanische Sagenkreis und andere griechische Sagen in der etruskischen Kunst* (Mainz 1974); M. Martelli, 'Prima di Aristonothos', *Prospettiva* 38 (1984), pp. 2–15. For the theory that Greek epic texts were circulating in archaic Etruria, R. Hampe and E. Simon, *Griechische Sagen in der frühen etruskischen Kunst* (Mainz 1964): it is instructing and amusing to read the reviews of this book, in *Parola del Passato* 19 (1964), pp. 428ff.; *Journal of Hellenic Studies* 85 (1965), p. 241; *Classical Review* 15 (1965), pp. 97–100; and *Gnomon* 37 (1965), p. 838. For myths on Etruscan gems, the best introduction in English remains G. M. A. Richter, *The Engraved Gems of the Greeks and Etruscans* (London 1968). On the Francois tomb, F. Buranelli (ed.), *La tomba François di Vulci* (Rome 1987), esp. pp. 225–33. For Herakles in temple decoration and on Athenian vases in Etruria, see respectively *Opuscula Romana* XVI (1987), pp. 7–41, and W. Moon, 'The Priam Painter: Some Iconographic and Stylistic Considerations', in W. Moon (ed.), *Ancient Greek Art and Iconography* (Wisconsin 1983), pp. 97–118. The best work on literacy in Etruria has been done by M. Cristofani: see his 'Rapporto sulla diffusione della scrittura nell'Italia antica' in *Scrittura e civiltà* 2 (1978) pp. 5–33; and 'Varieta linguistica e contesti sociali di pertinenza nell'antroponomia etrusca' in *Annali dell'Istituto Orientale* (Naples) 3 (1981), pp. 47–78. Social factors are discussed by S. K. F. Stoddart and J. Whitley, 'The social context of literacy in Archaic Greece and Etruria', in *Antiquity* 62 (1988), pp. 761–72. For comparison (and further general bibliography), see P. Burke, *The historical anthropology of early modern Italy* (Cambridge 1987), pp. 110–31. And for the end of the Etruscan language: J. Kaimio, 'The ousting of Etruscan by Latin in Etruria', in *Studies in the Romanisation of Etruria* (Acta Instituti Romani Finlandiae V 1975), pp. 85–246.

Chapter VI

For the general problems of learning about ritual from archaeology, see C. Renfrew *et al.*, *The Archaeology of Cult: the Sanctuary at Phylakopi* (London 1985), pp. 1–26 (the lucid introduction to fieldwork study). For Etruscan sanctuaries the best survey is G. Colonna (ed.), *I santuari d'Etruria* (Milan 1985); followed by I. M. Edlund, *The Gods and the Place* (Stockholm 1988). On the 'iconography of power', J. Cherry's contribution to J. M. Wagstaff (ed), *Landscape and Culture* (Oxford 1987), pp. 146–72, is useful. The latest work on the Iguvine Tables is A. Prosdocimi, *Le tavole Iguvine* (Florence 1984). The rituals of city-founding are nicely discussed by an architect in J. Rykwert, *The Idea of a Town* (London 1976). The standard account of the anthropological theory espoused here is E. Leach, *Culture and Communication* (Cambridge 1976). Some parallels for Etruscan eschatology may be sought in M. Bloch and J. Parry (eds.), *Death and the regeneration of life* (Cambridge 1982). For a fuller reading of Etruscan funerary art, see N. J. Spivey's essay in M. A. Rizzo (ed.), *Un artista etrusco e il suo mondo: il Pittore di Micali* (Rome 1988). Good contributions to our knowledge of Etruscan votives are contained in T. Linders and G. Nordquist (eds.), *Gifts to the Gods* (Proceedings of the Uppsala Symposium 1985: Uppsala 1987). The latest opinions on Pyrgi (with much preceding bibliography on the site) are in F. Coarelli, *Il Foro Boario* (Rome 1988). The Tarquinia excavations were published in M. Bonghi Jovino (ed.), *Gli Etruschi di Tarquinia* (Modena 1986); and further in M. B. Jovino/C. C. Trere (eds.), *Tarquinia: ricerche, scavi e prospettive* (Milan 1987).

Chapter VII

For warfare in its wider context, see C. Renfrew/J. Cherry (eds.), *Peer Polity Interaction and Socio-Political Change* (Cambridge 1986), pp. 8–9 and pp. 51–2. The most up-to-date account of Greek hoplite warfare is W. K. Pritchett's *The Greek state at war* (Berkeley 1971–85), in 4 vols.; still essential is A. M. Snodgrass,

'The Hoplite Reform and History', *Journal of Hellenic Studies* 85 (1965), pp. 110–22. For a military historian's view of what hoplite tactics involve, see M. van Crefeld, *Command in War* (Harvard 1985), pp. 17–57. The archaeological evidence: the most serious contribution is P. F. Stary's dissertation, *Zur eisenzeitlichen Bewaffnung und Kampfesweise in Mittelitalien, ca. 9. bis 6. Jh. v. Chr.* (Hamburg 1980), of which good digests appear as 'Foreign Elements in Etruscan Arms and Armour: 8th to 3rd centuries BC', *Proceedings of the Prehistoric Society* 45 (1979), pp. 179–206; and 'Orientalische und griechische Einflüsse in der etruskischen Bewaffnung und Kampfesweise', in *Die Aufnahme fremder Kultureinflüsse in Etrurien* (Mannheim 1980), pp. 25–40. Some of this material is covered less thoroughly in C. Saulnier, *L'Armee et la guerre dans le monde etrusco-romain, VIII–IVe s.* (Paris 1980) and P. Connolly, *Greece and Rome at War* (London 1981), pp. 91–7. For the Greek background, see A. M. Snodgrass, *Arms and Armour of the Greeks* (London 1967). Specialized examinations of Italo-Etruscan armour and weapons will be found in J. Swaddling (ed.), *Italian Iron Age Artefacts in the British Museum* (London 1986), pp. 3–36. Livy's account of the reforms of Servius see Bk I, 43; see also M. P. Nilsson, 'The Introduction of Hoplite Tactics at Rome', *Journal of Roman Studies* 19 (1929), pp. 1–11, and R. Thomsen, *King Servius Tullius* (Copenhagen 1980), pp. 162–3. For the armed dance, see R. Bloch, *The Origins of Rome* (London 1960), pp. 134–41, and N. J. Spivey, 'The Armed Dance on Etruscan Vases', *Proceedings of the Second Congress on Ancient Greek and Related Pottery* (Copenhagen 1989). War at sea: see M. Cristofani, *Gli etruschi del mare* (Milan 1983); *Idem*, 'Nuovi spunti sul tema della talassocrazia etrusca', *Xenia* 8 (1985), pp. 3–20.

Chapter VIII

An exemplary study of the way in which the archaeology of graves can demonstrate social organization is I. Morris, *Burial and Ancient Society* (Cambridge 1987): much more could be done on Etruscan material following the example set by Morris. A harbinger of the possibilities is given by B. d'Agostino, 'Comunità dei morti, società dei vivi: un rapporto difficile', in *Dialoghi di archeologia* 1985, 1, pp. 47–58. The most recent treatment of a Villanovan cemetery is by Judith Toms, 'The relative chronology of the Villanovan cemetery of Quattro Fontanili at Veii' in *Archeologia e Storia Antica* 8, (1988), pp. 44–97. For an overview of the historical development of Etruscan society, see T. W. Potter, 'Social Evolution in Iron Age and Roman Italy: an appraisal', in

J. Bintliff (ed.), *European Social Evolution* (Bradford 1984). For a stout attempt to define Etruscan offices of power, see M. Cristofani, *The Etruscans: a new investigation* (London/New York 1979), pp. 27–43. There is no satisfactory summary of the cemeteries ringing Cerveteri, but the most recent general book is G. Proietti, *Cerveteri* (Rome 1987). For Chiusi, R. Bianchi Bandinelli's survey remains valid: see *Monumenti Antichi* 30 (1925), pp. 210–578. A well-researched account of Populonia is given by F. Fedeli in his *Populonia: storia e territorio* (Florence 1983). The iconology of Etruscan art is under-developed. The new standard reference work for tomb-paintings is S. Steingräber's *Etruskisches Wandmalerei* (Mainz 1984), of which an English version is forthcoming under the curatorship of David Ridgway. Useful background to the significance of certain headgear etc. will be found in L. Bonfante, *Etruscan Dress* (Baltimore 1975). The latest evaluation of the terracotta plaques is by M. Cristofani, in M. Cristofani (ed.), *Etruria e Lazio arcaico* (Rome 1987), pp. 95-120; still essential is A. Andren, *Architectural Terracottas from Etrusco-Italic Temples* (Lund 1940).

General

The chapter bibliographies above are selective, added simply to enable readers to pursue certain themes and gain access to more comprehensive references, particularly in English: what follows here is also selective, and again intended to supply directions for directions in the territory of further reading. It is no reflection upon modern scholarship if we say that George Dennis' *Cities and Cemeteries of Etruria* (2 vols., best edition being the third, London 1883) still stands at the head of any bibliography of Etruscan Italy. Dennis was not a professional scholar (for his biography, see D. E. Rhodes, *Dennis of Etruria*, London 1973), with large libraries, grants and research students at his disposal: but he knew the land and the sites probably better than anyone ever since. If you jettison the camera and sit down to draw or verbally describe what is in front of you, the chances are that you look more closely at it.

Some things have been lost since the last century, but very many more have been discovered: and a discipline has been created, at least in Italy, of *Etruscologia*. Massimo Pallottino's handbook of that title goes into a new edition almost annually in his home country: well-translated, it is available in English as *The Etruscans* (revised and enlarged, Harmondsworth 1974). Italian universities have chairs in Etruscology: in Britain, only two institutions (Edinburgh University and St David's University College, Lampeter) offer courses on Etruscan matters, so it is hardly surprising that Italian scholarship dominates the present scene. The best of this is gathered in an outstanding volume, *Rasenna* (Milan 1986); it is also generously evident in the exhibition catalogue produced for the principal exhibition of the 'Year of the Etruscans', *Civiltà degli etruschi*, ed. M. Cristofani (Milan 1985). The momentum produced by this celebration carries on: see *National Geographic* 173, No. 6 (June 1988), pp. 696–743. A certain amount of Italian expertise is devolved in F. Coarelli (ed.), *Etruscan Cities* (London 1975), which also serves as a useful (if bulky) gazetteer of sites. The handiest guide-book is M. Torelli's *Etruria* in the Laterza series; those without Italian might look out for the thematic map/guide published in various languages by the Instituto Geografico De Agostini, *The Etruscans*, often available in tourist offices.

INDEX

(Compiled by Anna-Louise Lawrence)